AF605807

Linguistic Explorations in Translation Studies

Linguistic Explorations in Translation Studies

Analyses of English Translations of Ancient Chinese Poems and Lyrics

Written by Guowen Huang
Translated by Bo Wang and Yuanyi Ma

UNIVERSITY OF TORONTO PRESS
Toronto Buffalo London

Published by University of Toronto Press
Toronto Buffalo London
utorontopress.com
Printed in the USA

First published in Chinese in 2006 by Shanghai Foreign Language Education Press. This English edition, with a new a Preface written by the translators and an interview with the author, published in 2024 by University of Toronto Press.

ISBN 978-1-4875-6641-8 (cloth)
ISBN 978-1-4875-6643-2 (EPUB)
ISBN 978-1-4875-6642-5 (PDF)

Publication cataloguing information available from Library and Archives Canada.

Cover design: Mark Lee / hisandhers.design
Cover painting courtesy of the Palace Museum, China

We wish to acknowledge the land on which the University of Toronto Press operates. This land is the traditional territory of the Wendat, the Anishnaabeg, the Haudenosaunee, the Métis, and the Mississaugas of the Credit First Nation.

University of Toronto Press acknowledges the financial support of the Government of Canada, the Canada Council for the Arts, and the Ontario Arts Council, an agency of the Government of Ontario, for its publishing activities.

Canada Council for the Arts | Conseil des Arts du Canada

Funded by the Government of Canada | Financé par le gouvernement du Canada | Canada

Contents

List of figures and tables

Figures

Tables

Abbreviations and symbols

ASP	aspect marker
CNKI	China National Knowledge Infrastructure
DE	"的" (*de*)
MEAS	measurer
MOD	verbal particle: modal
SFG	Systemic Functional Grammar
SFL	Systemic Functional Linguistics
VPART	verbal particle
ø	ellipsis
|||	clause complex, boundary marker
||	clause (not rankshifted), boundary marker
|	phrase or group, boundary marker
/	line break

Acknowledgements

The interview transcript in Appendix 2 was previously published in the *Journal of World Languages*. We are grateful to the original publisher, Mouton de Gruyter, for permission to reprint the article in this book. The original publication detail is provided below:

> Huang, Guowen, Bo Wang & Yuanyi Ma. 2023. "Developing and contributing to systemic functional translation studies in China: An interview with Professor Guowen Huang". *Journal of World Languages* 9(2): 165–181. https://doi.org/10.1515/jwl-2022-0041

Bo Wang and Yuanyi Ma would like to take this chance to express their gratitude to Professor Guowen Huang for his trust and guidance. We are also grateful to Professor Christian M.I.M. Matthiessen, who has continued to be the semogenic source for us to produce more academic works. We thank Professor Chenguang Chang for his support all along, Janet Joyce, Sarah Lee and Valerie Hall from Equinox and copy editor Susan Jarvis for their generous help in producing this book, and Ms Xitong Wang for her help in typing in the poems in the appendix.

Translators' preface

About this book

This book is an English translation of Guowen Huang's monograph, which was originally written in Chinese and previously published in Mainland China in 2006. As a seminal work in Chinese academia, the book represents one of the first attempts of Chinese scholars to apply Halliday's Systemic Functional Linguistics (SFL) to translation studies in general and to English translations of ancient Chinese poems in particular. By offering comprehensive analyses of English translations of ancient Chinese poems, this book successfully illustrates how different aspects of the SFL theory can help to illuminate translation as a meaning-making process and also point out the choices in the originals and their translations.

As translators of this book, we are very honored to have translated this inspiring and important book we read in our linguistic "kindergarten" into English and to be able to introduce it to a wider readership around the globe. We believe the book is important in the literature of applying SFL to translation studies (or systemic functional translation studies – see Wang & Ma 2021, 2022) and that a translation of this book can serve the following purposes: (1) to introduce a groundbreaking book in the Chinese academia to a wider audience; (2) to illustrate how SFL can be applied to translation studies; (3) to provide a comprehensive framework for analysing ancient Chinese poems and their English translations; and (4) to offer directions for future research in applying SFL to translation studies.

Furthermore, we maintain that several features of the book make it an important reference for readers who are interested in SFL, translation, ancient Chinese poems and language comparison. First, the book includes a wide range of theoretical perspectives, such as the four different metafunctional modes of meaning, reported speech, tense, text structure and personal pronoun, delving into both the lexical and the grammatical ends of the lexicogrammatical continuum. Second, the analysis ranges across different ranks at the stratum of lexicogrammar, including not only the clause rank, but also the group/phrase and the word ranks. Three, six steps in applying SFL to translation are suggested in this book: observation, interpretation, description, analysis, explanation and evaluation. Moreover, the six steps are situated on a spectrum ranging from subjective to objective, with observation located at the objective end and evaluation at the subjective end. Fourth, the book helps to confirm that a linguistic analysis informed by SFL is capable of answering the two possible goals in text analysis suggested by Halliday (2001). Finally, this book also serves as an update of the original edition (Huang 2006). To highlight Guowen Huang's contributions to the research area, we have conducted an interview with him, the transcript of which is included in Appendix 2.

Locating this book in the context of SFL in China

In the Chinese academia, SFL was first introduced in the 1970s with the publication of an article titled "On the Three Systems in Modern English Grammar and Communicative Grammar" by Li Fang, Zhuanglin Hu and Kerong Xu (1977). The early 1980s saw the publication of two journal articles by Zongyan Wang, "The Linguistic Theories of J.R. Firth – Founder of the London School" (Wang 1980) and "A Review of Halliday's 'Grammatical Categories in Modern Chinese'" (Wang 1981), which evaluated SFL and played a significant role in introducing SFL to China (see Wang & Huang 2010; Hongyang Wang 2010). When Zhuanglin Hu graduated from University of Sydney under Halliday's supervision and returned to China, he published a series of papers on SFL (e.g. Hu 1983, 1984, 1986), covering topics such as Halliday's views on language and his systemic functional theories, and started to train junior scholars in the area. With scholars like Yongsheng Zhu, Delu Zhang, Yan Fang, Guowen Huang and Xinzhang Yang all returning to China after studying abroad, SFL became an important topic in linguistic research in China.

The earliest theoretical engagement of SFL with translation in China can be found in the co-authored textbook *A Survey of Systemic-functional Grammar*, by Zhuanglin Hu, Yongsheng Zhu, and Delu Zhang (1989), in which suggestions are proposed for applying SFL in the Chinese context. In the section on human translation and machine translation, the authors briefly modelled translation according to rank, metafunctional modes of meaning and stratification, explaining translation equivalence with literal and free translation strategies as well as highlighting the specificity of machine translation.

According to Wang and Huang (2010), there are three stages of SFL development in China. The first stage is from the late 1970s to the late 1980s, and studies in this period primarily focus on the introduction and the importation of SFL theory. The second stage, ranging from the 1980s to the mid-1990s, signals the continuous importation of SFL theory and the application and assessment of the theory. The third stage, from the mid-1990s, is characterized by the introduction, application, assessment and amendment of the theory. The application of SFL to translation has occurred mostly during the third stage. We can also note that the monographs in this area (including Huang 2006; see Table 0.1) were all published at the third stage of SFL development in China.

Table 0.1 Monographs on the application of Systemic Functional Linguistics to translation studies published in Mainland China

Year	Author	Title	Register involved	Language pair
2004	Jianguo Si	*Systemic Functional Linguistics and the Style of Novels – A Modified Functional Analysis of* In Cold Blood	Novel (recreating)	English–Chinese
2005	Yuanyuan Shang	*Translation Shifts in Political Texts from English into Chinese*	Political speeches (exploring)	English–Chinese
2005	Xianzhu Si	*Translation Studies: Theory, Method, and Evaluation*	Examples of various registers are selected.	–
2005	Meifang Zhang	*Functional Approaches to Translation Studies*	Examples of various registers are selected.	–
2006	Guowen Huang	*Linguistic Explorations in Translation Studies: Analyses of English Translations of Ancient Chinese Poems and Lyrics*	Ancient Chinese poems and lyrics (recreating)	Chinese (ancient Chinese)–English
2007	Fagen Li	*Interpersonal Meanings and Equivalence in Translation: A Functional Linguistic Analysis of "Shu Dao Nan" and Its English Version*	Ancient Chinese poem (recreating)	Chinese (ancient Chinese)–English

2007	Xianzhu Si	*Translation Studies: A Functional Linguistic Approach – Constructing a Translation Quality Assessment Model*	Examples of various registers are selected.	—
2007	Peng Wang	Harry Potter *and Its Chinese Translation: Analysis of* MODALITY *from the Perspective of Systemic Functional Linguistics*	Novel (recreating)	English–Chinese
2007	Dequan Zhao	*Transferring Metafunctions Between English and Chinese: A Functional Linguistic Approach to Translation Studies*	Examples of various registers are selected.	—
2008	Jianping Xie et al.	*Functional Context and ESP Discourse Translation*	Examples of various registers are selected.	—
2013	Jian Han	*A Comparative Study of Legal Texts in the Perspective of Functional Linguistics*	Legal text (enabling)	English–Chinese
2014	Zhenzhen Wang	*On the Effect of Systemic Functional Linguistic Analysis in Japanese-Chinese Translation*	Examples of various registers are selected.	Japanese–Chinese
2015	Xuqin Mu	*Attitudinal Meanings of Metaphors: A Systematic Study Based on English Poetry*	Poems (recreating)	English–Chinese
2015	Qianhua Ouyang	*Assessing the Quality of Interpreting: A New Perspective from Functional Linguistics*	Speeches in business context (exploring)	English–Chinese, Chinese–English
2015	Meifang Zhang	*Functional Approaches to English-Chinese Translation* (2nd ed. of Zhang 2005)	Examples of various registers are selected.	—

2016	Shengwen Gao	*Translation Studies from the Perspective of Register: Comparison Between the Translations of* Lun Yu (The Analects) *by James Legge and Ku Hung-ming*	*The Analects* (*Lun Yu*) (exploring & reporting)	Chinese (ancient Chinese)–English
2016	Xianzhu Si	*Translation Studies from the Perspective of Systemic-functional Linguistics – Constructing a Translation Quality Assessment Model*	Examples of various registers are selected.	–
2017	Jing Zhao	*Transitivity Translation Shifts in the Perspective of Interlingual Re-instantiation*	Novel (recreating)	English–Chinese
2017	Xianzhu Si, Yuhou Pang & Jintao Cheng	*Studies of Chinese into English Translation: A Systemic Functional Linguistic Approach*	Examples of various registers are selected.	–
2019	Honghui Hu	*A Study on the Equivalence of Projection in the* Lunyu (The Analects) *and Its Translations*	*The Analects* (*Lun Yu*) (exploring and reporting)	Chinese (ancient Chinese)–English
2019	Xianzhu Si & Yuhou Pang	*Studies of English into Chinese Translation: A Systemic Functional Linguistics Approach*	Examples of various registers are selected.	–
2020	Yang Chen	*A Functional Discourse Analysis of Translations of the* Lun Yu (The Analects of Confucius)	*The Analects* (*Lun Yu*) (exploring and reporting)	Chinese (ancient Chinese)–English
2020	Ying Chen	*A Functional Discourse Analysis of Variation in English Translations of* Lun Yu	*The Analects* (*Lun Yu*) (exploring and reporting)	Chinese (ancient Chinese)–English
2020	Jintao Cheng	*Translation Studies: A Systemic Functional Linguistics Approach*	–	–

2021	Haihu Zhao	*A Study of Tourism Translation from the Perspective of Systemic-functional Linguistics*	Tourism texts (reporting, enabling and recommending)	Chinese–English
2022	Dandan Chen	*Research on Translation of* Book of History *– a Pre-Qin Confucius Classic*	*Book of History* (reporting)	Chinese (ancient Chinese)–English
2023	Xi Li	*Research on the Patterns of Coherence in Literary Translation: Examples from* Hongloumeng *and Its English Translations*	*Hongloumeng* (recreating)	Chinese–English

Chronologically, Guowen Huang is one of the first scholars to have worked on the application of SFL to translation in China. From 2002, he began to publish papers on the translation of Chinese classical poems based on SFL analysis, covering a wide range of theoretical perspectives (see e.g. Huang 2002a, 2002b, 2002c, 2002d, 2002e). Many of these papers are collected in Huang (2006), illustrating the applicability of SFL to translation and exploring the potential of applying different aspects of SFL theory to translation.

In terms of tenor relationship, various authors of the monographs tabulated in Table 0.1 have semiotically engaged with Guowen Huang (see also Appendix 2). Authors such as Yuanyuan Shang (2005), Xianzhu Si (2005, 2007, 2016), Fagen Li (2005, 2007), Shengwen Gao (2016), Yang Chen (2020) and Ying Chen (2020) conducted their PhD research with Huang and became prominent scholars in this research area in China. Meifang Zhang (2005, 2015) used to be a colleague of Huang at Sun Yat-sen University. Honghui Hu (2019), who studied for her PhD with Lei Zeng – a student of Huang's – once worked as a visiting scholar with Huang and chose to investigate translation under Huang's influence. Furthermore, Honghui Hu, Yang Chen and Ying Chen are members of Huang's research group that investigates the translations of *Lun Yu* (*The Analects*) by Confucius and promotes the study of *Lun Yu* worldwide (cf. Huang 2014, 2017).

In addition, the registers involved in the monographs can be categorized in accordance with Matthiessen's (2014, 2015) functional text typology, as shown in Table 0.1. Among the 27 monographs, 16 involve comprehensive empirical analyses of texts from one specific register: seven monographs focus on recreating texts (e.g. novel, poem), four on exploring and reporting texts (i.e. *The Analects*), two on exploring texts (i.e. speech), one on reporting, enabling and recommending texts (i.e. tourism texts), and one each on enabling (legal texts) and reporting texts (*Book of History*). In terms of the selection of certain register for investigation, this book is also pioneering as an early attempt of applying SFL to the analysis of ancient Chinese poems and their translations.

Some conventions in this book

Throughout the book, there are terms with an initial upper-case letter (e.g. Carrier, Theme, and Subject), terms in small caps (also possible in all caps, e.g. MOOD, THEME and PROCESS TYPE) and terms in all lower-case letters (e.g. mood and process type). This is because we are following the conventions in Halliday's works (e.g. Halliday 1985; Halliday & Matthiessen 2014). For instance, when using the term "mood", MOOD (also MOOD) refers to the name of the major grammatical system of the clause – that is, the system for realizing the semantic system of SPEECH FUNCTION; Mood (with the first letter capitalized) indicates the structural function of a clause – that is, the element in the interpersonal structure of the English clause; mood (or mood type in all lower-case letters) is the name of this systemic term or feature, with quotation marks sometimes being put around the term (see Matthiessen et al. 2022: Ch. 4 for more discussion).

Moreover, a large number of examples of Chinese poems are provided in this book. For readers who cannot read Chinese characters, we present the examples with pinyin and interlinear glossing. As shown below, the pinyin in italics indicates how the poetic line can be pronounced when being read aloud in modern Chinese, and the interlinear glossing is a word-for-word literal translation for readers' careful examination:

洛阳 亲 友 如 相问，
luò yáng qīn yǒu rú xiāng wèn,
Luoyang relative friend if ask,

一 片 冰 心 在 玉 壶。
yí piàn bīng xīn zài yù hú.
one piece ice heart be in jade jar.

The names of poets who composed the ancient Chinese poems and lyrics are presented in the following style: BAI Juyi, LI Bai, SU Shi, JIA Dao and MA Zhiyuan, with the family names placed before the given names and the complete family names being capitalized. On the other hand, for the names of translators who produced their works in modern times, their names are presented in the following style: Yuanchong Xu, Dayu Sun, Changsheng Wan, Xianzhong Wang and Zuxin Ding, with their given names preceding their family names. A complete list of the poems and their translations discussed in this book can be found in Appendix 1. The relevant information about these poems and their translators is provided in Table 0.2 (see Appendix 1 for details).

Table 0.2 Ancient Chinese poems and their English translations discussed in this book

Poem no.	Author	Dynasty	Title of poem	Translators	Relevant chapters in this book
1	白居易 BAI Juyi	Tang	长相思 *Chang Xiang Si*	1. 龚景浩 Jinghao Gong 2. 许渊冲 Yuanchong Xu	Chapter 10
2	曹雪芹 CAO Xueqin	Qing	《红楼梦》卷头诗 *Hong Lou Meng Juan Tou Shi*	1. David Hawkes 2. 黄新渠 Xinqu Huang 3. 刘重德 Zhongde Liu 4. 杨宪益、戴乃迭 Xianyi Yang & Gladys Yang	Chapter 1
3	崔颢 CUI Hao	Tang	长干曲 *Chang Gan Qu*	1. Burton Watson 2. 吴钧陶 Juntao Wu 3. 许渊冲 Yuanchong Xu 4. 许渊冲 Yuanchong Xu	Chapter 12
4	崔护 CUI Hu	Tang	题都城南庄 *Ti Du Cheng Nan Zhuang*	1. Kenneth Rexroth 2. 孙大雨 Dayu Sun 3. 王大濂 Dalian Wang 4. 许渊冲 Yuanchong Xu	Chapter 13

5	杜牧 DU Mu	Tang	泊秦淮 *Bo Qin Huai*	1. 罗志野 Zhiye Luo 2. 王大濂 Dalian Wang 3. 许渊冲 Yuanchong Xu 4. 许渊冲 Yuanchong Xu 5. 杨宪益、戴乃迭 Xianyi Yang & Gladys Yang	Chapter 10
6	杜牧 DU Mu	Tang	遣怀 *Qian Huai*	1. 罗志野 Zhiye Luo 2. 王大濂 Dalian Wang 3. 许渊冲 Yuanchong Xu 4. 许渊冲 Yuanchong Xu 5. 傯仕 Shi Zong	Chapter 10
7	杜牧 DU Mu	Tang	清明 *Qing Ming*	1. 蔡廷干 Tinggan Cai 2. 丁祖馨 Zuxin Ding 3. 孙大雨 Dayu Sun 4. 万昌盛、王僩中 Changsheng Wan & Xianzhong Wang 5. 吴钧陶 Juntao Wu 6. 许渊冲 Yuanchong Xu 7. 杨宪益、戴乃迭 Xianyi Yang & Gladys Yang	Chapters 2, 3, 4, 5, 11
8	贺知章 HE Zhizhang	Tang	回乡偶书 *Hui Xiang Ou Shu*	1. Witter Bynner 、江亢虎 Witter Bynner & Kanghu Jiang 2. 刘重德 Zhongde Liu 3. 万昌盛、王僩中 Changsheng Wan & Xianzhong Wang 4. 王大濂 Dalian Wang 5. 吴钧陶 Juntao Wu	Chapter 13

9	贾岛 JIA Dao	Tang	寻隐者不遇 *Xun Yin Zhe Bu Yu*	1. Witter Bynner 2. 孙大雨 Dayu Sun 3. 万昌盛、王僩中 Changsheng Wan & Xianzhong Wang 4. 王大濂 Dalian Wang 5. Burton Watson 6. 吴钧陶 Juntao Wu 7. 许渊冲 Yuanchong Xu 8. 许渊冲 Yuanchong Xu	Chapters 6, 11, 13
10	李白 LI Bai	Tang	黄鹤楼送孟浩然之广陵 *Huang He Lou Song Meng Hao Ran Zhi Guang Ling*	1. Witter Bynner 、江亢虎 Witter Bynner & Kanghu Jiang 2. 孙大雨 Dayu Sun 3. 屠笛、屠岸 Di Tu & An Tu 4. 万昌盛、王僩中 Changsheng Wan & Xianzhong Wang 5. 王大濂 Dalian Wang 6. 王守义、诺弗尔 Shouyi Wang & John Knoepfle 7. 许渊冲 Yuanchong Xu 8. 许渊冲 Yuanchong Xu 9. 杨宪益、戴乃迭 Xianyi Yang & Gladys Yang 10. 张炳星 Bingxing Zhang	Chapter 10
11	李白 LI Bai	Tang	金陵酒肆留别 *Jin Ling Jiu Si Liu Bie*	1. 屠笛、屠岸 Di Tu & An Tu 2. 许渊冲 Yuanchong Xu	Chapter 10

12	李白 LI Bai	Tang	静夜思 *Jing Ye Si*	1. Witter Bynner 2. Arthur Cooper 3. L. Cranmer-Byng 4. W.J. Fletcher 5. Herbert A. Giles 6. 黄新渠 Xinqu Huang 7. Amy Lowell 8. 刘军平 Junping Liu 9. 马红军 Hongjun Ma 10. S. Obata 11. 孙大雨 Dayu Sun 12. 屠笛、屠岸 Di Tu & An Tu 13. 王大濂 Dalian Wang 14. 万昌盛、王僴中 Changsheng Wan & Xianzhong Wang 15. Burton Watson 16. 翁显良 Xianliang Weng 17. 许渊冲 Yuanchong Xu 18. 徐忠杰 Zhongjie Xu 19. 赵甄陶 Zhentao Zhao 20. 张炳星 Bingxing Zhang 21. 卓振英 Zhenying Zhuo	Chapter 13
13	李白 LI Bai	Tang	苏台览古 *Su Tai Lan Gu*	1. 王大濂 Dalian Wang 2. Burton Watson 3. 许渊冲 Yuanchong Xu	Chapter 13
14	李白 LI Bai	Tang	越中览古 *Yue Zhong Lan Gu*	1. 孙大雨 Dayu Sun 2. Burton Watson 3. 许渊冲 Yuanchong Xu	Chapter 13

15	李商隐 LI Shangyin	Tang	无题 *Wu Ti*	1. Innes Herdan 2. 万昌盛、王僩中 Changsheng Wan & Xianzhong Wang 3. 许渊冲 Yuanchong Xu 4. 许渊冲 Yuanchong Xu 5. 曾炳衡 Bingheng Zeng 6. 张廷琛、魏博思 Tingchen Zhang & Bruce M. Wilson	Chapter 12
16	柳宗元 LIU Zongyuan	Tang	江雪 *Jiang Xue*	1. Witter Bynner 2. Soame Jenyns 3. 孙大雨 Dayu Sun 4. 王大濂 Dalian Wang 5. 王守义、诺弗尔 Shouyi Wang & John Knoepfle 6. Burton Watson 7. 翁显良 Xianliang Weng 8. John C.H. Wu 9. 吴钧陶 Juntao Wu 10. 许渊冲 Yuanchong Xu 11. 许渊冲 Yuanchong Xu	Chapter 9
17	吕本中 LÜ Benzhong	Song	采桑子 *Cai Sangzi*	1. 龚景浩 Jinghao Gong 2. Robert Kotewell & Norman Smith 3. 裘小龙 Xiaolong Qiu 4. 许渊冲 Yuanchong Xu	Chapter 10
18	马致远 MA Zhiyuan	Yuan	天净沙 · 秋思 *Tian Jing Sha Qiu Si*	1. 丁祖馨、Burton Raffel Zuxin Ding & Burton Raffel 2. Wayne Schlepp 3. 翁显良 Xianliang Weng	Chapters 8, 14

19	苏轼 SU Shi	Song	题西林壁 *Ti Xi Lin Bi*	1. 万昌盛、王僩中 Changsheng Wan & Xianzhong Wang 2. 王守义、诺弗尔 Shouyi Wang & John Knoepfle 3. Burton Watson 4. 许渊冲 Yuanchong Xu	Chapters 1, 14
20	王昌龄 WANG Changling	Tang	芙蓉楼送辛渐 *Fu Rong Lou Song Xin Jian*	1. 陶洁 Jie Tao 2. 万昌盛、王僩中 Changsheng Wan & Xianzhong Wang 3. 王大濂 Dalian Wang 4. 许渊冲 Yuanchong Xu 5. 许渊冲 Yuanchong Xu	Chapters 7, 10, 11, 13
21	王建 WANG Jian	Tang	新嫁娘词 *Xin Jia Niang Ci*	1. W.J. Fletcher 2. 罗志野 Zhiye Luo 3. 王大濂 Dalian Wang 4. Burton Watson 5. 许渊冲 Yuanchong Xu	Chapters 6, 12, 13
22	王维 WANG Wei	Tang	鹿柴 *Lu Zhai*	1. C.J. Chen & Michael Bullock 2. Burton Watson	Chapter 12
23	王维 WANG Wei	Tang	送别 *Song Bie*	1. Witter Bynner 2. W.J. Fletcher 3. Herbert A. Giles 4. 孙大雨 Dayu Sun 5. 王宝童 Baotong Wang 6. 许渊冲 Yuanchong Xu 7. 杨宪益、戴乃迭 Xianyi Yang & Gladys Yang	Chapters 11, 12, 13

24	韦应物 WEI Yingwu	Tang	寄李儋元锡 *Ji Li Dan Yuan Xi*	1. 陆佩弦 Peixian Lu	Chapter 13
25	辛弃疾 XIN Qiji	Song	丑奴儿 *Chou Nu Er*	1. 龚景浩 Jinghao Gong 2. Robert Kotewell & Norman Smith 3. 许渊冲 Yuanchong Xu 4. 杨宪益、戴乃迭 Xianyi Yang & Gladys Yang	Chapter 13
26	张籍 ZHANG Ji	Tang	节妇吟 *Jie Fu Yin*	1. 裘小龙 Xiaolong Qiu 2. 许渊冲 Yuanchong Xu	Chapter 13
27	张继 ZHANG Ji	Tang	枫桥夜泊 *Feng Qiao Ye Bo*	1. 蔡廷干 Tinggan Cai 2. 王大濂 Dalian Wang 3. 许渊冲 Yuanchong Xu 4. 许渊冲 Yuanchong Xu	Chapters 10, 12

Chapter 1

Preamble: Towards a linguistic analysis of English translations of ancient Chinese poems and lyrics

1.1 Introduction

This book analyses English translations of ancient Chinese poems (including lyrics and verses) using a linguistic perspective. It is hoped that this exploration can shed some light on translation studies. Both in China and abroad, analyses and discussions of English translations of ancient Chinese poems using a linguistic perspective – especially Systemic Functional Linguistics – are rarely seen. The tentative discussions in this book are neither systematic nor detailed; however, the analysis here will certainly have a positive effect on comparative studies of English and Chinese discourse, as well as on translation studies.

In this chapter, we will investigate *Ti Xi Lin Bi* (题西林壁), written by SU Shi (苏轼), a poet in the Song Dynasty. We can draw the following insights from our exploration: (1) a linguistic analysis of English translations of ancient Chinese poems will not only raise some questions on translation studies and contrastive studies of Chinese-English discourse but will also have some important implications; and (2) it will become clear that an analysis of a poem can be multidimensional or very detailed.

In our following discussion, we will first interpret *Ti Xi Lin Bi* before stating our reasons for choosing it and its English translations as our data for analysis. We will then provide a brief introduction to the chapters in this book. Finally, based on the analysis of the four English translations, we will delineate the main points in Chapters 2 to 13.

1.2 Interpreting *Ti Xi Lin Bi*

Written by SU Shi in the Song Dynasty, *Ti Xi Lin Bi* is a four-line poem that includes seven characters in each line. The original poem is as follows:

题西林壁
tí xī lín bì
write Xilin (west-forest) wall

（宋）苏轼
(sòng) sū shì
(Song Dynasty) SU Shi

横看成岭侧成峰，
héng kàn chéng lǐng cè chéng fèng,
horizontal look become ridge side become peak,

远近高低各不同。
yuǎn jìn gāo dī gè bù tóng.
far near high low each not same.

不识庐山真面目，
bù shí lú shān zhēn miàn mù,
not recognize Lu-Mount real appearance,

只缘身在此山中。
zhǐ yuán shēn zài cǐ shān zhōng.
only because body be in this mountain in.

In appreciating this poem, Liyun Zhu (2000: 211–12, our translation) makes the following remarks: "This poem is about the poet's advancement in his understanding after he paid a visit to Mount Lu. To tell the true shape of Mount Lu, the poet must carry out an all-round observation, incorporating views from the front, from the side, from afar, from nearby, from above, and from below. If one merely views Mount Lu from one aspect, one side, or one direction, one cannot have an overall image of the mountain." In fact, as discussed by Haiou Zhang (2001: 134–35, our translation), "this poem is a breakthrough following the traditional paradigm of scenery depiction in landscape poetry. It opens a new path by integrating scenery depiction and elucidation of principles. Inspired by the scenery, the poet has expressed his feelings, comprehended a principle in human life and entailed a philosophical implication into his poem." Based on the fact that one has to observe in various dimensions and perspectives to ascertain the true shape of Mount Lu, the poet suggests a philosophy of life according to which a true investigation of an event or a person must be comprehensive, multi-level, multi-dimensional and multi-directional so as not to draw conclusions from partial observation. When involved, we may often make partial and subjective judgements rather than gaining a comprehensive and objective understanding of something or someone. As a saying goes, spectators often understand the chess game better than the players.

The philosophy of life indicated in this poem is simple and universal. Since it is possible for us to extend the meaning in this poem and draw an analogy from it, it is also possible for different translators to interpret this poem differently. The translators try to express the meaning encoded in one code with another code, thus they all have to elaborate and interpret the original from their own standpoints (which are also restricted by their knowledge and skills). As generally acknowledged, poetry translators and poetry translation researchers are all scholars in translation studies. Are their investigations and comments likely to be restricted by their standpoints, like viewing Mount Lu when being inside the mountain? This is why we attempt to explore and analyse English translations of ancient Chinese poems in a linguistic perspective (viz. from "out of the mountain"). We hope more scholars will now examine and analyse English translations of ancient Chinese poems in different perspectives and enlightened by different theories. In this way, it will be possible for us to obtain a comprehensive and objective analysis and evaluation of certain issues in translation.

1.3 Reasons for choosing *Ti Xi Lin Bi*

As discussed above, SU Shi's poem explicates a philosophy of life that gives us a reason for investigating English translations of ancient Chinese poems in a linguistic perspective. Since this book deals with issues relating to English translations of ancient poems, it is appropriate to adopt this poem to support our exploration in this book.

Another reason to discuss this poem in the introductory chapter of this book is that its four English translations serve as a starting point for our discussions in the following chapters, in which various issues related to the English translations are examined in detail. Our following analysis of the English translations provides an outline of the whole book and functions as a gateway to the analysis in the remaining chapters.

1.4 Four English translations of *Ti Xi Lin Bi*

We have collected four English translations of *Ti Xi Lin Bi*, including those by Changsheng Wan and Xianzhong Wang (2000: 212), Shouyi Wang and John Knoepfle (1989: 88), Burton Watson (see Wen 1989: 251) and Yuanchong Xu (2000a: 139). The four English translations are as follows:

***Changsheng Wan and Xianzhong Wang's (2000: 212) translation:** An Inscription on the Wall of Xilin Temple*
The sidelong ranges become steep peaks in a vertical view,
The scenes so vary when seen from high or low, from far or near.
The genuine features of Lushan Mountain are strange to you,
Because your situation is within this mountain's bounding sphere.

***Shouyi Wang and John Knoepfle's translation (1989: 88) (note that no capital letter is applied throughout the poem):** written on the wall of xilin monastery*
behold this world horizontally
and it appears all ranges
or stare at it vertically
and peaks scrape the clouds

high or low
far or near
all this individuality
teeming in diversity

how can we recognize
the real face of lushan
we who wander here
so deep in the mountains

***Burton Watson's translation (see Wen 1989: 251):** Written on the Wall of West Forest Temple*
From the side, a whole range; from the end, a single peak:
Far, near, high, low, no two parts alike.
Why can't I tell the true shape of Lu-shan?
Because I myself am in the mountain.

Yuanchong Xu's (2000a: 139) translation: *Written on the Wall of West Forest Temple*
It's a range viewed in face and peaks viewed from one side,
Assuming different shapes viewed from far and wide.
Of Lu Mountains we cannot make out the true face,
For we are lost in the heart of the very place.

The four translations above will serve as the data for our analysis in this chapter. Our analytical perspectives will meanwhile be related to our discussions in the other chapters. In the next section, we will first provide a short introduction to the chapters in this book.

1.5 A synopsis of the chapters in this book

Along with Chapter 1 (Introduction) and Chapter 14 (Epilogue), the remaining 12 chapters deal with the various issues involved in English translations of ancient Chinese poems. Chapter 2 (Experiential analysis), Chapter 3 (Logical analysis), Chapter 4 (Interpersonal analysis), and Chapter 5 (Textual analysis) respectively explore the English translations of *Qing Ming* (清明), a poem written by DU Mu (杜牧) from the Tang Dynasty in the perspectives of experiential, logical, interpersonal and textual metafunctions in Systemic Functional Linguistics.

Chapter 6 (Verbal process and text structure) analyses *Xun Yin Zhe Bu Yu* (寻隐者不遇), composed by JIA Dao (贾岛), a poet in the Tang Dynasty, in the perspectives of verbal process and text structure. One focus of analysis is how turns are defined.

Chapter 7 (A comparative study of Chinese and English discourse) attempts to compare Chinese and English discourse. It analyses and compares *Fu Rong Lou Song Xin Jian* (芙蓉楼送辛渐) by WANG Changling (王昌龄), a Tang Dynasty poet, with its English translations in the perspectives of cohesion, logico-semantic relation, thematic structure and information focus.

Chapter 8 (Formal equivalence in translation) compares *Tian Jing Sha Qiu Si* (天净沙·秋思), a short lyric composed by MA Zhiyuan [马致远] in the Yuan Dynasty, with its English translations, based on the principle of formal equivalence in translation studies. The purpose of the comparison is to investigate the significance of formal equivalence in the translation of poems and lyrics.

Chapter 9 (Translating dynamic and static meaning) studies *Jiang Xue* (江雪) by LIU Zongyuan (柳宗元), a Tang Dynasty poet, and its English translations. In the analysis, emphasis is given to the realization of dynamic and static meaning as well as the relationship between form and meaning.

Chapter 10 (Proper nouns and their English translations) explores the English translations of proper nouns in poetry by selecting ZHANG Ji's (张继) *Feng Qiao Ye Bo* (枫桥夜泊), WANG Changling's (王昌龄) *Fu Rong Lou Song Xin Jian* (芙蓉楼送辛渐), LI Bai's (李白) *Huang He Lou Song Meng Hao Ran Zhi Guang Ling* (黄鹤楼送孟浩然之广陵) and DU Mu's (杜牧) *Bo Qin Huai* (泊秦淮) as data.

Chapter 11 (Quoting-reporting in English translations) discusses quoting-reporting in poetry and how quoting-reporting is rendered in the English translations. Chapter 12 (Translating person into English) deals with the choice of person in ancient poems and their translations, involving issues such as the choice of personal pronoun. Chapter 13 (Choice of tense in English translations) investigates the selection of tense in the English translations of ancient poems, exploring how different choices in tense lead to different meanings.

Finally, Chapter 14 (Epilogue: A functional linguistic approach to translation studies) provides a survey of linguistic approaches to translation studies. It also illustrates the application of the various steps of functional discourse analysis to translation studies.

1.6 Analysis of the English translations of *Ti Xi Lin Bi*

In the previous section, we briefly sketched the main points to be discussed in this book. Here, we will examine SU Shi's *Ti Xi Lin Bi* and its English translations in terms of the perspectives to be discussed in the book. This analysis, which is comprehensive but not detailed, simply represents one attempt at exploring the English translations of a poem.

1.6.1 Experiential analysis

We can interpret the original poem – that is, "横看成岭侧成峰 / 远近高低各不同" (*héng kàn chéng lǐng cè chéng fēng / yuǎn jìn gāo dī gè bù tóng*; horizontal look become range side become peak / far near high low all not same), in the following way: If we/you see the mountain horizontally, it will be a whole range; however, if we/you see it from one side, it will become a peak; from far or near, high or low, it has many different looks. Thus, it would be better to construe the two lines in the original as a behavioral or mental process. In this respect, the four translations are all appropriate. We can first look at the translation by Shouyi Wang and John Knoepfle (1989):

Example (1)
behold this world horizontally
and it appears all ranges
or stare at it vertically
and peaks scrape the clouds

high or low
far or near
all this individuality
teeming in diversity

In Example (1), the two verbs – "behold" and "stare" – construe behavioral processes. In contrast, in Changsheng Wan and Xianzhong Wang's translation, we find a relational process realized by "become" and a change in the narrative perspective:

Example (2)
The sidelong ranges become steep peaks in a vertical view,
The scenes so vary when seen from high or low, from far or near.

In Example (2), Wan and Wang use a mental process realized by "(are) seen" in the second line of their translation. This choice is also appropriate. In comparison with Wang and Knoepfle's translation, although different choices are selected, both renditions are satisfactory. Similarly, in Yuanchong Xu's (2000a: 139) translation, "(are) viewed" is applied, which is a mental process and is thus also appropriate.

Furthermore, by following Shu Wen's (1989: 252) discussion, Watson applies an elliptical sentence in his translation. We can add the omitted parts back:

Example (3)
Seen from the side, *it is* a whole range; *seen* from the end, *it is* a single peak:
Far, near, high, low, no two parts *are* alike.

In Example (3), "seen", which is the same as "seen" in Wan and Wang's translation and "viewed" in Xu's translation, realizes a mental process and appropriately indicates the meaning in the original poem.

Although different choices are made in the selection of other process types in the four translations, they have all appropriately expressed the artistic conception in the original. For instance, "不识庐山真面目" (*bù shí lú shān zhēn miàn mù*; not recognize Lu-Mount real appearance) is rendered differently in the four translations:

Example (4) Wan and Wang's translation:
The genuine features of Lushan Mountain are strange to you

Example (5) Wang and Knoepfle's translation:
how can we recognize the real face of lushan

Example (6) Watson's translation:
Why can't I tell the true shape of Lu-shan?

Example (7) Xu's translation:
Of Lu Mountains we cannot make out the true face

In Example (4), a relational process is used, whereas in Examples (5), (6) and (7), mental processes are applied. We can also find differences in the participants involved in the processes. In terms of meaning and artistic conception, Example (4) is less appropriate compared with the other three examples, as it applies a relational process that cannot indicate how participants view things.

The fourth line of the original – that is, "只缘身在此山中" (*zhǐ yuán shēn zài cǐ shān zhōng*; only because body be in this mountain in) – provides the reason for the third line, "不识庐山真面目" (*bù shí lú shān zhēn miàn* mù; not recognize Lu-Mount real appearance). Relational processes are applied in three translations:

Example (8) Wan and Wang's translation:
Because your situation is within this mountain's bounding sphere.

Example (9) Watson's translation:
Because I myself am in the mountain.

Example (10) Xu's translation:
For we are lost in the heart of the very place.

Example (11) Wang and Knoepfle's translation:
we who wander here so deep in the mountains

In contrast, Watson's translation is the most appropriate, as it properly expresses the meaning in the original. For Wan and Wang's translation, its shortcoming lies in the fact that "your situation" rather than "you" (or "we" and "I") is adopted to function as the Carrier involved in the relational process. In Xu's translation, "lost" is used, which indicates a meaning not seen in the original. In Wang and Knoepfle's translation, a material process is selected, which is distant from the meaning in the original.

As revealed by our analysis above, although the same process type is used in different translations, variations can be caused by the different participants or the different verbs that realize the process; hence, the translations vary in the expression of meaning in the original.

1.6.2 Logical analysis

In terms of interdependency (taxis) and logico-semantic relation (see Section 3.2 for more discussion), the four lines in SU Shi's original have formed two clause complexes. Two logical relations are involved between the clauses in the clause complex, including both parataxis and hypotaxis.

Example (12)
横看成岭侧成峰，远近高低各不同。(*héng kàn chéng lǐng cè chéng fèng, yuǎn jìn gāo dī gè bù* tóng; horizontal look become ridge side become peak, far near high low each not same) (paratactic extension)

Example (13)
不识庐山真面目，只缘身在此山中。(*bù shí lú shān zhēn miàn mù, zhǐ yuán shēn zài cǐ shān zhōng*; not recognize Lu-Mount real appearance, only because body be in this mountain in) (hypotactic enhancement)

In translating Example (12), the same choices of tactic relation and logico-semantic type (i.e. paratactic extension) are selected in translations by Wan and Wang, Wang and Knoepfle, and Watson. Xu's translation is different from these three in selecting hypotactic enhancement:

Example (14) Xu's translation
It's a range viewed in face and peaks viewed from one side,
Assuming different shapes viewed from far and wide.

With the application of "assuming ..." in Xu's translation, the tactic relation between the two clauses is changed to hypotactic enhancement. The second clause is no longer an extension of the first clause, as seen in the original, but rather foregrounds the hypotactic relation and highlights the meaning in the first clause. In terms of logico-semantic relation, Xu's translation may not be as good as the other three translations.

For the English translations of Example (13), in the translations by Wan and Wang, Watson and Xu, a clause complex indicating reason is adopted to render the last two lines of the original poem. However, in terms of tactic relation, hypotaxis is applied in translations by Wan and Wang as well as by Watson, while parataxis is selected in Xu's translation. Such variation is caused by "cause" and "for", which serve connective purposes:

Example (15)
Wan and Wang's translation:
The genuine features of Lushan Mountain are strange to you,
Because your situation is within this mountain's bounding sphere.
Watson's translation:
Why can't I tell the true shape of Lu-shan?
Because I myself am in the mountain.

Example (16)
Xu's translation:
Of Lu Mountains we cannot make out the true face,
For we are lost in the heart of the very place.

In Wang and Knoepfle's translation, the third and fourth lines of the original – that is, "不识庐山真面目，只缘身在此山中" (*bù shí lú shān zhēn miàn mù, zhǐ yuán shēn zài cǐ shān zhōng*; not recognize Lu-Mount real appearance, only because body be in this mountain in) are rendered as follows:

Example (17)
how can we recognize
the real face of lushan
we who wander here
so deep in the mountains

In a strict sense, Example (17) is a clause rather than a clause complex. In terms of structure, however, "how can we recognize the real face of lushan" is the major part and the following part – that is, "we who wander here so deep in the mountains" – indicates an appended meaning, providing a semantic interpretation to "we" in the preceding line. In Wang and Knoepfle's translation, the reason is not stated as directly as in the translations by Wan and Wang or Watson. In Xu's translation, the reason indicated by "for", which serves to combine two clauses, is also not as direct as the translations by Wan and Wang or Watson; thus, the choice of "for" not only changes the tactic relationship between clauses, but also influences the expression of "reason" in terms of meaning.

1.6.3 Interpersonal analysis

In the process of communication, a speaker can choose their speech role according to their communicative purpose. For instance, they can state their opinion, ask a question or demand the addressee to do certain things. As we can see, there are three delicate choices in the system of MOOD.

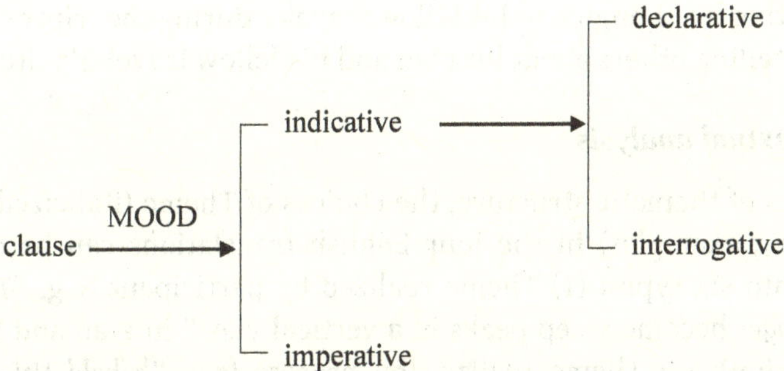

Figure 1.1. Basic choices in the system of MOOD (cf. Halliday & Matthiessen 2014: 24)

Differences are found in the choice of mood in the four English translations of the poem. First, in the translations by Wan and Wang, and by Xu, all clauses are of declarative mood. Second, in Watson's translation, declarative mood is applied in three lines, while in one line (i.e. the third line), interrogative mood is used. Third, in Wang and Knoepfle's translation, imperative mood is selected in two clauses: interrogative mood in one clause and declarative mood in the remaining clauses, as shown in Example (18):

Example (18)
imperative: behold this world horizontally / or stare at it vertically /
interrogative: how can we recognize / the real face of lushan / we who wander here / so deep in the mountains /
declarative: and it appears all ranges / and peaks scrape the clouds / high or low / far or near / all this individuality / teeming in diversity

The choice of mood in the translations can determine the expression of meaning and artistic conception. For instance, in the translations by

Wan and Wang, and by Xu, all clauses are of declarative mood, indicating the meaning of description. In Watson's translation, interrogative clause is seen in the third line, hence forming a pair of question and answer by the same interactant. In Wang and Knoepfle's translation, due to the choices of imperative and interrogative mood, the sense of interaction is highlighted. In translations by Wang and Knoepfle as well as by Watson, although interrogative mood is selected to render "不识庐山真面目" (*bù shí lú shān zhēn miàn mù*; not recognize Lu-Mount real appearance), the pronouns (i.e. "we" and "I") are different in terms of number, thereby indicating different interpersonal meanings. When "I" is used, the poet may want to inform his own situation to the addressee. When "we" is selected, two possibilities are involved: (1) the poet is recounting his thoughts to his fellow traveler during the trip; or (2) the poet is telling others about his own and his fellow traveler's situation.

1.6.4 Textual analysis

In terms of thematic structure, the choices of Theme (italicized in the following examples) in the four English translations can be categorized into six types: (1) Theme realized by participant (e.g. "*The side long ranges* become steep peaks in a vertical view" in Wan and Wang's translation); (2) Theme realized by process (e.g. "*behold* this world horizontally" in Wang and Knoepfle's translation); (3) Theme realized by circumstance – that is, circumstantial element (e.g. "*From the side*, a whole range; from the end, a single peak" in Watson's translation); (4) Theme realized by connective plus participant (e.g. "*Because your situation* is within this mountain's bounding sphere" in Wan and Wang's translation, "*and it* appears all ranges" in Wang and Knoepfle's translation); (5) Theme realized by connective plus process (verb) (e.g. "*or stare* at it vertically" in Wang and Knoepfle's translation); and (6) Theme realized by displaced modifier (e.g. "*Of Lu Mountains* we cannot make out the true face" in Xu's translation).

When Themes are realized by different elements, clauses will have different points of departure and different points of focus. With different points of departure in narration or description, the meaning and the information focus in the clause will also be different. For example, in the first line of Wan and Wang's translation, "the sidelong ranges" serves as the point of departure in narration, thus revealing the appearance of "the horizontal range" at the beginning of the clause; in Wang and Knoepfle's translation, the first clause selects "behold" as its Theme and asks readers to look at the scenery before their eyes. Such different thematic structures convey completely different meanings. Take the third line in Xu's translation – that is, "Of Lu Mountains we cannot make out the true face" – as another example, a displaced modifier – that is, "Of Lu Mountains" – here functions as the Theme of the clause. (One can compare this line with "We cannot make out the true face of Lu Mountains"). The reason for selecting a marked rather than an unmarked thematic choice in this line is perhaps to place "face" at the end of this line, forming a rhyme with the word "place" at the end of the fourth line. Therefore, the motivation for placing "Of Lu Mountains" in the position of Theme is likely to achieve beauty in sound.

In terms of cohesion, the application of "it" in some English translations deserves our attention. For instance, in Wang and Knoepfle's translation, the two instances of "it" both belong to the category of "endophoric reference: anaphoric reference", with "it" referring to "this world" in the first line, whereas in Xu's translation, "it" is categorized as "exophoric reference" and refers to "the mountain" – an object outside language (or discourse).

1.6.5 Verbal process and text structure

Among the four English translations, verbal process is only seen in Wang and Knoepfle's translation, as well as that by Watson. We find projected clauses of verbal processes in both the last stanza of Wang and Knoepfle's translation – "how can we recognize / the real face of lushan / we who wander here / so deep in the mountains" – and the third and fourth lines in Watson's translation – "Why can't I tell the true shape of Lu-shan? / Because I myself am in the mountain." – while the projecting clauses of these verbal processes are not seen. In this way, we can conclude that the two projected clauses are in fact quoted speeches, which function differently compared with other narrative (and descriptive) clauses in the translation. Further, we can consider the first stanza in Wang and Knoepfle's translation – "behold this world horizontally / and it appears all ranges / or stare at it vertically / and peaks scrape the clouds" – as a projected clause, since it is very likely to be said by the poet to his fellow traveler.

In terms of discourse structure, SU Shi's original poem is a narration and description; translations by Wan and Wang, and by Xu, are the same as the original and also function as narrations and descriptions.

However, the structure of Wang and Knoepfle's translation deserves our attention: its first stanza – "behold this world horizontally / and it appears all ranges / or stare at it vertically / and peaks scrape the clouds" – contains the poet's words to his fellow traveler, while its second stanza – "high or low / far or near / all this individuality / teeming in diversity" – serves as a description, and the third stanza – "how can we recognize / the real face of lushan / we who wander here / so deep in the mountains" – functions as a question, which can be either used between the poet and others or said by the poet to himself. Despite being similar to Wang and Knoepfle's translation, Watson's translation is merely composed of two parts, with the first two lines providing a description of the behavior and the third and fourth lines serving as the questions and answer uttered by the poet himself.

1.6.6 A comparative study of Chinese and English discourse

Various discussions in this book are related to the comparative study of discourse, as highlighted in Chapter 7. The four English translations of *Ti Xi Lin Bi* have interpreted the original in different perspectives: some interpretations are identical or similar to the original, while some differ significantly from the original. By comparing the original with its translations, we find that some variations are caused by the differences between English and Chinese. For example, as suggested by various scholars, Chinese is a meaning-oriented language, while English is a form-oriented language; thus, some forms not used in Chinese, such as personal pronouns, must be added back into the English translations (see Section 3.5).

Some observations based on the comparison between the original and its translations deserve our attention. Take the third and four lines in the original for example: "不识庐山真面目，只缘身在此山中" (*bù shí lú shān zhēn miàn mù zhǐ yuán shēn zài cǐ shān zhōng*; not recognize Lu-Mount real appearance, only because body be in this mountain in). The four English translations vary in terms of meaning:

Example (19) Wan and Wang's translation
The genuine features of Lushan Mountain are strange to you,
Because your situation is within this mountain's bounding sphere.

Example (20) Wang and Knoepfle's translation
how can we recognize
the real face of lushan

we who wander here
so deep in the mountains

Example (21) Watson's translation
Why can't I tell the true shape of Lu-shan?
Because I myself am in the mountain.

Example (22) Xu's translation
Of Lu Mountains we cannot make out the true face,
For we are lost in the heart of the very place.

Some points need to be made regarding to the third and fourth lines and their translations: First, "真 面目" (*zhēn miàn mù*; real appearance) in the original is respectively translated as "the genuine features", "the real face", "the true shape" and "the true face". Second, in translations by Wang and Knoepfle, Watson and Xu, it is "we" who cannot tell the real face of Lu Mountain – we cannot differentiate which genuine face belongs to Lu Mountain; whereas Wan and Wang render this line as "The genuine features of Lushan Mountain are strange to you", leading to differences not only in the pronouns "I/we" and "you", but also in the point of departure of discourse (i.e. Theme) (see Chapter 5) and in process type (see Chapter 2). In contrast, among the four translations, Wan and Wang's is distant from the original in meaning, and differences between the translations are found not only in the starting point of narration, but also in the choice of participant. Third, the fourth line of the original is translated in a similar way compared with the third line; apart from Wan and Wang's translation, the other three translations all indicate the meaning of "I am (we are) in the mountain". However, the three translations differ in terms of realization: Watson adopts a relational process (realized by "am') to indicate the original meaning in a simple manner; Wang and Knoepfle adopt a material process (realized by "wander') to describe the action conducted by the participant "we" rather than the state of the participant; Xu also applies a relational process, but the Attribute is realized by "lost in the heart of the very place", thus increasing the meaning of "losing one's way" in the translation. Despite all the differences, these three translations are more appropriate than Wan and Wang's, as Wan and Wang merely discuss "your situation" rather than the state the participant is in.

The nouns in the original are not marked by plurality; however, when translated into English, the translators have to take the single or plural forms into consideration. For instance, "岭" (*lǐng*; ridge), "峰"

(*fēng*; peak) and "山" (*shān*; mountain) in the original are translated as nouns in both singular and plural forms:

Example (23)
"岭" (*lǐng*; ridge)
plural: "ranges" (Wan and Wang's translation), "ranges" (Wang and Knoepfle's translation)
singular: "a whole range" (Watson's translation), "a range" (Xu's translation)

Example (24)
"峰" (*fēng*; peak)
plural: "peaks" (Wan and Wang's translation), "peaks" (Wang and Knoepfle's translation), "peaks" (Xu's translation)
singular: "a single peak" (Watson's translation)

Example (25)
"山" (*shān*; mountain)
plural: "mountains" (Wang and Knoepfle's translation), "the mountain" (Watson's translation)
singular: "this mountain" (Wan and Wang's translation)

In the original, the object – Phenomenon – that is "looked at horizontally" is not mentioned, while different words are used to refer to it in the translations: in Wang and Knoepfle's translation, "this world" is used; in Xu's translation, "it" is adopted to indicate exophoric reference; in Watson's translation, the object is omitted, which is the same choice compared with the original; in Wan and Wang's translation, "the sidelong ranges" is selected as the given information or shared knowledge, serving as the point of departure – that is, Theme – of the clause. We would here consider Watson's choice as a better translation.

1.6.7 Formal equivalence in translation

In translation studies, "formal equivalence" and "functional equivalence" are sometimes regarded as standards of translation quality assessment. The issue of "formal equivalence" will be explored further in Chapter 8. In this section, to compare SU Shi's original poem and its four English translations in the perspective of "formal equivalence", two points can be made.

The first involves the issue of form, which is related to the "beauty in form" suggested by scholars regarding translation. The original consists of four lines, each of which has seven characters. In translations by Wan and Wang, and by Xu, a four-line style is adopted to render the four lines in the original and the numbers of syllable in each line are basically the same. Although Watson's translation is not equivalent to the original in form compared with translations by Wan and Wang, and by Xu, a similar four-line style is adopted, with one line in the translation being adopted to render one line in the Chinese original. In Wang and Knoepfle's translation, equivalence in form is abandoned: the first line in the original is rendered as four lines that constitute a stanza; similarly, the second line in the original is rendered as four lines, constituting the second stanza; the final two lines in the original are translated as four lines and form one stanza. A careful examination of Wang and Knoepfle's translation will reveal its inappropriateness. The two translators, taking Arthur Waley's (1938) approach, paraphrase the original and aim to convey meaning. Although their translation is arranged like a poem, much revision is needed both in the equivalence of line arrangement and in their faithfulness to the original. In simple terms, Wang and Knoepfle's translation is not equivalent to the original in form; however, as pointed out by Weng (1982: 47), we cannot regard a poem that is inequivalent to the original in form as a bad translation (see Chapter 8).

Second, we need to consider the "beauty in sound" and one of such considerations is the end rhyme in each line. In translations by Wan and Wang, and by Xu, end rhymes are found, with the pattern being a^b^a^b in Wan and Wang's translation and a^a^b^b in Xu's translation. No choice of end rhyme is found in the other two translations, despite the fact that rhyming also contributes to formal equivalence in translation.

1.6.8 Translating dynamic and static meanings

In the first and second lines of SU Shi's original, we find a hint of "dynamic" meaning, encompassing the variation from ridge to peak and the change of height. In Wan and Wang's translation, such "dynamic" meaning is expressed through verbs – "become" and "vary'; in contrast, in Watson's translation, elliptical sentences are applied (see Section 1.6.1), which lead to the omission of verbs in the structure, thus the "dynamic" meaning cannot be expressed.

In Wang and Knoepfle's translation, "dynamic" meaning is indicated by "it appears all ranges" and "peaks scrape the clouds". Same as Wan and Wang's translation, in these two translations, the meaning in the original is rendered appropriately.

1.6.9 Translating proper nouns

In SU Shi's original, two proper nouns are applied, namely "西林" (*xī lín*; Xilin [west-forest]) and "庐山" (*lú shān*; Mount Lu). As suggested by Haiou Zhang (2001: 134), "西林" (*xī lín*; Xilin [west-forest]) is the name of a temple, which was located in Mount Lu in Jiangxi. It was built in the Jin Dynasty and changed its name to Qianming Temple (乾明寺) in the Song Dynasty. The translations of "西林" (*xī lín*; Xilin [west-forest]) include three types: (i) "Xilin Temple" (Wan and Wang's translation), (ii) "Xilin Monastery" (Wang and Knoepfle's translation; note that no capitalized letter is used in their translation, with this proper noun being included), and (iii) "West Forest Temple" (Watson's translation, Xu's translation). The differences among these three choices are as follows: firstly, whether "寺" (*sì*; temple) should be translated as "temple" or "monastery'; secondly, whether "西林" (*xī lín*; Xilin [west-forest]) should be translated as Xilin based on pinyin or as "West Forest" based on its meaning.

In terms of the strategy of translating "庐山" (*lú shān*; Lu-Mount), the different translations include: (i) "Lushan Mountain" (Wan and Wang's translation), (ii) "Lushan" (Wang and Knoepfle's translation, Watson's translation), and (iii) "Lu Mountains" (Xu's translation). Their differences are as follows: Firstly, which is a better choice among "Lushan", "Lushan Mountain", and "Lu Mountain"? Secondly, if adopting mountain to translate "山" (*shān*; mountain), whether singular form or plural form should be used? Regarding the translation of proper nouns, it is sometimes difficult to make choices (see also Pan 1994).

1.6.10 Translating quoting-reporting

The issue of quoting-reporting has already been explored in Section 1.6.5. Based on our previous discussion, in Wang and Knoepfle's translation, "how can we recognize the real face of lushan we who wander here so deep in the mountains" is a projected clause and functions as the quoted part; in Watson's translation, "Why can't I tell the true shape of Lu-shan? Because I myself am in the mountain." also serves as the quoted part. However, these two instances are not typical examples of quoting-reporting, as there is neither projected clause (the quoting-reporting sentence) nor a marker of quoting-reporting in the translations.

1.6.11 Choice of person

In terms of the choice of person, three forms of person (highlighted in italics) are applied in the four English translations:

Example (26)
Second person
Wan and Wang's translation:
The genuine features of Lushan Mountain are strange to *you*,
Because *your* situation is within this mountain's bounding sphere.

Example (27)
First person plural
Wang and Knoepfle's translation:
how can *we* recognize
the real face of lushan
we who wander here
so deep in the mountains
Xu's translation:
Of Lu Mountains *we* cannot make out the true face,
For *we* are lost in the heart of the very place.

Example (28)
First person singular
Watson's translation:
Why can't *I* tell the true shape of Lu-shan?
Because *I myself* am in the mountain.

Variation in the choice of personal pronoun and number has indicated different meanings. For instance, second person is applied in Wan and Wang's translation, as seen in the third line, i.e. "Because *your* situation is within this mountain's bounding sphere", the narrator (i.e. the poet) adopts a condescending manner. In contrast, when first person is applied, the poet is then recounting his own situation, leading to a completely different meaning compared with second person. For example, the third line of Watson's translation – "Why can't *I* tell the true shape of Lu-shan" is very different from Wan and Wang's "The genuine features of Lushan Mountain are strange to *you*". Further, we note that the choice of "I" or "we" will also lead to differences in meaning, as previously discussed in Section 1.6.3.

1.6.12 Choice of tense

On a surface level, the four translations have all applied simple present tense; however, a careful examination suggests that the instances of simple present tense can be categorized into the following three types:

1. Simple present tense used in narration

In this way, an individual's experience restricted by time and space has become a universal and constant experience. We can also change the simple present tense in these instances to simple past tense. One can compare the following choices:

> *Example (29) Wan and Wang's translation*
> The sidelong ranges *become* steep peaks in a vertical view,
> The scenes so *vary* when seen from high or low, from far or near.
>
> *Example (30)*
> The sidelong ranges *became* steep peaks in a vertical view,
> The scenes so *varied* when seen from high or low, from far or near.

Naturally, by changing the tense, the meaning indicated is also changed because form is the realization of meaning (see Huang 1999: 106–15).

2. Simple present tense used in imperative clause

Tense choices of this category cannot be changed to simple past tense because the simple present tense here indicates future behaviors. The first stanza in Wang and Knoepfle's translation is an example of this type.

3. Simple present tense used in quotation

One example of this kind is the third and fourth lines in Watson's translation: "Why can't I tell the true shape of Lu-shan? / Because I myself am in the mountain." These instances of simple present tense can be changed to simple past tense to indicate conditions at a certain time in the past. Different from the first type of tense, this type of simple present tense is not adopted to indicate universal and constant experiences.

1.6.13 Summary

The previous sub-sections serve to analyse SU Shi's *Ti Xi Lin Bi* and its English translations in 12 different perspectives, which will be elaborated further in the remainder of the book. Our analyses are simple and introductory. However, due to limited space, the theories and discussions are only presented in a brief way. Despite being simple, our exploration of English translations of SU Shi's *Ti Xi Lin Bi* has revealed all the topics to be examined in the following chapters. We also find that the analyses in different perspectives have not identified the best translations. To cite the poem we analyse, the translations indeed "vary when seen from high or low, from far or near" (Wan & Wang 2000: 212).

1.7 Conclusion

As an introduction to the book, this chapter has selected SU Shi's *Ti Xi Lin Bi* and its four English translations as data by conducting simple analyses using the perspectives to be discussed in this book. We hope our preliminary and introductory analyses can reveal the scope, method and framework of this book. In addition, we select *Ti Xi Lin Bi* for our discussion with special purposes. As informed by this poem, without a comprehensive, multi-perspective and multi-faceted investigation, we cannot truly understand a phenomenon and will often reach a partial and subjective conclusion. In terms of the translation of ancient Chinese poems, if we merely investigate this research area by drawing on traditional research paradigms in translation studies, we may be very likely to overlook some key issues, hence not being able to gain a clear picture of the scene. In this way, our linguistic explorations of English translations of ancient Chinese poems indeed have some positive significance and are very likely to illuminate translation studies.

We began this chapter with SU Shi's *Ti Xi Lin Bi*. Let us end the chapter with the opening poem in CAO Xueqin's (曹雪芹) *Hongloumeng* (红楼梦)[1] and Xinqu Huang's (2002: 197) English translation:

满 纸 荒唐 言，
mǎn zhǐ huāng táng yán,
full paper absurd word,

一 把 辛酸 泪！
yì bǎ xīn suān lèi!
one handful bitter tear!

都 云 作者 痴，
dōu yún zuò zhě chī,
all say author foolish,

谁 解 其中 味？
shuí jiě qí zhōng wèi?
who understand inside message?

Pages full of absurd words
Soaked with bitter tears;
All say he is a fool in love,
But who his message hears!

We hope our readers can apply the methods we introduce in this book to an analysis of this poem and its English translations (see Appendix 1 for other English translations (Cao 1973; Liu 2003; Yang & Yang 2001a, 2001b).

Note

1. Translators" note: *Hongloumeng* (红楼梦, also known as *A Dream of Red Mansions* or *The Stone of the Stone*), written by CAO Xueqin (曹雪芹), is regarded as one of the four great classic novels in China. Hailed as an encyclopaedia of feudal society in eighteenth-century Beijing, the novel provides a chronicle of the noble family. It begins with how a sentient stone reincarnates as Jia Baoyu – the capricious heir of the Jia clan – and depicts his emotional entanglements with his frail cousin Lin Daiyu. After composing 80 chapters of the book, CAO Xueqin passed away and left his manuscript unfinished. The remaining 40 chapters were then composed by GAO E (高鹗).

Chapter 2

Experiential analysis

2.1 Introduction

In Chinese academia, valuable discussions have taken place about the translation of ancient Chinese poems into English. However, it seems that scholars have not reached a consensus on the standards of translation. One widely discussed topic is whether poetry translation should follow Yuanchong Xu's (e.g. 1979a, 1979b, 1987, 1990a) standards of "the three beauties" (i.e. "beauty in meaning", "beauty in sound" and "beauty in form"). Some scholars are in favor of these standards (e.g. Chu 1992), while some dispute them (e.g. Liu 1982, 1986, 1989). There is therefore no unified standard for translating ancient Chinese poems into English.

When commenting on the English translations of ancient Chinese poems, Chinese scholars mainly argue from angles of literary criticism and literary translation. Such analyses are largely subjective and the discussions are based mainly on impressions and experiences. In this book, we will not deal with the advantages and disadvantages of this kind of analysis since there will always be a fair public opinion on this issue. In this chapter, we approach poetry translation in the perspective of Halliday's (1994) Systemic Functional Linguistics (SFL) by conducting an experiential analysis of *Qing Ming* (清明), a poem written by DU Mu (杜牧) in the Tang Dynasty, and its English translations. Our analysis is based on the experiential metafunction – one of the metafunctions in SFL (see Chapters 3, 4 and 5 for analyses based on the logical, interpersonal and textual metafunctions; for the basics and methods of SFL analysis, see Halliday 1994; Hu 1994; Hu, Zhu & Zhang 1989; Huang 2001a; Thompson 1996).

2.2 A sketch of the experiential metafunction

Metafunction is a very important organizing principle in Halliday's Systemic Functional Grammar (SFG). The experiential metafunction, one of the metafunctions, deals with how people use language to (1) talk about their experiences of the world (including both the outside real world and their inner world) and (2) describe the event or situation that takes place around them. As a reflection of people's world views, language deals with issues that express such world views – for example, going-on and state, thing, attribute, and background.

The experiential metafunction involves various systems, with the most important one being TRANSITIVITY. The TRANSITIVITY system functions to indicate the experiences of the outside world and the inner world with several processes and to point out the participants and circumstances involved in the processes. Halliday (1994) differentiates six major process types in the grammar of English: material process, mental process, relational process, verbal process, behavioral process and existential process. Halliday (1994: 143) also suggests that there is a meteorological process – a special process type dealing with weather phenomena, which is located between existential process and material process.

2.3 Experiential analysis of the original version of *Qing Ming*

In terms of transitivity, which models on the experiential metafunction, four process types are identified in the original of *Qing Ming*:

1. meteorological process: "清明 时节 雨 纷纷" (*qīng míng shí jié yǔ fēn fēn*; Qingming season rain succession),
2. relational process: "路 上 行人 欲 断 魂" (*lù shàng xíng rén yù duàn hún*; road on pedestrian will lose soul),
3. verbal process: "借 问 酒家 何 处 有" (*jiè wèn jiǔ jiā hé chù yǒu*; may ask tavern what place have),
4. material process: "牧 童 遥 指 杏 花 村" (*mù tóng yáo zhǐ xìng huā cūn*; herd child far point apricot flower village).

When carrying out a transitivity analysis by following the procedures of functional text analysis (see Huang 2001a, 2001b; see also Hu 1994), we need to determine the participants and circumstances once the process types are identified.

(1) In the clause with meteorological process, "清明 时节" (*qīng míng shí jié*; Qingming season) functions as a circumstance and "雨 纷纷" (*yǔ fēn fēn*; rain succession) functions as the process. It is also possible to analyse "雨" (*yǔ*; rain) as the process, and "纷纷" (*fēn fēn*; succession), which provides elaboration to the process, as an expanding or extending element of the process. There are also scholars who treat "纷纷" (*fēn fēn*; succession) as a circumstance.

(2) In the clause with relational process, "路 上 行人" (*lù shàng xíng* rén; road on pedestrian) is the Carrier and "欲 断 魂" (*yù duàn hún*; will lose soul) is the process and Attribute.

(3) In the clause with verbal process, "借" (*jiè*; may) functions as a circumstance indicating interpersonal meaning, "问" (*wèn*; ask) is the process, while the invisible Sayer is not stated in the poem. "酒家 何 处 有" (*jiǔ jiā hé chù yǒu*; tavern what place have), as a projected clause, includes an existential process, with "酒家" (*jiǔ jiā*; tavern) being the Existent, "何 处" (*hé chù*; what place) being a circumstance and "有" (*yǒu*; have) being the process.

(4) In the clause with material process, "指" (*zhǐ*; point) functions as the process, "牧 童" (*mù tóng*; herd child) as the Actor, "杏 花 村" (*xìng huā cūn*; apricot flower village) as the Goal, and "遥" (*yáo*; far) as a circumstance.

When interpreting the original of *Qing Ming*, the following points need clarification, as they can become obstacles to translating the poem:

- Does "清明 时节" (*qīng míng shí jié*; Qingming season) refer to the specific day of Qingming Festival (Ching Ming Festival, Tomb-Sweeping Day) or the rainy spring season that includes Qingming Festival in general?
- Who does "路 上 行人" (*lù shàng xíng* rén; road on pedestrian) refer to? Some scholars hold that "行人" (*xíng* rén; pedestrian) indicates "travelers that are away from home" (see Xiao et al. 1983: 1101 for Ruchang Zhou's discussion), while some scholars think that it indicates "the author himself" (Chen & Huang 2000: 76; Ji 2001: 54). However, if "行人" (*xíng* rén; pedestrian) does not refer to the author himself, should its English translation be in singular form or plural form?
- Who is performing the action of "借 问" (*jiè wèn*; may ask)? Could it be "行人" (*xíng* rén; pedestrian) or the author himself? If it

were "行人" (*xíng* rén; pedestrian), could it be one pedestrian or many? What, then, is the relationship between "行人" (*xíng* rén; pedestrian) and the author?

- Is there one "酒家" (*jiǔ jiā*; tavern) or several?
- Is "牧童" (*mù tóng*; herd child) a cow-herd or a shepherd boy? Is he riding a cow or a horse?
- Is "杏花村" (*xìng huā cūn*; apricot flower village) a specific village or a village located amid apricot flowers? Following Ruchang Zhou's (see Xiao et al. 1983: 1102, our translation) explanation, "'杏花村' (*xìng huā cūn*; apricot flower village) is not necessarily the name of a real village and it may not refer to a tavern." Thus, "杏花村" (*xìng huā cūn*; apricot flower village) may refer to "a village located amid apricot flowers" (Chen & Huang 2000: 76; Li & Zhang 2001: 239, our translation), "a village deep in the blossoming apricot woods" (Min Xu 1990: 17, our translation), or "a village where apricot flowers blossom" (Sanqin Press 2000: 108, our translation).

In Section 2.5, we will answer these queries based on our analysis of the English translations.

2.4 Experiential analysis of the English translations

Six English translations of *Qing Ming* will be discussed in this chapter. The translators include Juntao Wu (see Zhang 1996: 30), Tinggan Cai (see Wen 1989: 174), Dayu Sun (1997: 435), Xianyi Yang and Gladys Yang (2001a: 266), Changsheng Wan and Xianzhong Wang (see Zhu 2000: 166) and Yuanchong Xu (2000b: 537).

2.4.1 Experiential analysis of the translations of sentence 1

We will first analyse the translations in terms of process type. For the convenience of comparison, Sections 2.4.1 to 2.4.4 will each deal with the translations of one of the four sentences in the poem. In Table 2.1, we tabulate the experiential analysis of the first sentence.

Table 2.1. Experiential analysis of the first sentence in the English translations of *Qing Ming*

Translator(s)	Process	Participant	Circumstance
Wu	meteorological process: "drizzles"		Quality: "thick" Time: "on the Pure Brightness Day"
Cai	material process: "falls"	Actor: "the rain"	Time: "on All Soul's festive day" Quality: "thick and fast"
Sun	material process: "drizzleth"	Actor: "the rain"	Time: "upon the Clear-and-Bright Feast of spring"
Yang & Yang	meteorological process: "drizzles"		Manner: "endlessly" Time: "during the rainy season in spring"
Wan & Wang	material process: "drips"	Actor: "the ceaseless drizzle"	Time: "all the dismal day"
Xu	material process: "falls"	Actor: "a drizzling rain"	Manner: "like tears" Time: "on the Mourning Day"

We will now analyse the six English translations tabulated in Table 2.1 in terms of process type, participant and circumstance.

Process type and participant

In terms of process type, material processes are found in four of the six translations, while meteorological processes are applied in the other two translations. For the four clauses with material processes, only one participant is involved, namely "the rain", which is realized by "rain" (i.e. "the rain" and "a drizzling rain") in three translations and by "drizzle" (i.e. "the ceaseless drizzle") in the other translation. For meteorological process, there is no participant – "it" here only functions as subject rather than participant (see Halliday 1994: 143); thus, only the process ("drizzle") is involved (see translations by Wu, and by Yang and Yang). In Sun's translation, "drizzle" is also used to function as a process, whereas "the rain" in this clause serves as a participant, hence the process is analyzed as a material rather than a meteorological one.

In terms of the realizations of the processes, we find that "drizzle" (in translations by Wu, Sun, and Yang and Yang) and "drip" (in translation by Wan and Wang) are better choices than "fall" (in translations by

Cai and by Xu) in terms of the expression of artistic conception. When lexical choices of "rain" (in translations by Cai and by Sun: "the rain", translation by Wan and Wang: "the ceaseless drizzle", translation by Xu: "a drizzling rain") are applied as subjects of the clauses, they more vividly describe the scene of the drizzling rain in spring, compared with the non-participant "it" (in translations by Wu and Yang and Yang) that functions as the subject in the clause.

Circumstance

In DU Mu's original, "清明 时节" (*qīng míng shí jié*; Qingming season) functions as a circumstance; while in the six English translations, it is also rendered as circumstances. In the four translations by Wu, Cai, Sun and Xu, "清明时节" (*qīng míng shí jié*; Qingming season) is translated as a proper noun, with the first letters of the content words being capitalized; whereas in the other two translations, it is translated as a common noun (see also discussions in Chapter 10).

However, among the four translations where "清明 时节" (*qīng míng shí jié*; Qingming season) is rendered as a proper noun, the meanings of the circumstances would also vary.

"清明 时节" (*qīng míng shí jié*; Qingming season), as one of the 24 solar terms, falls around 5 April. On this day, the Chinese people follow the custom of sweeping their ancestors' tombs and having an outing in the countryside. The translations by Wu (i.e. "the Pure Brightness Day"), Sun (i.e. "the Clear-and-Bright Feast [of spring]") and Xu (i.e. "the Mourning Day") all have their own characteristics: the first two translators adopt the method of literal translation, with their meanings being less straightforward; the last translator adopts the method of free translation and expresses a more direct meaning. When adopting the method of literal translation, it is also possible to render "清明" (*qīng míng*; Qingming) as "the Clear and Bright Day", "the Qingming Festival" or "the Late Spring Festival Day"; when adopting the method of free translation, choices such as "Day of Tomb-worship" (see Wen 1989: 174–175) and "the Tomb-visiting Day" (as seen in the title of Wan and Wang's translation) are involved. It can further be noted that in Sun's translation, in addition to applying the method of literal translation, notes are added to the translation of "the Clear-and-Bright Feast".

In Cai's translation, "清明" (*qīng míng*; Qingming) is translated as "All Souls' Day". According to Wen (1989: 174, our translation), All Souls' Day, a festival in the Western culture, falls on 2 November and refers to "a festival of the Roman Catholic for people to pray for the souls and to release them from suffering". In terms of remembering the dead, All Souls' Day is similar to the Qingming Festival in China. However, in terms of time, they take place in November and April respectively; "All Souls' Day" also carries a strong religious connotation (see Wen 1989: 174). Thus, the method applied in Cai's translation is domestication.

In translations by Wan and Wang, as well as by Yang and Yang, "清明" (*qīng míng*; Qingming) is rendered as a common noun. On the one hand, in the first line of their translation, Wan and Wang translate the title as "The Tomb-visiting Day" and the festival as "the dismal day", which can be seen as adopting the free translation method. On the other hand, Yang and Yang adopt "the rainy season in spring" to describe the weather in spring in general, while Wan and Wang focus on one particular dismal day. The definite article "the" is applied in both translations, indicating that the narrator is aware of the fact that readers will know which season the rainy season is in (or which day the dismal and gloomy day occurs on). In addition, it can be noted that in the other translation by Xu (2000a: 123), "清明" (*qīng míng*; Qingming), is not translated as a proper noun, but instead as a common noun (i.e. "the mourning day").

"纷纷" (*fēn fēn*; succession) in the original indicates how raindrops have fallen and is depicted by circumstances in four English translations, namely "thick" (Wu's translation), "thick and fast" (Cai's translation), "in spray" (Sun's translation) and "endlessly" (Yang and Yang's translation). However, in Wan and Wang's translation, the action of "雨 纷纷" (*yǔ fēn fēn*; rain succession) is rendered as a nominal group (i.e. "the ceaseless drizzle"). Similarly, in Xu's translation, this action is rendered as a nominal group (i.e. "a drizzling rain"). Moreover, Xu applies "like tears" to elaborate on the scene of the rain, thus emphasizing the desolate nature of the rain in spring.

In Sun's translation, "down" is used to describe "drizzle", while in Xu's translation, "like tears" is adopted to describe "fall". We find that the two structures are applied due to consideration of meter in verse, whereas in a semantic perspective, both "down" and "like tears" can be considered redundant.

In four English translations, prepositions of "on" or "upon" are placed before Qingming Festival. In one translation, "during" is used. In fact, the different word choices have led to variations in meaning, with "on" or "upon" indicating one point in time (*viz.* a certain day) and "during" indicating a period of time (*viz.* a season).

2.4.2 Experiential analysis of the translations of sentence 2

In Table 2.2, we provide an experiential analysis of the six translations of the second sentence in the original – "路上行人欲断魂" (*lù shàng xíng* rén yù duàn hún; road on pedestrian will lose soul).

Table 2.2. Experiential analysis of the second sentence in the English translations of *Qing Ming*

Translator(s)	Process	Participant	Circumstance
Wu	material process: "travel"	Actor: "I"	Manner: "with my heart lost in dismay"
Cai	material process: "move"	Actor: "the men and women"	Manner: "sadly" Place: "along the way"
Sun	material process: "are pining away"	Actor: "pedestrians on countryside ways"	Manner: "in gloom"
Yang & Yang	relational process: "look"	Carrier: "travelers along the road" Attribute: "gloomy and miserable"	
Wan & Wang	material process: "fares"	Actor: "the traveler"	Place: "on the way" Quality: "so broken-hearted"
Xu	material process: "is going to break"	Actor: "the mourner's heart"	Place: "on his way"

From Table 2.2, we find that different choices are made in the six translations. Our analysis will be carried out using three perspectives: process type, participant and circumstance.

Process type

Five translations apply material processes: three of them use verbs indicating "walking and moving" (i.e. "travel" in Wu's translation, "move" in Cai's translation and "fare" in Wan and Wang's translation) and the other two use verbs indicating "weakening and breaking" rather than "walking and moving" (i.e. "pine away" in Sun's translation and "break" in Xu's translation). Yang and Yang, however, choose a relational process by adopting the verb "look" to realize the process.

A relational process is applied in DU Mu's original (see Section 2.3), whereas among the six translations, only Yang and Yang choose a relational process. In terms of the expression of artistic conception, relational process indicates "static" meaning, which possibly plays a more effective role in expressing the emotion and the status of the pedestrians.

Participant

In the five translations (except for that of Xu) using material processes, the participants in four of them are realized by human beings, with different realizations being found. In Wu's translation, the first-person pronoun "I" is used. In the other three translations, nominal groups indicating third-person meaning are applied, of which two are in plural form (Cai's translation: "the men and women", Sun's translation: "pedestrians on countryside ways") and one is in singular form (i.e. Wan and Wang's translation: "the traveler").

In Xu's translation, the Actor in the material clause is not realized by a human being, but by part of the human body (i.e. "the mourner's heart").

Yang and Yang choose a relational process, the Carrier is realized by "travelers along the road" that refers to a human being, and the Attribute is realized by an adjectival group indicating the state of the Carrier (i.e. "gloomy and miserable").

Circumstance

In the original, "路上" (*lù shàng*; road on) serves to modify "行人" (*xíng rén*; pedestrian). Hence, two translations use "路上" (*lù shàng*; road on) as part of the participant, namely as a postmodifier of the head word (Head) in the nominal group (Sun's translation: "[pedestrians] on countryside ways"; Yang and Yang's translation: "[travelers] along the road"). In these two translations, prepositional phrases function as post-modifiers in nominal groups, thus leading to the identical structures of "head word" + "modifier" in the two translations and the original.

In translations by Cai, Wan and Wang, as well as Xu, prepositional phrases that indicate the meaning of "路上" (*lù shàng*; road on) are found (Cai's translation: "along the way"; Wan and Wang's translation: "on the way"; Xu's translation: "on his way"). In these translations, prepositional phrases indicate circumstantial meaning (Place) and do not function as modifiers. It is noted that "on the way" in Wan and Wang's translation can also be analyzed as the postmodifier of "the traveler" rather than as a circumstance. Indeterminacy is involved in the analysis because the word order in this sentence is reversed.

In Wan and Wang's translation, "欲 断 魂" (*yù duàn hún*; will lose soul) is translated as "so broken-hearted" – a circumstance (i.e. Quality) that describes the state of the participant/subject. Such a usage is the same as "thick" in "It drizzles thick on the Pure Brightness Day" (Wu's translation) and "thick and fast" in "The rain falls thick and fast on All Souls' Day" (Cai's translation).

Among the six translations, it is only in Wu's translation that the meaning of "路 上" (*lù shàng*; road on) is not explicitly stated, whereas the application of "travel" has already implied such a meaning.

In terms of the expression of artistic conception, the translations with relational processes (e.g. Yang and Yang's translation) are best at expressing the meaning in the original.

2.4.3 Experiential analysis of the translations of sentence 3

This section focuses on the experiential meaning in the translations of the third sentence in the original – "借 问 酒家 何 处 有" (*jiè wèn jiǔ jiā hé chù yǒu*; may ask tavern what place have).

Scholars have different opinions on whether this sentence is an indirect or direct question. Some scholars (e.g. Ruchang Zhou – see Fei 2001: 94; Ji 2001: 54; Li & Zhang 2001: 239; Sun 1997: 437; Xiao et al. 1983: 1101) apply a comma at the end of this sentence to treat it as an indirect question, while some scholars (e.g. Chen & Huang 2000: 76; Sanqin Press 2000: 108; Wen 1989: 173; Xu 2000b: 536; Yang & Yang 2001a: 264; Zhu 2000: 165) apply a question mark at the end, signalling that it is a direct question.

Among the six translations we collected, three – translations by Cai, Yang and Yang, as well as Wan and Wang – treat this sentence as an indirect question. Wu renders it as a direct question; Xu takes it as a mixture of free direct speech and free indirect speech; Sun translates it as a structure between direct speech and indirect speech (i.e. "When asked 'Where a tavern fair for rest is hereabouts to be found'"), which is different from direct speech (e.g. "When asked 'Where is a tavern fair for rest hereabouts to be found'").

In a strict sense, in all six translations, this sentence is rendered as quoted speech, with verbal processes being applied. In Wu's translation, only direct speech is applied, with the structure of verbal process such as "I ask the boy" (i.e. the projecting clause) being omitted. Similarly, in Xu's translation, a mixture of free direct speech and free indirect speech is applied, with structures of verbal processes (i.e. the projecting clause), such as "when someone asks" and "when asked" being omitted. Following this logic, we find quoted speeches (i.e. questions) being applied in the six translations, among which four – translations by Cai, Sun, Yang and Yang, as well as Wan and Wang – apply indirect speech and two – translations by Wu and Xu – apply a mixture of free direct speech and free indirect speech.

In verbal clauses, three participants are involved: Sayer, Receiver and Verbiage. In the following discussion, we will treat the processes in the six translations as verbal ones.

Wu's translation

"Is there a public house somewhere, cowboy?"

This sentence is a direct speech and functions as the Verbiage. The Sayer could be "I" in the last sentence, while the Receiver is "cowboy" in the direct speech. Such direct speech is a clause with an existential process, with "is" being the process, "a public house" being the Existent and "somewhere" being a circumstance. The use of "cowboy" in the quoted speech serves as the Vocative, which indicates interpersonal meaning.

Cai's translation

"They ask where wineshops can be found or where to rest –"

This sentence includes a verbal process from an indirect speech. The Sayer ("they") refers to "the men and women" in the last sentence; the Receiver refers to "herdboy" in the next sentence, while the Verbiage is the projected clauses – "where wineshops can be found or where to rest". Within the projected clauses, the first process is a mental one found in a passive clause, with "wineshop" – a participant – functioning as the Phenomenon, and the Senser indicating the previously used "they" being invisible; there is also a second process, which is a material one.

Sun's translation

"When asked 'where a tavern fair for rest is hereabouts to be found',"

In terms of syntax, this is a dependent clause (i.e. a subordinate clause) that forms a hypotactic relation with the next clause. The Sayer could be "pedestrians on countryside ways" in the previous sentence, the Receiver is "the shepherd boy" in the following sentence, and the Verbiage is a direct speech – "where a tavern fair for rest is hereabouts to be found". Further, this direct speech is a projected clause, which not only involves a mental process but is also in passive form (i.e. "be found"); the Senser, which is "pedestrians on countryside ways", is not stated explicitly; the Phenomenon is "a tavern fair for rest hereabouts"; and "where" functions as a circumstance.

Yang and Yang's translation

"When I ask a shepherd boy where I can find a tavern,"

In the perspective of syntax, this clause is also a dependent clause, which forms a hypotactic relation with the subsequent clause. The Sayer (i.e. "I") is explicitly stated, which may refer to one of the "travelers" rather than "travelers along the road" in the preceding sentence. Also, in this clause with a verbal process, the Sayer (i.e. "a shepherd boy") is stated explicitly and the Verbiage is an indirect speech – "where I can find a tavern" – which is a projected clause that involves a mental process, with "I" being the Senser and "a tavern" being the Phenomenon.

Wan and Wang's translation

"When asked where could be found a tavern bower,"

This clause is also a dependent one that forms a hypotactic relation with the preceding clause. In this clause with a verbal process, the Sayer is "the traveler" in the previous sentence, the Receiver is "a cowboy" in the following sentence and the Verbiage is a projected clause – "where could be found a tavern bower". This projected clause involves a mental process and is in passive form. In the projected clause, the Senser is implicit and can be traced to "the traveler" in the second sentence, the Phenomenon is "a tavern bower" and the Place is realized by "where" – a circumstance.

Xu's translation

"Where can a wineshop be found to drown his sad hours?"

As discussed previously, Xu here applies a mixture of free direct speech and free indirect speech. We can compare Xu's translation with the following two sentences: (1) "Where *could* a wineshop be found to drown his sad hours?" (free indirect speech); and (2) "Where can a wineshop be found to drown *my* sad hours?" (free direct speech). The quoted speech in Xu's translation is realized by a clause complex. The first process is a mental one, with the Senser referring to "the mourner" in the last sentence, the Phenomenon being "a wineshop" and "where" functioning as the Place. The second process is a material one, with the Actor being realized by "a wineshop" as previously seen and the Goal being realized by "his sad hours".

The analysis of participants involved in clauses of verbal processes can help us to explore the dialogue in the poem.

2.4.4 Experiential analysis of the translations of sentence 4

This section examines the six translations of the last sentence in the original: "牧 童 遥 指 杏 花 村" (*mù tóng yáo zhǐ xìng huā cūn*; herd child far point apricot flower village).

Wu's translation

"He points at Apricot Bloom Village faraway."

This clause involves a material process, which is realized by "points", with "he" being the Actor and "Apricot Bloom Village faraway" being the Goal ("faraway" here serves as the postmodifier of "Apricot Bloom Village"). "杏 花 村" (*xìng huā cūn*; apricot flower village) is here treated as a proper noun, which may not be appropriate.

Cai's translation

"And there the herdboy's fingers Almond-Town suggest."

A material process, which is realized by "suggest", is also applied in Cai's translation. The Actor of the clause is not a human being, but part of the human body – "the herdboy's fingers" – and the Goal is "Almond-Town there", which is a nominal group. In addition, the application of "fingers" (in plural form) rather than "finger" (in singular form) deserves our attention, because a person normally uses one finger to point to a faraway place – see also Ding's (2001: 267) translation of this line: "A cow boy replies pointing his finger." In addition, Cai's translation is similar to Wu's in rendering "杏 花 村" (*xìng huā cūn*; apricot flower village) as a proper noun, which can be an inappropriate choice.

Sun's translation

"The shepherd boy the Apricot Bloom Vill doth point to afar and say."

The syntactic structure of this sentence is to a large extent reversed. The sentence includes two processes. For the clause with the first process (i.e. "point"), the Actor (i.e. "the shepherd boy") and the Goal ("Apricot Bloom Vill") are juxtaposed, with "afar", which serves to modifier the Goal, being located after the process (i.e. "doth point") and being separated from the Head of the group (i.e. "the Apricot Bloom Vill"). One can compare Sun"s translation with "The shepherd boy doth point to the Apricot Bloom Vill afar and say" to observe the differences. The second process, which is realized by "(doth) say", is a verbal process, with the Sayer being "the shepherd boy" at the beginning of this sentence, the Receiver being the questioner in the last sentence (i.e. "The pedestrians on countryside ways"), and the Verbiage being unseen. In Sun's translation, which is the same as translations by Wu and Cai, "杏 花 村" (*xìng huā cūn*; apricot flower village) is rendered as a proper noun. In DU Mu's original, the cowherd does not say anything, whereas the addition of "and say" in Sun's translation is perhaps due to considerations of the number of syllables and of making up a certain rhyme. In the perspective of the expression of artistic conception, the clause realized by "and say" is rather redundant.

Yang and Yang's translation

"He points at a distant hamlet nestling amidst apricot blossoms."

A material process realized by "points" is applied, with the Actor "he" referring to "a shepherd boy" in the last sentence and the Goal being realized by "a distant hamlet nestling amidst apricot blossoms".

Wan and Wang's translation

"A cowboy points to yonder village of the apricot flower."

Wan and Wang also adopt "points" to realize a material process; whereas it can be noted that the Actor, "a cowboy", is indeterminate (cf. "the cowboy"). If the third sentence of the poem is a question raised to "a cowboy", it would be a better choice to change "a cowboy" to "the cowboy".

Xu's translation

"A cowherd points to a cot 'mid apricot flowers."

In Xu's translation, which is similar to the other translations, "points" is selected to realize a material process, thus "a cowherd" at the beginning of the sentence is the Actor and "a cot 'mid apricot flowers" is the Goal. Also, like Wan and Wang's translation, an indefinite article is used in Xu's translation to signal the Actor (see Chapter 5 for discussions on the use of article).

To translate "指" (*zhǐ*; point), the choice of "point" in Xu's translation is obviously more appropriate than "suggest" in Cai's translation. Different from the other translators, Cai perhaps chooses "suggest" to rhyme with the previous sentence (i.e. "They ask where wineshops can be found or where to rest – "). In our opinion, "where to rest" is redundant and "suggest" is not a choice as appropriate and natural as "point".

2.5 Some clarifications

As discussed in Section 2.3, some issues must be clarified when interpreting *Qing Ming*. We will now explore these issues based on our analysis of the English translations.

2.5.1 "Qingming season"

Does "清明 时节" (*qīng míng shí jié*; Qingming season) refer to the specific day of the Qingming Festival (i.e. Ching Ming Festival or Tomb-Sweeping Day) or the rainy spring season that includes the Qingming Festival in general? Both explanations are reasonable. Based on the whole poem, it may be more appropriate to translate "清明 时节" (*qīng míng shí jié*; Qingming season) not only as the day of the Qingming Festival but also as a proper noun. Following this explanation, Yang and Yang's translation would seem inappropriate. For the other five translations, however, different translation strategies have been adopted: translations by Wu and Sun apply the strategy of literal translation, while translations by Wan and Wang, and Xu, apply the strategy of free translation. The method of foreignization is used in the four translations, while the method of domestication is used in Cai's translation. We hold that the foreignizing method can play a better role in expressing the connotation and artistic conception of the original; by adopting the foreignizing method, the strategy of literal translation will be better at conveying the information and implication in the original.

2.5.2 "Pedestrian on the road"

As pointed out previously in the analysis, scholars in China and abroad have not reached a consensus on the understanding of "路 上 行人" (*lù shàng xíng* rén; road on pedestrian). Based on the artistic conception of the whole poem, if we were to depict the sadness and loneliness of an independent traveler walking in the spring rain, it would be better to treat "行人" (*xíng* rén; pedestrian) as a determinate person rather than as several indeterminate persons. Therefore, the translations by Wu (i.e. "I travel with my heart lost in dismay"), Wan and Wang (i.e. "So broken-hearted fares the traveler on the way") and Xu (i.e. "The mourner's heart is going to break on his way") are better than the others.

2.5.3 "Asking about the tavern"

In three of the six translations, the question is raised by one person, namely "me" (in translations by Wu as well as by Yang and Yang) and "a traveler" (in Wan and Wang's translation). In Cai's translation, the question is raised by several people: "them". In Sun's translation, the questioner is implicit. In Xu's translation, the questioner is difficult to identify. According to the preceding text in Xu's translation, the questioner should be "the mourner" in the second sentence, whereas the use of "his" has falsified our inference. However, if we changed "his" in Xu's translation to "my", the questioner would then be "the mourner" in the second sentence, thus making this sentence more appropriate.

In five of the six translations, "酒家" (*jiǔ jiā*; tavern) is rendered as words in singular form, while it is only translated as "wineshops" in plural form in Cai's translation. Based on our speculation, the plural form in Cai's translation can be due to the consideration of form since the singular choice (i.e. "a wineshop") will add up an additional syllable and thus destroy the beauty of arranging twelve syllables in each line. In this way, meaning is abandoned due to the choice of rhyme.

In addition, Wu applies the domesticating method in translating "酒家" (*jiǔ jiā*; tavern) as "a public house", which is an inappropriate choice. This is because "酒家" (*jiǔ jiā*; tavern) and "public house" vary significantly in terms of their denotative, connotative and associative meanings.

2.5.4 "Herdboy"

"牧 童" (*mù tóng*; herd child) is translated in the six translations in the following ways: "cowboy" (translations by Wu as well as Wan and Wang); "shepherd boy" (translations by Sun as well as Yang and Yang);

"herdboy" (Cai); and "cowherd" (Xu). In terms of connotative meaning, "cowboy" and "牧 童" (*mù tóng*; herd child) do not refer to the same group of people. "Cowboy" indicates a person who rides horses and looks after cowherds in the west of the United States, and it differs significantly from "牧 童" (*mù tóng*; herd child) in the Chinese culture (see Zhang 1996: 30). "Shepherd boy", which refers to a person who looks after sheep, does not involve riding a cow and is not identical with "牧 童" (*mù tóng*; herd child) in the Chinese culture. "Herdboy" refers to a person who looks after a group of animals and is also not identical with "牧 童" (*mù tóng*; herd child), who only takes care of one ox. "Cowherd", which is synonymous to "cowhand", refers to people who are hired to look after cows, whereas "牧 童" (*mù tóng*; herd child) only looks after one ox that is used for farming. Therefore, the four nouns in the six translations cannot appropriately express the denotative and connotative meanings of "牧 童" (*mù tóng*; herd child) in the Chinese culture, while the associative meanings of these words are also far from that of "牧 童" (*mù tóng*; herd child). By contrast, "herdboy" in Cai's translation is a better choice.

2.5.5 "Apricot Bloom Village"

Based on the literature, it is widely accepted in the Chinese literary circle that "杏 花 村" (*xìng huā cūn*; apricot flower village) is not a real village name, but is rather "a village where apricot flowers blossom" (Sanqin Press 2000: 108, our translation). Nowadays, in various places in China, such as Pingyang in Shanxi Province, we can find villages called "杏 花 村" (*xìng huā cūn*; apricot flower village), which are "named after the poem by people in the later generations" (Li & Zhang 2001: 239, our translation). Therefore, we believe it is inappropriate to translate "杏 花 村" (*xìng huā cūn*; apricot flower village) as a proper noun (in translations by Wu, Cai and Sun). In translations by Yang and Yang and by Wan and Wang, the herdboy points at a hamlet (or village) with apricot flowers, whereas in Xu's translation, the herdboy points at a cot. By contrast, translations by Yang and Yang as well as Wan and Wang, are more appropriate and credible in this respect. It can further be estimated that "cot" is applied in Xu's translation to reduce a syllable, whereas the number of syllables in the first three lines is in fact different from the number of syllables in the fourth line.

2.6 Conclusion

This chapter provides an analysis of DU Mu's *Qing Ming* and its six English translations in the perspective of transitivity that models on the experiential metafunction. In an interview, Baohong Zhang, a scholar who works on poetry translation in China, has shared his interpretation of this poem. He points out that the lexical choices of "欲" (*yù*; will) in "路 上 行人 欲 断 魂" (*lù shàng xíng* rén yù duàn hún; road on pedestrian will lose soul) and "遥 指" (*yáo zhǐ*; far point) in "牧 童 遥 指 杏 花 村" (*mù tóng yáo zhǐ xìng huā cūn*; herd child far point apricot flower village) have played significant roles in the poem, whereas he feels it is a pity that they are not rendered properly in several translations. In the perspective of SFL, "欲" (*yù*; will) indicates modal meaning, and by evaluating the choice of process type in terms of modal meaning, "is going to" in Xu's translation (i.e. from "The mourner's heart is going to break on his way") has already expressed such a meaning. In this way, our analyses and discussions in different chapters are merely carried out in one perspective and cannot provide an overall account of the English translations, hence we cannot tell which translation is better than all the other translations in all respects.

This chapter applies metafunction in Halliday's SFL as a theoretical basis and provides a preliminary exploration of DU Mu's *Qing Ming*. Some analyses may be helpful to translation studies, while some may play a guiding role in text analysis. Besides carrying out an experiential analysis of the poem and its English translations, some related issues are also discussed in this chapter. There were in fact two purposes for writing this chapter: based on a linguistic analysis of translated texts, we aim at: (1) reinvestigating some issues in translation studies in a new perspective; and (2) building an analytical framework for describing poems and their translations.

Chapter 3

Logical analysis

3.1 Introduction

In Chapter 2, we conducted an experiential analysis of DU Mu's (杜牧) *Qing Ming* (清明) and its English translations. Here, we will explore this poem in a logical perspective. Following Halliday's Systemic Functional Linguistics (SFL), the logical metafunction and the experiential metafunction are collectively known as the ideational metafunction, with the logical metafunction being paralleled with the experiential, interpersonal and textual metafunctions (see also Thompson 1996).

3.2 A sketch of the logical metafunction

The logical metafunction deals with the relationship between one message and other messages. In terms of realization, the logical metafunction involves how clauses are combined – that is, the coordination or subordination between one clause and another in a clause complex. By carrying out a logical analysis, we can identify the semantic relationship between clause complexes.

When two or more clauses are combined, they will become a clause complex and there will be certain logical relationships between one clause and another. In light of Systemic Functional Grammar (SFG), we can conduct a logical analysis in two perspectives. First, we can investigate the tactic relation between clauses that form a clause complex. These relations include hypotaxis and parataxis, which reveal the interdependent relation between clauses. For instance, in Example (1), paratactic relation is seen between the two clauses; while in Example (2), hypotactic relation is applied.

Example (1)
Henry is rich || but he is sad.

Example (2)
Henry is sad || although he is rich.

Second, we can study the logico-semantic type – that is, the relationship between a primary clause and a secondary clause, which involves expansion or projection (see Thompson 1996: 196–211). For instance, in Example (3), the secondary clause – "he ran away" – is an expansion of the primary clause – "John didn't wait". Specifically, the secondary clause – "he ran away" – is an elaboration of the primary clause – "John didn't wait".

Example (3)
John didn't wait; he ran away.

Example (4)
Helen said, "I'm very happy."

In Example (4), the secondary clause — "I'm very happy" – is a projection of the primary clause – "Helen said." In this case, "Helen said" is the projecting clause and "I'm very happy" is the projected clause.

In terms of logico-semantic type, expansion means that one clause serves to add and explain the meaning of another clause. There are three subtypes of expansion: (1) elaboration, (2) extension and (3) enhancement. The three subtypes can be used in both hypotactic and paratactic relations.

1. Elaboration means that the second clause further develops or explains the first clause. The paratactic elaborating clause expresses a meaning that is close or similar to the first clause, as previously shown in Example (3).
2. Extension means that the second clause adds a certain meaning to the first clause; most paratactic elaborating clauses involve the structure of coordination studied in traditional grammar, as shown in Example (5).

Example (5)
Helen came into the room, and she saw Henry playing chess with Alan.

3. Enhancement refers to the addition of a secondary clause to the primary clause in perspectives such as time, place, manner and reason. In hypotactic relations, enhancing clauses are usually adverbial clauses in traditional grammar, as illustrated in Example (6).

Example (6)
George no longer felt lonely after he met Michelle.

In a paratactic combination, clauses indicating enhancing relations are often marked by words such as "so", "and then" and "and yet".

In terms of projection, direct speech and indirect speech in traditional grammar are mainly involved. In normal cases, projection in a clause complex indicates that the projected clause has already been said/thought before being projected. For instance, in Example (4), "I'm very happy" is the projected clause and it has already been said by Helen before the reporter says "Helen said". In terms of the nature of projection, it can be either a quote or a report. In Example (4), "I'm very happy" is a quote because it is exactly what Helen has said. In Example (7), "she was very happy" is a report, because it is not exactly what Helen has said.

Example (7)
Helen said she was very happy.

What Helen has actually said is in fact "I am very happy", while in Example (7), it is reported as "she was very happy".

3.3 Logical analysis of the original of *Qing Ming*

Written by DU Mu during the Tang Dynasty, *Qing Ming* is a popular poem. The original is as follows:

清明时节雨纷纷，
qīng míng shí jiē yǔ fēn fēn,
Qingming season rain succession,

路上行人欲断魂。
lù shàng xíng rén yù duàn hún.
road on pedestrian will lose soul.

借问酒家何处有，
jiè wèn jiǔ jiā hé chù yǒu,
may ask tavern which place have,

牧童遥指杏花村。
mù tóng yáo zhǐ xìng huā cūn.
herd child far point apricot flower village.

In the logical perspective, the four clauses in *Qing Ming* have formed two clause complexes. The first and the second clauses are paratactically related and the relationship is extension – that is, the second clause adds some meaning to the first clause. The poet not only informs his readers about the weather during the Qingming season (i.e. circumstance), but also introduces the persons (participants) and their mental states under such a circumstance. Therefore, the second clause is an extension to the first clause. The third and fourth clauses, which form one clause complex, are hypotactically related, with their relationship being enhancement – the third clause provides a reason for the fourth clause: the reason for the cowherd to point to the Apricot Bloom Village is that somebody has asked about the location of a tavern. Naturally, this relationship can also be interpreted as a "time" relation – when someone asks the cowherd about where to find a tavern, the cowherd answers with an action of pointing to the Apricot Bloom Village. Whether a causal or time relationship is applied between the third and fourth clauses, the logico-semantic type will still be analysed as enhancement.

Seen in the traditional perspective of text structure, the four sentences in *Qing Ming* respectively reflect the four steps in ancient Chinese poem composition: (1) "opening", (2) "developing", (3) "changing' and (4) "concluding". As pointed out by Ruchang Zhou (see Xiao et al. 1983: 1102, our translation):

> The text structure of this poem is a natural one in that the sequential steps are applied in its composition. Its first sentence discusses the situation, environment, and atmosphere, hence functioning as the "opening"; the second sentence is the "developing" stage in its depiction of the characters and their perplexed state of mind; the third sentence is the "changing" stage, which proposes a solution to extricate from the state of mind; the fourth sentence, triggered by the third sentence, marks the "concluding" stage and represents the highlight of the poem.

Although similarities are found between the views on text structure from traditional Chinese rhetoric and the logical analysis in this chapter, the two views are different in nature.

3.4 Logical analysis of the English translations

There are several English translations of *Qing Ming*. Six of them are analysed here: those by Juntao Wu (see Zhang 1996: 30); Tinggan Cai (see Wen 1989: 174); Dayu Sun (1997: 435); Xianyi Yang and Gladys Yang (2001a: 266); Changsheng Wan and Xianzhong Wang (see Zhu 2000: 166); and Yuanchong Xu (2000b: 537).

In Table 3.1, we chunk the clause complexes in the six translations into clauses. As the English translations are in written language, the use of punctuation marks hence serves as the basis in clause chunking.

Table 3.1. Chunking clause complexes in the six English translations into clauses

<table>
<tr><th>Line / Translator(s)</th><th>1</th><th>2</th><th>3</th><th>4</th></tr>
<tr><td>Wu</td><td colspan="2">/ It drizzles thick on the Pure Brightness Day; / I travel with my heart lost in dismay. /
• One clause complex
• Paratactic structure
• Relation of expansion: extension between the two clauses</td><td>/ "Is there a public house somewhere, cowboy?" /
• One clause
• A projected clause, with the projecting clause being unseen</td><td>/ He points at Apricot Bloom Village faraway. /
• One clause</td></tr>
<tr><td>Cai</td><td colspan="2">/ The rain falls thick and fast on All Souls' Day, / The men and women sadly move along the way. /
• One clause complex
• Paratactic structure
• Relation of expansion: extension between the two clauses</td><td colspan="2">/ They ask where wineshops can be found or where to rest – / And there the herdboy's fingers Almond-Town suggest. /
• One clause complex
• Paratactic structure
• Relation of expansion: extension between the two clauses</td></tr>
<tr><td>Sun</td><td>/ Upon the Clear-and-Bright Feast of spring | The rain drizzleth down in spray. /
• One clause</td><td>/ Pedestrians on country-side ways | In gloom are pining away. /
• One clause</td><td colspan="2">/ When asked "Where a tavern fair for rest | Is hereabouts to be found", | The shepherd boy the Apricot Bloom Vill | Doth point to afar and say. /
• One clause complex
• Hypotactic structure
• Relation of expansion: enhancement between the two clauses</td></tr>
</table>

Yang & Yang	/ It drizzles endlessly during the rainy season in spring, / Travelers along the road look gloomy and miserable. / • One clause complex • Paratactic structure • Relation of expansion: extension between the two clauses	/ When I ask a shepherd boy where I can find a tavern, / He points at a distant hamlet nestling amidst apricot blossoms. / • One clause complex • Hypotactic structure • Relation of expansion: enhancement between the two clauses	
Wan & Wang	/ The ceaseless drizzle drips all the dismal day, / So brokenhearted fares the traveler on the way. / • One clause complex • Paratactic structure • Relation of expansion: extension between the two clauses	/ When asked where could be found a tavern bower, / A cowboy points to yonder village of the apricot flower. / • One clause complex • Hypotactic structure • Relation of expansion: enhancement between the two clauses	
Xu	/ A drizzling rain falls like tears on the Mourning Day; / The mourner's heart is going to break on his way. / • One clause complex • Paratactic structure • Relation of expansion: extension between the two clauses	/ Where can a wineshop be found to drown his sad hours? / • One clause • A projected clause, with the projecting clause not being found	/ A cowherd points to a cot 'mid apricot flowers. / • One clause

As shown in Table 3.1, the six English translations basically share the same relations between the clauses. Except for Sun's translation, the relations between the first two clauses in the other translations are all paratactic, and the logico-semantic types are those of expansion: extension, with the second clause adding certain meanings to the first clause. Similarly, the logico-semantic type between the two free clauses in Sun's translation is also expansion: extension.

For the third and fourth clauses, direct speech is used in Wu's translation (i.e. "Is there a public house somewhere, cowboy?"). A mixture of free direct speech and free indirect speech is seen in Xu's translation (i.e. "Where can a wineshop be found to drown his sad hours?"); quoted (projected) clauses are not used in these two translations and all the clauses are simple ones. In the other four translations, these two lines are rendered as one clause complex. Cai uses a paratactic relation, with the second clause adding certain meanings to the previous one, forming the logico-sematic relation of expansion: extension (i.e. "/ They ask where wineshops can be found or where to rest – / And there the herdboy's fingers Almond-Town suggest. /"). In translations by Sun (i.e. "/ When asked "Where a tavern fair for rest | Is hereabouts to be found", / The shepherd boy the Apricot Bloom Vill | Doth point to afar and say. /"), Yang and Yang (i.e. "/ When I ask a shepherd boy where I can find a tavern, / He points at a distant hamlet nestling amidst apricot blossoms. /") and Wan and Wang (i.e. "When asked where could be found a tavern bower, / A cowboy points to yonder village of the apricot flower. /"), these two clauses are rendered as clause complexes, with hypotactic relations being selected; further, as the dependent (secondary) clauses serve to elaborate on the primary clause in terms of time, the logico-semantic relation of expansion: enhancement is hence applied.

It can be noted that the third sentence in Cai's translation (i.e. "They ask where wineshops can be found or where to rest –" is a clause complex: "they ask" is the projecting clause and "where wineshops can be found or where to rest" is the projected clause, with indirect quoting being used. In a strict sense, the projected clause can also be regarded as a clause complex, with elaborating relation being used between the two clauses (i.e. "where wineshops can be found' and "where to rest"). In translations by Sun (i.e. "When asked 'Where a tavern fair for rest | Is hereabouts to be found'"), Yang and Yang (i.e. "When I ask a shepherd boy where I can find a tavern") and Wan and Wang (i.e. "When asked where could be found a tavern bower"), the third sentences are also clause complexes, which include projected clauses (i.e. "(he is) asked", "I ask" and "(he is) asked").

In Sun's translation, the projected clause ("Where a tavern fair for rest is hereabouts to be found") is a direct quote, while the projected clauses in the other three translations by Cai ("where wineshops can be found or where to rest –"), Yang and Yang ("where I can find a tavern") and Wan and Wang ("where could be found a tavern bower") are indirect quotes, which serve to repeat what others have said directly, with quotation marks being adopted to signal the quote.

Furthermore, the fourth sentence in Sun's translation (i.e. "The shepherd boy the Apricot Bloom Vill | Doth point to afar and say") is another clause complex: the first clause has a material process (realized by "point") and the second clause has a verbal process (realized by "say"), with paratactic relation and logico-semantic type of expansion:

extension being applied. Also, in Sun's translation, the second clause within the fourth sentence (i.e. "and say") is an elliptical clause, with the Verbiage not being stated. This usage could be due to the considerations of "beauty in form" and "beauty in sound"; however, in terms of the expression of artistic conception, this clause seems somewhat redundant.

3.5 A meaning-oriented and form-oriented analysis

As is generally acknowledged, English is a "form-oriented" language, while Chinese is a "meaning-oriented" language (see Lian 1993: 48–63; Liu 1994: 163–78; Wu 1994: 152–62). English is oriented towards form because English words and structures that serve connecting purposes are often adopted to indicate the logico-semantic relations between linguistic structures. Chinese is oriented towards meaning because the semantic relations between words or clauses in Chinese are often not realized by words or structures that serve connecting purposes, but by the logico-semantic relations determined by language users based on the context of situation and the co-text.

Based on the analysis of the original and the English translations of *Qing Ming*, we can observe the differences between the meaning-orientated Chinese language and the form-oriented English language. In the English translations, we find various instances of (1) reference (e.g. applications of personal pronouns and demonstrative pronouns), (2) ellipsis and (3) conjunction (see also Huang 2002c).

3.5.1 Reference

Wu's translation: "cowboy" ← "he" ("/ 'Is there a public house somewhere, cowboy?' / He points at Apricot Bloom Village faraway. /")

Cai's translation: "the men and women" ← "they" ("/ The men and women sadly move along the way. / They ask where wineshops can be found or where to rest – /")

Yang and Yang's translation: "a shepherd boy" ← "he" (/ When I ask a shepherd boy where I can find a tavern, / He points at a distant hamlet nestling amidst apricot blossoms. /)

Xu's translation: "the mourner's" ← "his" (/ The mourner's heart is going to break on his way. / Where can a wineshop be found to drown his sad hours? /)

Cai's translation: "there" → "Almond-Town" (/ And there the herdboy's fingers Almond-Town suggest. /)

3.5.2 Ellipsis

The same ellipsis of "he is" is seen in translations by Sun as well as by Wan and Wang.

Sun's translation: "/ When ø asked 'Where a tavern fair for rest | Is hereabouts to be found'"

Wan and Wang's translation: "/ When ø asked where could be found a tavern bower /"

3.5.3. Conjunction

A coordinating conjunction "and" that indicates connecting meaning is used in Cai's translation (i.e. "/ And there the herdboy's fingers Almond-Town suggest /'). The application of this conjunction is possibly due to the consideration of form in poetry translation.

The purpose of adopting reference, ellipsis and conjunction is to clearly signal the relationship between the different sentences in the poem; these cohesive devices have reflected the form-oriented nature in English.

Since Chinese is not a form-oriented language, there thus arise questions such as (1) "Who is the person asking the way?" and (2) "Are the pedestrian and the person asking the way in fact the same person?"

Since English is form-oriented and Chinese is meaning-oriented, the connections between words or between sentences in the English translations are different from those in the original. However, with the help of our analysis, we can point out the logico-semantic relations in the original and the translations, compare these choices and hence identify that the original and the translations are very similar in this respect; in certain perspectives, these choices between the original and the translations are even identical.

3.6 Conclusion

By carrying out a logical analysis, this chapter provides a preliminary exploration into DU Mu's *Qing Ming* and its six English translations. From the analysis, we can point out the semantic relations between clauses and observe how such relations are realized by linguistic forms; however, the realizations in Chinese and English are not identical. Although different translators may apply different strategies in translation, they tend to choose the same semantic relation between clauses. For example, in Sun's translation, although the first and second sentences of the original are translated as simple clauses, the hypotactic expanding: extending relation is still found between the clauses. In another example, it is observed that in both translations by Wu and by Xu, the third and fourth sentences are rendered as simple clauses; whereas the same hypotactic expanding: enhancing relations are found in both translations.

Chapter 4

Interpersonal analysis

4.1 Introduction

In Chapters 2 and 3, we explored the English translations of DU Mu's (杜牧) *Qing Ming* (清明) in the experiential and the logical perspectives. In this chapter, we attempt to analyse the English translations in light of the interpersonal metafunction. This chapter is composed of three parts: (1) an overview of the interpersonal metafunction, (2) an interpersonal analysis of *Qing Ming* and (3) an interpersonal analysis of the English translations.

4.2 A sketch of the interpersonal metafunction

Following Halliday's (1994) Systemic Functional Grammar (SFG), the interpersonal metafunction deals with how people use language to communicate with each other, to establish and maintain interpersonal relationship, to influence others' behaviors, to express their views on the world – both the real outside world and the inner world – and even to change the world.

As discussed previously, in daily life people use language to establish and maintain interpersonal relationships. During interactions, they continuously change their interaction roles. However, no matter how such roles are changed, only two major roles are involved: "giving" and "demanding". Moreover, what has been given or demanded can be either information or goods-&-services. In this way, by intersecting the interaction role and the commodity being exchanged (i.e. information and goods-&-services), we can identify the four speech functions (see Table 4.1; see also Halliday 1994: 68–69; Thompson 1996: 39–40).

Table 4.1. The four speech functions

interaction role \ commodity	information	goods-&-services
giving	statement	offer
demanding	question	command

For the speech functions of "statement", "question" and "command", there are often congruent realizations between these speech functions and certain lexicogrammatical choices. For instance, "statement" is usually realized by declarative clauses, "question" by interrogative clauses, and "command" by imperative clauses.

4.3 Interpersonal analysis of the original of *Qing Ming*

Our analysis will focus on the original poem written by DU Mu:

清明时节雨纷纷，
qīng míng shí jiē yǔ fēn fēn,
Qingming season rain succession,

路上行人欲断魂。
lù shàng xíng rén yù duàn hún.
road on pedestrian will lose soul.

借问酒家何处有，
jiè wèn jiǔ jiā hé chù yǒu,
may ask tavern what place have,

牧童遥指杏花村。
mù tóng yáo zhǐ xìng huā cūn.
herd child far point apricot flower village.

When analysing a literary work, it is necessary for us to differentiate the writer and the narrator. DU Mu, as the author of *Qing Ming*, does not have to be the narrator of this poem. However, in studies on *Qing Ming*, it seems that most scholars have equated the poet with the narrator. For the convenience of discussion in this chapter, we will also adopt this view.

In terms of mood, declarative mood is used in the first, second and fourth clauses, while the third sentence can be of either interrogative or declarative mood in indirect speech.

In the third clause, "借" (*jiè*; may) indicates modal meaning, which suggests that the speaker is talking in a polite way. The third and fourth clauses could be regarded as an adjacency pair, with the third clause being a question and the fourth an answer realized by action rather than by language.

The author of *Qing Ming* is Du Mu and the readers are the up-coming generations in the different eras. The people involved include "行人" (*xíng rén*; pedestrian) and "牧 童" (*mù tóng*; herd child), and the background involved includes time (e.g. "清明 时节" [*qīng míng*; Qingming season]), scene (e.g. "雨 纷纷" [*yǔ fēn fēn*; rain succession]), status of the characters (e.g. "欲 断 魂" [*yù duàn hún*; will lose soul]) and place (e.g. "酒家" [*jiǔ jiā*; tavern] and "杏 花 村" [*xìng huā cūn*; apricot flower village]). Also, "行人" (*xíng rén*; pedestrian) in this poem could refer to the author, the outsiders or both the author and the outsiders.

As the phenomenon of reporting is identified, the following concepts are involved in this poem: (1) speaker – the person who produces a certain sentence or a passage, (2) listener – the person the speaker talks to, (3) reporter – the person who reports on the other's utterance, and (4) report – the content being reported, which could be direct speech, indirect speech or both (see Thompson 2000: vi–vii).

4.4 Interpersonal analysis of the English translations

As stated previously, there are several English translations of *Qing Ming*, six of which will be discussed in this chapter. The translators are Juntao Wu (see Zhang 1996: 30), Tinggan Cai (see Wen 1989: 174), Dayu Sun (1997: 435), Xianyi Yang and Gladys Yang (2001a: 266), Changsheng Wan and Xianzhong Wang (see Zhu 2000: 166) and Yuanchong Xu (2000b: 537).

In the following sub-sections, we will discuss the six English translations of *Qing Ming* in several perspectives, modelling on the interpersonal metafunction.

4.4.1 Mood

Scholars have adopted different views on whether the third clause in the original (i.e. "借 问 酒家 何 处 有" [*jiè wèn jiǔ jiā hé chù yǒu*; may ask tavern what place have]) should be analysed as an indirect interrogative or a direct interrogative. In terms of graphology, some people apply a comma at the end of the sentence, indicating that it is an indirect interrogative, while some use a question mark at the end, suggesting that it is a direct interrogative.

In three of the six English translations, the third clause in the original is translated as an indirect interrogative (i.e. Cai's translation: "They ask where wineshops can be found or where to rest –"; Yang and Yang's translation: "When I ask a shepherd boy where I can find a tavern"; Wan and Wang's translation: "When asked where could be found a taver bower"). In one translation, this clause is rendered as a direct interrogative (i.e. Wu's translation: "Is there a public house somewhere, cowboy?"). In another translation, this clause is translated as a mixture of free direct speech and free indirect speech (i.e. Xu's translation: "Where can a wineshop be found to drown his sad hours?"). However, in Sun's translation (i.e. "When asked 'Where a tavern fair for rest is hereabouts to be found'"), this clause is rendered as a structure between direct speech and indirect speech.

As the narrator, the poet produces his speech in declarative mood, aiming to provide information to his readers. As the reporter, the poet then reports the speech produced by "行人" (*xíng rén*; pedestrian). In the English translations by Cai, Yang and Yang, and Wan and Wang, the indirect speech has been quoted, whereas Sun's translation is special in that the sentence is translated as a structure between direct speech and indirect speech. In the translations by Wu and by Xu, the third clause in the original is translated as direct speech. Hence, one can say that the interrogative is not applied by the poet as a narrator but is used as a direct question by the questioner in the poem (i.e. "行人" [*xíng rén*; pedestrian]).

4.4.2 Question and answer

In the original poem, the questioner remains unclear. In Wu's translation (i.e. "Is there a public house somewhere, cowboy?"), projection of direct speech is not found and the speaker is not clearly stated. However, in the second sentence (i.e. "I travel with my heart lost in dismay"), "行人" (*xíng rén*; pedestrian) only refers to one person (namely "I", who can be either the poet or the narrator); we can thus infer that the speaker is in fact "I". Further, in Wu's translation, the hearer is revealed by the vocative – "cowboy"; therefore, in this translation, the speaker is "I", the hearer is the "cowboy", and the reporter is the poet (or the narrator of the poem), with the reported speech being the interrogative – "Is there a public house somewhere?"

In Xu's translation, we only find two characters: "the mourner" and "a cowherd". Based on common sense, the speaker should be "the mourner", while the listener should be "a cowherd". However, the use of "his" in the interrogative (i.e. "Where can a wineshop be found to drown his sad hours?") has explicitly indicated that the questioner is not "the mourner" in the last sentence (i.e. "The mourner's heart is going to break on his way") for the reason that "his" in "his sad hours" is adopted to refer to "the mourners". If we changed "his" to "my", the questioner would undoubtedly be "the mourner". Also, we should identify not only the questioner in Xu's translation, but also the target of the question. We further need to point out to whom the question is raised, because an indefinite article "a" is applied before "cowherd". If the question is addressed to "cowherd", "a cowherd" in the fourth line should then be changed to "the cowherd".

In Wan and Wang's translation, there involves the issue of the choice of article. An omission has taken place in the third sentence (i.e. "When asked where could be found a tavern bower"), while the questioner and the answerer are not revealed. Based on co-text, it can be inferred that the speaker is "the traveler" from the second sentence (i.e. "So broken-hearted fares the traveler on the way") and the hearer is the "cowboy" from the fourth sentence (i.e. "A cowboy points to yonder village of the apricot flower"). However, since "a cowboy is" is omitted in the third sentence, with its complete form being "when a cowboy is asked where could be found a tavern bower", one should not use "a cowboy" but "he" or "the cowboy" in the fourth sentence. Furthermore, in the fourth sentence, the use of the indefinite article "a" suggests that "cowboy" is for the first time referred to in the exchange, which is contradictory to the fact. It can also be noted that in Wan and Wang's translation, "could" in "when a cowboy is asked where could be found a tavern bower" should have been changed to "can" so as to remain consistent in the selection of tense throughout the poem.

In translations by Cai (i.e. "They ask where wineshops can be found or where to rest –") as well as by Yang and Yang (i.e. "When I ask a shepherd boy where I can find a tavern"), the questioners are made explicit. In Cai's question, the hearer – that is, "the herdboy" – is not explicitly pointed out but can be inferred from the co-text.

In Sun's translation (i.e. "When asked 'Where a tavern fair for rest is hereabouts to be found'"), both the questioner and the hearer are not found. From the co-text, it can be inferred that "pedestrians on countryside ways" in the second line (i.e. "Pedestrians on countryside ways in gloom are pining away") is the questioner and "the shepherd boy" in the fourth line (i.e. "The shepherd boy the Apricot Bloom Vill doth point to afar and say") is the hearer. However, the issue of identifying the questioner has arisen in the analysis. Normally, the several pedestrians (namely "pedestrians on countryside ways" from the second line) will not serve as the questioner. In other words, it is impossible for several pedestrians to simultaneously raise their questions to the cowherd.

4.4.3 Identifying the questioner

In the translations by Wu, Wan and Wang, and Xu, the instances of "行人" (*xíng rén*; pedestrian) are rendered as singular nouns (nominal groups); therefore, the questioner should in fact be the individual "行人" (*xíng rén*; pedestrian), namely "I" in Wu's translation, "the traveler" in Wan and Wang's translation, as well as "the mourner" in Xu's translation. In Yang and Yang's translation, however, "行人" (*xíng rén*; pedestrian) is rendered as a nominal group in plural form – "travelers along the road", whereas the questioner – "I" – is explicitly stated. There is thus no difficulty in identifying the questioner.

In Cai's translation (i.e. "They ask where wineshops can be found or where to rest –"), the questioner is "they", which should refer to "the men and women" in the last sentence. However, the problem is whether it is one person or several persons raising the question. If the question is raised by one person, "they" should not be used. If the question is raised by several persons, then how is the question raised? It seems unlikely that several people would raise the question unanimously.

4.4.4 Use of vocative

In English, the application of vocative is governed by rules. According to Biber et al. (1999: 1112), when used at the end of a sentence, a vocative often serves to identify someone as an addressee or to maintain or enhance an existing social relation.

In Wu's translation (i.e. "Is there a public house somewhere, cowboy?"), a vocative – "cowboy" – is used to determine the hearer but is not used to either maintain or enhance an existing social relation.

Based on our understanding, the speaker "I" and the hearer ("cowboy") do not know each other, therefore the vocative cannot be adopted to maintain or enhance a social relation that never exists.

In terms of language use, sentences with vocatives are normally regarded as informal. Suppose the two interactants originally do not know each other; the use of vocatives such as "cowboy" will thus be infrequent and improper. As a result, it could be inappropriate to use vocatives in the English translations of poems such as *Qing Ming*.

4.4.5 Who is "asking about the location of the tavern"?

In the original, the person who asks about the location of the tavern remains unclear. Among the six translations in our study, three regard the questioner as one person. In translations by Wu and by Yang and Yang, it is "I" that asks the question. In Wu's translation, "I" is the only participant; hence only "I" can be the questioner. In Yang and Yang's translation, the questioner is stated explicitly in "I ask a shepherd boy where ..." In Wan and Wang's translation, the question is asked by "the traveler", who is also the only participant in the translation. In Cai's translation, the question is raised by various people, as seen in "They ask where ..." In Sun's translation, the questioner is not clearly stated, but it can be inferred that the question is asked by various people. In Xu's translation (i.e. "Where can a wineshop be found to drown his sad hours?"), the questioner is difficult to be identified; based on the previous sentences, the questioner should be "the mourner" in "The mourner's heart is going to break on his way." However, such an inference is proved to be false due to the choice of "his" in the question. In this case, it is necessary to identify the questioner as the relationship between the questioner and the cowherd is a reflection of the interpersonal relationship.

4.4.6 Relationship between questioner and "passenger"

In four of the six English translations (i.e. translations by Wu, Cai, Sun, and Wan and Wang), "行人" (*xíng rén*; pedestrian) is rendered as questioner. However, the case is different in Yang and Yang's translation (i.e. "... / Travelers along the road look gloomy and miserable. / When I ask a shepherd boy where I can find a tavern, / ..."), in which two possibilities exist: (1) "I" am one of the "travelers" walking in the street and "I" want to find a tavern to have some rest, so that "I" am asking the cowherd about the location of the tavern; and (2) "行人" (*xíng rén*;

pedestrian) is translated as one of the "travelers" in the second line, while "I" am a bystander that helps others to ask the way rather than one of the "travelers" mentioned in the second line. However, the possibility of adopting the second interpretation is rather small.

In Xu's translation ("... / The mourner's heart is going to break on his way. / ..."), the questioner is in singular form, whereas the question – "Where can a wineshop be found to drown his sad hours?" – has left the readers the impression that there is another questioner besides "the mourner" and "a cowherd", as the use of "his" in the question has indicated that the question is not raised by "the mourner". However, as seen from the co-text, the sudden appearance of a question would be awkward and unimaginable. It would also be impossible to interpret this sentence as a voiceover.

4.4.7 *Speaker, hearer and reporter*

Based on the above analysis, we find that the translators have interpreted and rendered the speaker in the poem differently. Some translators regard the narrator – "I" – as the speaker (i.e. Wu's translation: "... / I travel with my heart lost in dismay. / ..." and Yang and Yang's translation: " ... / When I ask a shepherd boy where I can find a tavern, / ..."); some translators treat a third person – "行人" (*xíng rén*; pedestrian) – as the speaker (i.e. Cai's translation: "... / They ask ..."; Sun's translation: "they"; Wan and Wang's translation: "he"); in Xu's translation, it is possible that the translator has also interpreted a third person as the speaker. Additionally, in terms of the hearer, "牧童" (*mù tóng*; herd child) is rendered as the hearer in all the six English translations. The reporter is then DU Mu, as he is the poet who composed this poem. It can also be noted that, in translations by Wu and by Yang and Yang, the instances of "I" have functioned as both the speaker and the reporter.

4.5 Conclusion

Interpersonal analysis is not only capable of helping us to identify the characters involved in the poem and their relationships; it can also help us to determine the accuracy of the English translations. For instance, based on our common knowledge, we know that it is generally impossible for several people to ask the way together in one voice; thus the choices of translating the questioners in plural form are debatable.

According to the interpersonal analysis, indirect speech is on the one hand used in two translations (i.e. Wu's translation: "Is there a public house somewhere?" and Sun's translation: "Where a tavern fair for rest is hereabouts to be found"). Wu applies a direct interrogative and Sun applies a structure between direct speech and indirect speech. On the other hand, in the original poem, DU Mu applies indirect speech, which can obviously give readers more imaginary space compared with direct speech.

Chapter 5

Textual analysis

5.1 Introduction

In Chapters 2 to 4, we analysed DU Mu's (杜牧) *Qing Ming* (清明) and its six English translations using the experiential, logical and interpersonal perspectives. This chapter now approaches *Qing Ming* and its English translations in the textual perspective.

5.2 A sketch of the textual metafunction

Textual metafunction deals with the organization of message in language use. It meanwhile indicates the relationship between one message and other messages. Three systems are involved in the textual metafunction: THEME (Theme–Rheme), INFORMATION (given–new) and COHESION. More discussion of the three systems will be provided when needed.

5.3 Theme analysis of the original

In terms of thematic structure, the choices of Theme and Rheme in the original of *Qing Ming* are shown in Table 5.1.

Based on the analysis, we find that the Themes in clauses 1, 2 and 4 are all realized by nominal groups, while the Theme in clause 3 is realized by a verbal group. "清明 时节" (*qīng míng shí jié*; Qingming season) functions as a circumstance, "路 上 行人" (*lù shàng xíng* rén; road on pedestrian) and "牧童" (*mù tóng*; herdboy) function as participants and "(借) 问" (*jiè wèn*; may ask) functions as process.

In terms of INFORMATION, except for "清明 时节" (*qīng míng shí jié*; Qingming season), which indicates given information (for the reason that the title of the poem is "清明" [*qīng míng*; Qingming]), the Themes in the other three clauses all serve to indicate new information. Such a structure of presenting new information is commonly seen in poetry.

Table 5.1. Theme and Rheme choices in the original of *Qing Ming*

Theme	Rheme
清明时节 *qīng míng shí jié* Qingming season	雨纷纷 *yǔ fēn fēn* rain succession
路上行人 *lù shàng xíng rén* road on pedestrian	欲断魂 *yù duàn hún* will lose soul
借问 *jiè wèn* may ask	酒家何处有 *jiǔ jiā hé chù yǒu* tavern what place have
牧童 *mù tóng* herd child	遥指杏花村 *yáo zhǐ xìng huā cūn* far point apricot flower village

5.4 Textual analysis of the English translations

When using language, we organize linguistic structures with textual strategies to indicate the relationship between different clauses or elements. In Systemic Functional Grammar (SFG), the textual metafunction involves (1) the organization of linguistic elements to present a text and (2) the composition of linguistic structures to express meaning.

There are several English translations of DU Mu's *Qing Ming*. As in the previous chapters, six English translations will be discussed here: those by Juntao Wu (see Zhang 1996: 30), Tinggan Cai (see Wen 1989: 174), Dayu Sun (1997: 435), Xianyi Yang and Gladys Yang (2001a: 266), Changsheng Wan and Xianzhong Wang (see Zhu 2000: 166) and Yuanchong Xu (2000b: 537).

5.4.1 Theme analysis

In simple terms, a clause can be divided into Theme and Rheme, with Theme being the departure of message and the beginning element of a clause. After we identify the Theme of a clause, the rest of the clause will be the Rheme. Moreover, a Theme can be differentiated as marked or unmarked: in a declarative clause, a Theme realized by Subject will be unmarked, and that realized by other elements – for example, Complement and Adjunct – will be marked. In addition, a Theme can be differentiated as simple or multiple: a Theme realized by experiential elements – for example, process, participant, and circumstance – will be a simple Theme; while a Theme realized by experiential, interpersonal and/or textual elements will be a multiple Theme.

The following discussion will focus on the analysis of Theme in the English translations.

Among the six translations of the first sentence, three types of thematic structure are identified. First, a Theme can be realized by "it" (Subject), which does not function as a participant in the clause (as seen in both Wu's translation and Yang and Yang's translation). Second, a Theme can be realized by Actor (Subject): "the rain" (Cai's translation), "the ceaseless drizzles" (Wan and Wang's translation) and "a drizzling rain" (Xu's translation). Third, a Theme can be realized by circumstance: "upon the Clear-and-Bright Feast of spring" (Sun's translation) (see Table 5.2).

Table 5.2. Theme and Rheme choices in the English translations of the first sentence in *Qing Ming*

Translator(s)	Theme	Rheme
Wu	It	drizzles thick on the Pure Brightness Day
Cai	The rain	falls thick and fast on All Souls' Day
Sun	Upon the Clear-and-Bright Feast of spring	the rain drizzleth down in spray
Yang & Yang	It	drizzles endless during the rainy season in spring
Wan & Wang	The ceaseless drizzle	drips all the dismal day
Xu	A drizzling rain	falls like tears on the Mourning Day

In Chinese, it is very common for time phrases, which indicate circumstantial meaning, to function as Theme. "清明 时节 雨 纷纷" (*qīng míng shí jié yǔ fēn fēn*; Qingming season rain succession) is an example. However, in English such instances of Theme are analysed as marked choices. In his translation, Sun places "upon the Clear-and-Bright Feast of spring" at the beginning of a clause as a marked Theme, thus making the clause somehow top-heavy. This choice may be due to the need to place "spray" at the end of the clause to rhyme with "away" in the second clause (i.e. "Pedestrians on country-side ways in gloom are pining away ") and "say" in the fourth clause (i.e. "The shepherd boy the Apricot Bloom Vill doth point to afar and say").

For the second sentence in Chinese, five of the six translations have adopted participants as Themes, including "I" (Wu's translation), "the men and women" (Cai's translation), "pedestrians on countryside ways" (Sun's translation), "travelers along the road" (Yang and Yang's translation) and "the mourner's heart" (Xu's translation). Except for Yang and Yang's translation, in which the Theme is realized by Carrier (i.e. a participant in a clause with relational process), in the other four translations Themes are all realized by Actors in clauses with material processes. In Wan and Wang's translation, the Theme is realized by a circumstance: "so broken-hearted" (see also Huang 2002a) (see Table 5.3).

Table 5.3. Theme and Rheme choices in the English translations of the second sentence in *Qing Ming*

Translator(s)	Theme	Rheme
Wu	I	travel with my heart lost in dismay
Cai	The men and women	sadly move along the way
Sun	Pedestrians on countryside ways	in gloom are pining away
Yang & Yang	Travelers along the road	look gloomy and miserable
Wan & Wang	So broken-hearted	fares the traveler on the way
Xu	The mourner's heart	is going to break on his way

In Wan and Wang's translation, a circumstance – "so broken-hearted" – is chosen as a marked topical Theme, which seems abrupt and unnatural. It can be estimated that the aim of choosing a circumstance as the marked topical Theme is to rhyme "way" at the end of this line with "day" at the end of the previous line (i.e. "The ceaseless drizzle drips all the dismal day").

For the third sentence in Chinese, single Themes are used in two translations, namely "they" (as Subject) in Cai's translation and "where" (as Adjunct) in Xu's translation. In the other four translations, multiple Themes are applied – "is there" (Finite + Subject) in Wu's translation, "when ..." in Sun's as well as Wan and Wang's translations and "When I" in Yang and Yang's translation. The Themes in these four translations are multiple because they include interpersonal and/or textual elements (see Table 5.4).

Table 5.4. Theme and Rheme choices in the English translations of the third sentence in *Qing Ming*

Translator(s)	Theme	Rheme
Wu	"Is there	a public house somewhere, cowboy?"
Cai	They	ask where wineshops can be found or where to rest –
Sun	When	asked "Where a tavern fair for rest is hereabouts to be found"
Yang & Yang	When I	ask a shepherd boy where I can find a tavern
Wan & Wang	When	asked where could be found a tavern bower
Xu	Where	can a wineshop be found to drown his sad hours?

In Wu's translation, the Theme is realized by Subject and Finite ("is there"). According to Halliday (1994), "there" functions as an experiential element and "is" as an interpersonal element. Therefore, "is there" is analysed as a multiple Theme (see Huang 1999: 135–46 for discussions on Theme in "there be" structure). In translations by Yang and Yang, Sun, and Wan and Wang, the Themes are all realized by "when" to indicate textual meaning, and by "I" and "he" to indicate experiential meaning. However, in translations by Sun and by Wan and Wang, the instances of "he" are omitted. In Table 5.5, we analyse the multiple Themes that consist of textual and experiential elements.

Table 5.5. Analysis of multiple Themes consisting of textual and experiential elements

<table>
<tr><td>Yang & Yang's translation:
Sun's translation:
Wan & Wang's translation:</td><td>when
when
when</td><td>I
(he)
(he)</td><td>ask ... a tavern
(is) asked "where ... found"
(is) asked where ... bower</td></tr>
<tr><td rowspan="3"></td><td>structure</td><td>topic</td><td rowspan="3">Rheme</td></tr>
<tr><td>textual Theme</td><td>topical (experiential) Theme</td></tr>
<tr><td colspan="2">(multiple) Theme</td></tr>
</table>

In a syntactic perspective, it has to be pointed out that the translations of this sentence by Sun, Yang and Yang, as well as by Wan and Wang, are dependent clauses. When these clauses do not function as independent poetic lines, the instances of the textual "when" plus the experiential "I" or "he" will not be analysed as multiple Themes.

Instead, the complete dependent clause will be considered as Theme (i.e. dependent clause as Theme), as shown in Table 5.6 (see Thompson 1996: 132).

Table 5.6. Analysis of dependent clause as Theme

When I was there	he was out of the country.
Theme	Rheme

Due to the fact that dependent clauses beginning with "when" are treated as dependent lines in the three translations by Sun, Yang and Yang, and Wan and Wang, we have modified our method of Theme analysis accordingly.

Among the six translations of the fourth sentence, Actors serve as Themes in five of the translations, including "he" (Wu's translation and Yang and Yang's translation), "the shepherd boy" (Sun's translation), "a cowboy" (Wan and Wang's translation) and "a cowherd" (Xu's translation). These elements function as Subjects in the clauses and are thus analysed as unmarked topical Themes, which are also single Themes (because they are only realized by experiential elements).

Table 5.7. Theme and Rheme choices in the English translations of the fourth sentence in *Qing Ming*

Translator(s)	**Theme**	**Rheme**
Wu	He	points at Apricot Bloom Village faraway
Cai	And there	the herdboy's fingers Almond-Town suggest
Sun	The shepherd boy	the Apricot Bloom Vill doth point to afar and say
Yang & Yang	He	points at a distant hamlet nestling amidst apricot blooms
Wan & Wang	A cowboy	points to yonder village of the apricot flower
Xu	A cowherd	points to a cot 'mid apricot flowers

In Cai's translation, the Theme is realized by "and there", which is both a marked topical Theme and a multiple Theme (see Table 5.8). It is a multiple Theme because it includes a textual element, "and", which indicates structural meaning; it is a marked topical Theme because it includes an experiential element, "there", which does not function as the Subject of the clause.

Table 5.8. Marked topical (and multiple) Theme in Cai's translation

And	there	the herdboy's fingers Almond-Town suggest
structural	topical	Rheme
textual Theme	experiential Theme	
(multiple) Theme		

The use of "and" in Cai's translation is largely due to the consideration of form. The first three sentences all include 12 syllables. With the addition of "and" in this sentence, the translator has then made up the 12 syllables. It can also be noted that "where to rest" from the third sentence in Cai's translation is added not only to make up the 12 syllables, but also to rhyme "rest" with "suggest" in the following sentence. Such a practice mainly reflects the considerations of "beauty in form" and "beauty in sound", whereas it may not be appropriate to the expression of meaning.

As shown in the analysis above, in terms of artistic conception, the translations with marked topical Themes (i.e. Sun's translation: "Upon the Clear-and-Bright Feast of spring the rain drizzleth down in spray", Wan and Wang's translation: "So broken-hearted fares the traveler on the way", and Cai's translation: "And there the herdboy's fingers Almond-Town suggest", with the Themes being underlined) may not be better choices compared with the other translations applying unmarked Themes.

5.4.2 Cohesion analysis

Cohesion refers to the relationship between the linguistic elements in a text. In the perspective of cohesion, cohesive relations can be observed when the interpretation of one element is dependent on another element. For instance, the interpretation of "he" in the fourth sentence in Wu's translation is dependent on "cowboy" in the previous sentence, thus a linkage is constructed between the two elements.

There are different cohesive devices, which Halliday and Hasan (1976) categorize into five major types: reference, omission, substitution, conjunction and lexical cohesion (see also Hu 1994; Huang 1988). In the English translations analysed in this chapter, we have identified three cohesive devices: reference, ellipsis and conjunction.

1. Reference

The instances of reference fall into two categories: (1) personal reference; and (2) demonstrative reference.

Uses of personal reference are seen in "cowboy" ← "he" (Wu's translation), "the men and women" ← "they" (Cai's translation), "a shepherd boy" ← "he" (Yang and Yang's translation) and "the mourner's" ← "his" (Xu's translation). The other instance of "his" (in "on *his* way") in Xu's translation does not play a cohesive role between the sentences and will not be discussed here.

Demonstrative reference is used in "there" → "Almond-Town" (Cai's translation). In the English translations, the uses of "he", "they" and "his" belong to anaphoric reference, while the use of "there" belongs to cataphoric reference (see Halliday & Hasan 1976; Hu 1994; Huang 1988).

The uses of reference discussed here are all endophoric, while instances of exophoric reference such as "I" (Wu's translation, Yang and Yang's translation) will not be explored.

2. Ellipsis

The same omissions (e.g. "he is") are seen in the translations by Sun as well as Wan and Wang. For ellipsis, it is necessary to take co-text into consideration to determine the elements being omitted. In translations by Sun as well as by Wan and Wang, "he" is omitted because "the shepherd boy" or "a cowboy" is seen in the preceding text; "is" is omitted because passive voice is used in this sentence; further, "is" rather than "was" is omitted because the other verbs in the translation are all in present tense.

3. Conjunction

Among the six translations, only Cai's has used "and" – a coordinating conjunction. As previously stated, the choice of this conjunction is mainly due to the consideration of form. Naturally, as a conjunction, "and" serves to cohesively link the two clauses and to express the additive meaning. In a logical perspective, the use of "and" indicates that a clause complex is constructed by paratactically linking "And there the herdboy's fingers Almond-Town suggest" to the following clause.

5.4.3 Use of article

Since we have already discussed the choice of article and the expression of meaning, in this section we will analyse the use of article in relation to our analysis of theme and information.

As previously shown in theme analysis, for Themes realized by nominal groups, some begin with indefinite articles, some with definite articles, while two apply no article (i.e. zero article):

1. indefinite article: "a cowboy" (Wan and Wang's translation), "a drizzling rain" (Xu's translation), and "a cowboy" (Xu's translation)
2. definite article: "the rain" (Cai's translation), "the men and women" (Cai's translation), "the shepherd boy" (Sun's translation), "the ceaseless drizzle" (Wan and Wang's translation), and "the mourner's heart" (Xu's translation).
3. no article: "pedestrians" (Sun's translation) and "travelers" (Yang and Yang's translation).

In terms of the use of article in the English translations, nominal groups with indefinite articles indicate indefinite specific reference; those with definite articles indicate definite specific reference; while those with no article play the same role as those with indefinite article and indicate indefinite specific reference.

As Theme is the departure of message, the nominal groups that realize Theme should normally indicate definite specific reference. In the perspective of linguistic realization, such a (common) nominal group should include a definite article. Therefore, in normal cases, a nominal group including a definite article will function as Theme.

In terms of information distribution, a message is normally composed of "given information + new information". The basic communicative function of definite article is to indicate a definite reference. In the English translations, this kind of definite reference does not depend on co-text, but rather on context, and is hence named as situational specific reference (see Zhang 1997: 228–33). As a result, based on the choices of definite and indefinite articles in the English translations we analysed, definite articles normally indicate given information, while indefinite articles (zero article) indicate new information. Following this logic, we can say that the choices of "a" in "a cowboy" (Wan and Wang's translation), "a drizzling rain" and "a cowherd" (Xu's translation) are not as natural and appropriate as "the".

The uses of zero article also indicate indefinite specific reference, as seen in "pedestrians" (Sun's translation) and "travelers" (Yang and Yang's translation). However, these are plural forms located in sentences that serve to describe the persons in an event and to function as referential and scene-painting sections in a poem. Therefore, choices of zero article are also natural and appropriate.

5.5 Conclusion

By offering a preliminary investigation of DU Mu's *Qing Ming* in the perspective of textual metafunction following Halliday's Systemic Functional Linguistics (SFL), this chapter represents one attempt at functional text analysis (see Huang 2001a, 2001b, 2002h). By conducting linguistic analyses, all chapters in this book have revealed that analyses of translated texts can help us to investigate some difficult problems in translation in a new perspective. Moreover, the discussion in this chapter has to some extent tested the applicability and operability of SFL in text analysis.

Chapter 6

Verbal process and text structure

6.1 Introduction

In Chapters 2 to 5, we analysed DU Mu's (杜牧) *Qing Ming* (清明) in the perspective of metafunctions. In this chapter, we conduct a functional discourse analysis of *Xun Yin Zhe Bu Yu* (寻隐者不遇), written by Jia Dao [贾岛] in the Tang Dynasty, and its English translations in terms of verbal process and text structure.

We will first briefly review the two terms in Systemic Functional Linguistics (SFL) – that is, verbal process and text structure. Then we will analyse JIA Dao's *Xun Yin Zhe Bu Yu* in these two perspectives and raise some questions worthy of discussion based on the analysis. We will then analyse the English translations of this poem in these two perspectives. Finally, we will discuss two issues identified in our analysis.

6.2 Two terms in Systemic Functional Linguistics

6.2.1 Verbal process

Following Halliday's (1994) Systemic Functional Grammar (SFG), verbal process is one of the six process types in the TRANSITIVITY system that models on the ideational metafunction. Verbal process serves to exchange information through verbal activities. In English, verbs such as "tell", "ask", "question", "answer" and "say" are often used to realize verbal processes. The participants involved in verbal process include Sayer, Receiver, Verbiage and so on.

Example (1)
Henry [Sayer] told [Process: verbal] Helen [Receiver] the news [Verbiage].

In certain situations, participants involved in the verbal processes are invisible – that is, they are not realized verbally.

Example (2)
Ask [Process: verbal] him [Receiver].

In terms of the realization in form, there is only one participant in Example (2) – that is, the Receiver. The Sayer (i.e. "you") is invisible and can be added back, whereas the Verbiage is uncertain and cannot be added back.

In the two examples above, the participants are all realized by nominal groups, including "Henry", "Helen", "the news" and "him". However, participants can also be realized by prepositional phrases, as seen in the following example:

Example (3)
She [Sayer] asked [Process: verbal] about his health [Verbiage].

In Example (3), the Verbiage is realized by a prepositional phrase – that is, "about his health". Based on our functional syntactic analysis, "She" functions as Subject, "asked" as Finite + Predicator and the prepositional phrase "about his health" as Complement. Such an analytical approach is different from traditional grammar, according to which a prepositional phrase cannot serve as complement or object.

6.2.2 Projection

In terms of logico-semantic relation, the relation of expansion or projection is found among two or more clauses in a clause complex. When the relation of projection is seen between two clauses in a clause complex, one of the clauses is the projecting clause and the other is the projected clause.

Example (4)
Henry said, "Helen is lovely."

Example (5)
John said Mary was ugly.

The relation of projection is found in the two examples above, with "Henry said" and "John said" being the projecting clauses and "Helen is lovely" and "Mary was ugly" being the projected clauses. In Example (4), the projected clause is a quote; in Example (5), the projected clause is a report. In traditional grammar, we refer to the former as direct speech and the latter as indirect speech. Quoting means to repeat what others have said once again, which indicates that before we use Example (4),

Henry has already said "Helen is lovely" and we are repeating the same sentence that Helen has said. Reporting means to say what others have said in one's own words. For reporting, one can repeat the words or structures used by others, while one can also express the meaning of the others in one's own words. For instance, the quote in Example (5) is based on "Mary is ugly", said by John, with "Mary" and "ugly" being repeated and "is" being changed to "was". In another example, suppose George said "Hello!" to me in the office and I want to indirectly quote his greeting, I can then use Example (6):

Example (6)
George greeted me.

In the report in Example (6), neither the word nor the structure used by George is repeated. In addition, suppose Michael said "Let me do this for you" to me; I can then report it, as in Example (7):

Example (7)
Michael offered to do that for me.

In Example (7), only two words ("do" and "for") are from the original, while other words and the complete sentence structure are reorganized based on the meaning of the original.

6.3 Analysis of JIA Dao's original

The following poem by JIA Dao serves as the source text in our analysis:

寻 隐者 不 遇
xún yǐn zhě bú yù
seek hermit not encounter

贾岛
jiǎ dǎo
JIA Dao

松 下 问 童子，
sōng xià wèn tóng zǐ,
pine under ask boy,

言 师 采 药 去。
yán shī cǎi yào qù.
say master gather herb go.

只在此山中，
zhǐ zài cǐ shān zhōng,
only be in this mountain in,

云深不知处。
yún shēn bù zhī chù.
cloud deep not know place.

In this short poem, consisting of 20 Chinese characters, the poet has depicted the following scene: In a quiet pinewood far from the madding crowd, the poet asked a boy, "Is your master home?" The boy answered: "My master went to gather herbs." Upon hearing this, the poet felt disappointed and went on asking, "Do you know where he went to gather herbs?" The boy then pointed to a distant place with his finger and said: "Right in this mountain." Wondering about the master's whereabouts in the mountain, the poet hoped that the boy could provide some more accurate information, but the boy did not know that either. Therefore, the boy said it was the place where the white clouds slowly rose.

The above explanation may be used by a Chinese teacher when interpreting this poem. However, by looking up a dictionary on Tang poems, we find the following discussion:

> The feature of this poem lies in its embeddedness of question in answer. By saying "松下问童子" (*sōng xià wèn tóng zǐ*; pine under ask boy), there must certainly be a question, which is here omitted. In the boy's reply, i.e. "师采药去" (*shī cǎi yào qù*; master gather herb go), we can tell that the question asked under the pine tree is in fact "师往何处去" (*shī wǎng hé chù qù*; master to what place go). It follows with another omission of the question "采药在何处" (*cǎi yào zài hé chù*; gather herb be at what place) by merely providing the boy's answer "只在此山中" (*zhǐ zài cǐ shān zhōng*; only be in this mountain in), which incorporates the question. In the final sentence, i.e. "云深不知处" (*yún shēn bù zhī chù*; cloud deep not know place), the boy further answers the question about where the master gathered herbs and whether the place was at the front, back, top, or foot of the mountain. To recount the questions and answers, there require at least six sentences, whereas JIA Dao has incorporated the questions in the answers and simplified the poem into twenty Chinese characters. Such a technique of wording is thus not seen at the level of words or phrases. (Xiqian Shen, see Xiao et al. 1983: 968, our translation).

Following Xiqian Shen's argument, the first sentence in JIA Dao's poem is a projecting clause. "问" (*wèn*; ask) is a verbal process, with "童子"

(*tóng zǐ*; boy) being the Receiver. "松 下" (*sōng xià*; pine under) is a circumstance, while Sayer and Verbiage are not seen. The last three sentences of the poem, except for the verb "言" (*yán*; say) in the second line, are projected by the first sentence and are thus projected clauses. The three projected clauses all have their implicit projecting clauses (e.g. "童子 答" [*tóng zǐ dá*; boy answer]) and the structures that include projected clauses are also answers to the implied questions.

6.4 Analysis of the English translations

There are various English translations of JIA Dao's *Xun Yin Zhe Bu Yu*. We have collected eight of them: Witter Bynner (see Wen 1989: 166–67), Burton Watson (see Wen 1989: 167), Yuanchong Xu (also referred to as Xu [1]) (i.e. Xu's first translation; see Xu, Lu & Wu 1988: 308), Juntao Wu (1997: 621), Dalian Wang (1997: 129), Dayu Sun (1997: 427), Changsheng Wan and Xianzhong Wang (2000: 160) and Yuanchong Xu (also referred to as Xu [2]) (i.e. Xu's second translation; see Xu 2000b: 479).

In the following sub-sections, we will discuss the English translations sentence by sentence.

6.4.1 Title

The title in the origina is "寻 隐者 不 遇" (*xún yǐn zhě bú yù*; seek hermit not encounter), which is rendered in the eight translations as follows (see Table 6.1):

Table 6.1 Translations of the title *Xun Yin Zhe Bu Yu*

Title / Translations	寻 隐者 不 遇 **xún yǐn zhě bú yù** **seek hermit not encounter**
Bynner's translation	A Note Left for an Absent Recluse
Watson's translation	Looking for a Recluse but Failing to Find Them
Xu's first translation	Looking for a Hermit without Finding Him
Wu's translation	Missing the Hermit when Visiting Him
Wang's translation	An Unsuccessful Visit to an Absent Recluse
Sun's translation	A Call on the Recluse Who Is Just Out
Wan and Wang's translation	A Hermit Visited but Not Encountered
Xu's second translation	For an Absent Recluse

In terms of form, the eight translations of the title can be categorized into three types: (1) nominal group (translations by Bynner, Wang, Sun, as well as Wan and Wang); (2) clause (Watson's translation, Xu's first translation, and Wu's translation); and (3) prepositional phrase (Xu's second translation). In terms of meaning, nominal groups realize things, clauses realize situations and prepositional phrases indicate that "the note is left for somebody". In the perspective of the target reader, Bynner's translation and Xu's second translation belong to one category, while the other six translations belong to the other category, with the former being composed for the "hermit" and the latter not being composed for the "hermit".

6.4.2 Sentence 1

In all the eight translations, verbal processes are used to indicate the meaning in this sentence. Two verbs that realize verbal processes are applied, namely "question" and "ask" (Table 6.2).

Table 6.2. Translations of the first sentence in *Xun Yin Zhe Bu Yu*

Line / Translations	松 下 问 童子 *sōng xià wèn tóng zǐ* pine under ask boy
Bynner's translation	When I questioned your pupil, under a pine tree
Watson's translation	Under the pines I questioned the boy
Xu's first translation	I ask your lad 'neath a pine-tree
Wu's translation	"Where is your Master?" under pines I ask a lad
Wang's translation	Beneath pine trees I asked your lad nearby
Sun's translation	I asked the boy beneath the pine tree
Wan and Wang's translation	About the hermit I ask a boy under a pine
Xu's second translation	I ask your lad "neath a pine tree

The eight translations in Table 6.2 share a very similar structure: "松 下" (*sōng xià*; pine under) is realized by prepositional phrases (i.e. "under a pine tree", "under the pines", "under pines", "under a pine", "beneath a pine-tree", "beneath pine trees", "beneath the pine tree" and "beneath a pine tree"), "问" (*wèn*; ask) is realized by verbs (i.e. "questioned" and "ask/asked"), and "童子" (*tóng zǐ*; boy) is realized by nominal groups (i.e. "your pupil", "your lad", "the boy", "a lad" and "a boy"). All translations select the first-person singular pronoun "I" to realize the Sayer of the verbal process.

As discussed above, there is an omitted question for "松下问童子" (*sōng xià wèn tóng zǐ*; pine under ask boy). For the boy's answer "师采药去" (*shī cǎi yào qù*; master gather herb go), we find that the question raised under the pine tree is "师往何处去" (*shī wǎng hé chù qù*; master to which place go). In Wu's translation, the implied question is realized by way of quoting: "Where is your Master?", which is a projected clause, with "under pines I ask a lad" being the projecting clause. In Wan and Wang's translation, the meaning of "about the hermit" is similar to the projected clause in Wu's translation: both directly present the implied details with language. "Where is your Master?" suggests one "situation", while "about the hermit" deals with a "thing" (a "person").

In terms of the artistic conception of poetry, the translations by Wu and by Wan and Wang are over-explicit by indicating the omitted words, thus leaving little imaginary space for readers and being incompatible with the organization of the whole poems. The other six translations have adopted a more appropriate method.

6.4.3 Sentence 2

A verbal process is found in the original poem, with "言" (*yán*; say) realizing the process and "师采药去" (*shī cǎi yào qù*; master gather herb go) being the projected clause. Among the eight translations, seven apply quoting, while only one translation applies reporting.

Quoting

Bynner's translation: "My master," he answered, "went for herbs,"

Watson's translation: "My master's off gathering herbs."

Xu's first translation: "My master's gone for herbs," says he,

Wu's translation: "He's gathering medicinal herbs," so he says,

Wang's translation: "My master's gone for herbs," was the reply.

Sun's translation: Who said, "The master's gone herbs to pick;"

Xu's second translation: "My master's gone for herbs," says he. (same as Xu's first translation)

Reporting

Wan and Wang's translation: And he answers that his master is gone out,

Among the seven translations that apply quoting, five – translations by Bynner, Xu [1], Wu, Sun, and Xu [2] – adopt verbal processes (realized by verbs including "answered", "says" and "said"), thus projecting clauses are applied; one translation omits the projecting clause; one translation adopts a relational process (the quoted clause "My master's gone for herbs" serves as Carrier in a clause with relational process, with "was" being the Process and "the reply" being the Attribute). In contrast, translations by Bynner, Xu [1], Wu, Sun and Xu [2] are more appropriate. In Wang's translation, a relational rather than a verbal process is used, so the first and the second sentences can rhyme with each other (as seen in "Beneath pine trees I asked your lad nearby; / 'My master's gone for herbs,' was the reply.").

Although Wan and Wang apply reporting in their translation ("And he answers that his master is gone out"), the process involved is still a verbal one, which is realized by the verb "answers". In this respect, this sentence is rendered appropriately. Also, in Wan and Wang's translation, "has" may be a better choice compared with "is". It is due to the organization of the whole poem that quoting is not applied. By translating in this way, the translated poem is much closer to the style of the original.

In general, the second sentence in the original is mostly equivalent to its eight translations in terms of both form and meaning. In some translations, we also find choices that are inappropriate to the style of the original in certain respects.

6.4.4 Sentences 3 and 4

Among the eight translations, seven – with the exception of Xu's second translation – have treated sentences 3 and 4 as the same turn with "师 采 药 去" (*shī cǎi yào qù*; master gather herb go) in the previous sentence. Thus, two turns are identified in these seven translations:

turn 1: raising a question to the boy (line 1 of the original poem)

turn 2: the boy answering the question (lines 2, 3, and 4 of the original poem).

In terms of structure, seven translations have treated the last three lines as the quoted part, which is realized by two clause complexes, with line 2 itself forming one clause and lines 3 and 4 being realized either by a clause complex or by two clauses.

Five translations have adopted one clause complex to render lines 3 and 4 (see Table 6.3)

Table 6.3. Translations that render lines 3 and 4 as one clause complex

Line / Translations	只在此山中，云深不知处 *zhǐ zài cǐ shān zhōng, yún shēn bù zhī chù* only be in this mountain in, cloud deep not know place
Bynner's translation	but toward which corner of the mountain," How can I tell, through all these clouds?"
Watson's translation	All I know is he's here on the mountain – clouds are so deep, I don't know where ...
Xu's first translation	"Amid the hills I know not where, For clouds have veiled them here and there."
Wu's translation	"Deep in the mountains, where all the things are clad. With clouds, and no one can grope out the ways."
Sun's translation	He must be somewhere around these cliffs, Concealed unseen in the clouds thick."

According to Wen (1989: 167, our translation), Bynner treats the second, third, and fourth lines as one clause complex: "The normal order of the second, third, and fourth lines should be as follows: 'Through all these clouds, how can I tell toward which corner of the mountains my teacher[1] went for herbs?' he answers."[2] Following Wen's analysis, the quoted part in the second line of Bynner's translation (i.e. "My master went for herbs") is the clause projected by "tell" in the fourth line, while the whole clause complex also serves as one projected clause, as shown in Table 6.4.

Table 6.4. Analysis of lines 3 and 4 in Bynner's translation

<table>
<tr><td>Through all these clouds</td><td>how</td><td>can</td><td>I</td><td>tell</td><td>toward which corner of the mountain my master went for herbs?</td><td>he</td><td>answered</td></tr>
<tr><td>Cause (circum-stance)</td><td>Manner (circum-stance)</td><td>part of Process 2: modality</td><td>Sayer 2</td><td>Process 2: verbal</td><td rowspan="2">projected clause 2</td><td rowspan="2">Sayer 1</td><td rowspan="2">Process 1: verbal</td></tr>
<tr><td colspan="5">projecting clause 2</td></tr>
<tr><td colspan="6">projected clause 1</td><td colspan="2">projecting clause 1</td></tr>
</table>

As shown in Table 6.4, Bynner's translation of lines 2–4 consists of a projecting clause and a projected clause. In the original, these three lines constitute one turn, which is the answer to the question raised in the first line of the poem. In translations by Watson, Xu [1], Wu and Sun, the third and fourth lines in the original are rendered as a clause complex (see Table 6.3).

In Wang's translation, the third and fourth lines of the original are rendered as two clauses:

> He's only in this mountain somewhere 'round.
> In heavy mists he's nowhere to be found.

In terms of semantic and structural equivalence, the two lines translated by Wang are better than the other seven English translations in terms of meaning expression and artistic conception.

In Wan and Wang's translation, which is similar to Bynner's, the second, third and fourth lines of the original are rendered as one sentence in English:

> And he answers that his master is gone out,
> Into the mountains to gather herbs for medicine,
> Yet for the heavy clouds he knows not his whereabout.

However, translations by Bynner as well as by Wan and Wang are different in that Bynner adopts quoting in his translation, whereas Wan and Wang apply reporting.

It can also be noted that, in Xu's second translation, the third and fourth lines in the original are rendered as words said by the poet to the hermit:

> You hide amid the mountains proud,
> I know not where deep in the cloud.

In the above-cited lines, "you" refers to the hermit, "I" refers to the poet who looks for the hermit and the two sentences are spoken by the poet to the hermit, who he has never met. In this respect, Xu's second translation is written by the poet, who cannot find the hermit and has therefore left this poem for him. This translation is different from the other seven translations, which regard the third and fourth lines of the original as the boy's answer to the questioner (i.e. the poet or "I" in the poem). Instead, the poet speculates on the whereabouts of the hermit and informs the hermit about this speculation.

Except for translations by Wang and by Xu [2], the other six translations have all "broken up" the lines when translating the third and fourth lines of the original. Therefore, we cannot treat these two lines as two independent answers. In this respect, we find that Wang's translation not only considers the semantic equivalence between the source language and the target language, but also maintains the equivalence in form.

In Xu's second translation, by treating the third and fourth lines as a visitor's note to the hermit, the meaning in these two lines has departed from those in the other translations. It can also be noted that in Xu's first translation, "只在此山中，云深不知处" (*zhǐ zài cǐ shān zhōng, yún shēn bù zhī chù*; only be in this mountain in, cloud deep not know place) is rendered as the boy's reply, whereas in Xu's second translation, these two lines are regarded as the poet's words to the hermit. Within a short period, the same translator has adopted two completely different strategies in translating the same ancient Chinese poem, which perhaps does not have a fixed interpretation.

6.5 Discussion

Several topics on the eight English translations of JIA Dao's *Xun Yin Zhe Bu Yu* are worthy of discussion. Due to limited space, only two points will be made here.

6.5.1 "Three questions and three answers" vs "one question and one answer"

According to Xiqian Shen (in Xiao et al. 1983: 968; see also Shen's discussion in Section 6.3), JIA Dao's poem has embedded questions in answers, with three rounds of questions and answers being involved and the questions being incorporated into the answers. In this way, the original poem only includes three answers (i.e. "师采药去" [*shī cǎi yào qù*; master gather herb go], "只在此山中" [*zhǐ zài cǐ shān zhōng*; only be in this mountain in], and "云深不知处" [*yún shēn bù zhī chù*; cloud deep not know place]), which include the questions in an implicit manner.

The eight English translations all involve one question and one answer. Except for Xu's second translation, the other seven translations all render the second, third and fourth lines of the original as the answer to the first line, hence adopting the style of "one question and one answer". In Xu's second translation, although the third and fourth lines in the original are not treated as the answer, the style of "one question and one answer" is still adopted, as in the other seven translations. Therefore, we have observed the pattern of "one question and one answer" in all eight translations.

In terms of the artistic conception in the original poem, the styles of "three questions and three answers" as well as "embedding questions in answers" may provide readers with more imaginary space. Following this logic, what kind of English translation can entail the poetic splendor of incorporating "three questions and three answers" and "incorporating questions in answers"? In Wang's translation, we suggest that if we add quotation marks at the end of the third line and at the beginning of the fourth line, questions will then be incorporated in answers:

An Unsuccessful Visit to an Absent Recluse
By JIA Dao
Beneath pine trees I asked your lad nearby;
"My master's gone for herbs," was the reply.
"He's only in this mountain somewhere 'round.
In heavy mists he's nowhere to be found."

In Wang's translation, the third and fourth lines constitute two sentences in one turn. However, by adding quotation marks in the third and fourth lines, these lines then become independent answers, which constitute two different turns. If we add the answer in the second sentence, there will be in total three turns that aim at answering the questions:

Turn 1: Question: (Where is your master?)
Turn 2: Answer: My master's gone for herbs.
Turn 3: Question: (Where did he go?)
Turn 4: Answer: He's only in this mountain somewhere around.
Turn 5: Question: (Where exactly is he now?)
Turn 6: Answer: In heavy mists he's nowhere to be found.

Based on our hypothesis discussed above, we find that the revised version of Wang's translation is equivalent to the original in terms of both form and meaning. In this respect, Wang's translation is perhaps more appropriate compared with the other seven translations.

In fact, the techniques of "embedding questions in answers" and "incorporating questions in answers" are frequently seen in poems written in both Chinese and English.

The following poem, written by Roger McGough, has applied such techniques. Due to the limited space in this book, however, we will merely cite the first 11 lines of the poem (see Tao 2002: 123–24 for the whole poem):

Conversation on a Train
Roger McGough
I'm Shirley, she's Mary.
We're from Swansea
(If there was a horse there
It'd be a one-horse town
But there isn't even that).
We're going to Blackpool.
Just the week. A bit late I know.
But then there's the Illuminations.
Isn't there? No, never been before.
Paris last year, didn't like it.
Too expensive and nothing there really.

In his analysis, Tao (2002) regards this poem as a conversation, in which the questions are not stated verbally. For the first 11 lines, we can add back the questions (in italics) to reconstruct the poem:

Conversation on a Train
May I know your names?
I'm Shirley, she's Mary.
Where are you from?
We're from Swansea
(If there was a horse there
It'd be a one-horse town
But there isn't even that).
Where are you going?
We're going to Blackpool.
How long will you stay there?
Just the week.
Don't you think it's too late for a holiday?
A bit late I know. But then there's the Illuminations.
Isn't there?
Have you ever been there?
No, never been before.

Where did you go for your holiday last year?
Paris last year, didn't like it.
Why?
Too expensive and nothing there really.

We agree with Tao's (2002) analysis and also hold that all the turns contributed by the other interactant in Roger McGough's original poem are implicit. Although further revisions can still be made to the italicized lines, it is convincing that the discourse contributed by the other interactant is omitted in the poem.

6.5.2 Narrator and addressee

In literary studies, the "author" of a literary work and the "narrator" tend to be separated, with the "author" indicating the writer (or the composer) of the work and the "narrator" being the person who tells the story in the work (see Goddard 1998: 28–29). Following this distinction, the author of a work can be a male, while its narrator can be a female. For instance, in *Xin Jia Niang Ci* (新嫁娘词), the author is WANG Jian (王建), a male Tang poet, and the narrator is a newly wedded woman:

新 嫁 娘 词
xīn jià niáng cí
newly wedded bride lyric

王建
wáng jiàn
WANG Jian

三 日 入 厨 下，
sān rì rù chú xià,
three day go to kitchen,

洗 手 作 羹汤。
xǐ shǒu zuò gēng tang.
wash hand make broth-soup.

未 谙 姑 食 性，
wèi ān gū shí xìng,
not know mother-in-law food habit,

先 遣 小姑 尝。
xiān qiǎn xiǎo gū cháng.
first dispatch sister-in-law taste.

If we strictly distinguish the author and the narrator of a poem, we can find that for some works, the author and the narrator are the same person, while for others, this would not be the case. Under certain circumstances, it is easy to differentiate the author and the narrator, while in other cases, it may not be so easy. For *Xun Yin Zhe Bu Yu*, JIA Dao, the author of the poem, can be regarded either as the narrator or not as the narrator. However, most people are likely to equate the poet as the narrator. Therefore, for the sake of convenience, we will also adopt this view.

In this poem, the narrator recounts the events of the poem in the first-person perspective, which is accepted by all the eight English translations. Thus, the narrator of "松 下 问 童子" (*sōng xià wèn tóng zǐ*; pine under ask boy) is "我" (*wǒ*; I):

I questioned (translations by Bynner and Watson)
I ask (translations by Xu [1], Wu, Wan and Wang, and Xu [2])
I asked (translations by Wang and Sun).

When analysing the narrative perspective of a poem, we also have to differentiate the "intended receiver" and the "actual receiver". In simple terms, the intended receiver refers to the target receiver in the addresser's (or author's) mind and the actual receiver refers to the people who actually read (or hear) certain text/discourse. In some cases, the intended receiver and the actual receiver are the same person, while in other cases, the intended receiver and the actual receiver are different persons. For instance, if Zhang writes a letter to Li, then Li receives the letter and reads it, Li will both be the intended receiver and the target receiver. However, if Zhang writes a letter to Li, but the letter is received and read by Wang rather than Li, Li will then be the intended receiver and Wang will be the actual receiver. Different from letters, the intended receiver of a literary work is not one person, so it is sometimes difficult to determine the intended receiver and the actual receiver.

Moreover, the narratee is involved, which is related to narrative perspective and refers to the audience of the narrator's narration in the story. Narratee is equivalent to the intended receiver in a story. In a literary work, a narratee is fictional and is different from an actual receiver, whereas in certain cases the two roles can be taken by one person (see Wang & Zhang 1996: 304).

The following discussion will focus on the eight translations of JIA Dao's *Xun Yin Zhe Bu Yu*.

In the translations by Bynner, Xu [1], Wang, and Xu [2], the hermit is the narratee. The narrator reports on the dialogue between him and the boy to the absent hermit. The poet is the narrator and the boy is the third person in the narration. We have reached this conclusion based on the usage of personal pronouns:

> Bynner's translation: I asked your pupil ... he answered ...
> Xu's first translation: I ask your lad ... says he ...
> Wang's translation: I asked your lad ...
> Xu's second translation: I ask you lad ... says he ...

In these four translations, "I" refers to JIA Dao – the narrator – while "your" indicates the hermit who is previously mentioned in the title and "he" refers to the boy the narrator has met.

In the other four translations, however, the case is somehow different. The narrator is the poet, while the narratee is an undefined person – that is, the narratee is hard to determine. We can say that in these four translations, "I" refers to JIA Dao – the narrator – while "he" indicates the boy; no second-person pronoun is used:

> Watson's translation: ... I questioned the boy ...
> Wu's translation: ... I ask a lad ...
> Sun's translation: ... I asked the boy ...
> Wan and Wang's translation: ... I asked a boy ...

Among the four translations, the choices of definite and indefinite articles before "boy" (or "lad") are purposely made. The definite article "the" indicates that both the narrator and narratee know whom "boy" (or "lad") refers to. However, when the indefinite article "a" is applied, it suggests that both parties in the communication (especially the narratee) do not know who "boy" (or "lad") is. Hence, based on the meaning in the selection of definite and indefinite articles, we can tell that the narratee in the translations by Watson and Sun is the hermit, as only the hermit knows whom "the boy" refers to.

We can note the usage of pronoun (e.g. "he" and "his") in quoting (e.g. translations by Bynner, Watson, Xu [1], and Wu) and reporting (e.g. Wan and Wang's translation) in the English translations:

> my master (in translations by Bynner, Watson, Xu [1], Wang, and Xu [2])
> your master (in Wu's translation)
> his master (in Wan and Wang's translation).

We also find that "my master" is said by the boy, "your master" is said by the narrator and "his master" is said by the reporter (narrator). Since the words are said by different persons, it is natural that different personal pronouns such as "my", "your" and "his" are applied.

6.6 Conclusion

In this chapter, we explore the English translations of JIA Dao's *Xun Yin Zhe Bu Yu* in terms of verbal process and projection. By analysing the text structure of the poem, we hypothesize the numbers of questions and answers. Based on the hypothesis, we further analyze and comment on the English translations. As the focus of this chapter is functional discourse analysis, our discussion centres on discourse analysis (especially on determining the turns) and has to ignore certain perspectives. In my personal correspondence with Professor Baohong Zhang (10 January 2003), he expressed his views on the number of questions and answers in the poem and pointed out the problem of lexical choices in the English translations that serve as the data in this chapter. However, as this chapter does not deal with the choices of certain words, we will not comment on the appropriateness of the choices of words or sentences in the translations. In this respect, the chapters of this book all aim to focus on one or several issues in the English translations rather than to carry out an exhaustive analysis of the translations. In a theoretical perspective, such exhaustive analysis is possible, whereas in practice it is not economical and can sometimes even be meaningless or impossible (see Huang 1988: 37; 2001b).

Notes

1. "Teacher" can also be "master".
2. If taking tense into consideration, "answers" should be changed to "answered".

Chapter 7

A comparative study of Chinese and English discourse

7.1 Introduction

Written by WANG Changling (王昌龄), a Tang poet, *Fu Rong Lou Song Xin Jian* (芙蓉楼送辛渐) is a well-liked poem, which include an extremely popular line, "一 片 冰 心 在 玉 壶" (*yí piàn bīng xīn zài yù hú*; one piece ice heart be in jade jar). In this chapter, we conduct a functional discourse analysis of this poem and its English translations in the perspectives of cohesion, logico-semantic relation, thematic structure and information focus. By comparing Chinese and English discourse, we hope our analysis can shed light on the comparative studies between English and Chinese as well as on translation studies.

Various works on discourse analysis have discussed the concepts of cohesion and coherence (e.g. Halliday 1994; Halliday & Hasan 1976; Hu 1994; Huang 1988; Zhang 1998; Zhu & Yan 2001) and some have provided relatively in-depth discussions (e.g. Zhu & Yan 2001). For the sake of convenience, we will first review the concepts of cohesion and coherence in Section 7.2.

7.2 A sketch of cohesion and coherence

According to Halliday and Hasan (1976: 4), cohesion as a semantic concept refers to the relations of meaning that exist in discourse. Cohesion is constructed when the explanation of a certain element in discourse is dependent on another element:

Example (1)
Catherine is a friend of mine. She is from Russia.

In this example, the explanation of "she" is dependent on "Catherine" in the first clause complex; thus, "she" and the prepositive "Catherine" both indicate the same person. Suppose we changed "Catherine" to

"Helen", then "she" and "Helen" would refer to the same person. Such cohesive relation is realized through the use of pronoun and is referred to as reference. Besides reference, there are also other grammatical devices such as substitution, ellipsis and conjunction, as well as lexical devices such as lexical repetition, synonymy, antonymy and collocation. All these devices can be adopted to realize the semantic relation of cohesion (see Halliday & Hasan 1976).

As a psychological phenomenon, coherence exists in the minds of the author (speaker) and reader (hearer). It refers to the relationship between various units of meaning in discourse. The construction of the relationship of coherence is mainly dependent on the shared knowledge of the two parties in communication. Each discourse must have its own texture, otherwise it will not be regarded as a discourse. Therefore, each discourse is coherent. Between the various elements, there can be no cohesive relation, but there must be coherence. Widdowson (1978: 29) provides a famous example of a text that has coherence rather than cohesion:

A: That's the phone.
B: I'm in the bath.
A: Okay.

Since cohesion and coherence are both semantic concepts, then what are their differences? This is a relatively complicated question that will not be explored in this book (see Zhu & Yan 2001: 66–95 for more discussion). A simple characterization of the two concepts is that both coherence and cohesion are regarded as semantic concepts. On the one hand, texture makes a text/discourse coherent and the degree of coherence is determined by the shared knowledge of the two parties in communication; on the other hand, whether or not the phenomenon of cohesion is found in a discourse is dependent upon the existence of cohesive devices (e.g. reference, ellipsis, substitution and repetition). A text/discourse must be coherent, but it may not necessarily involve the phenomenon of cohesion.

7.3 No choice of cohesion in the original vs choices of cohesion in the translations

The poem we analyse here is *Fu Rong Lou Song Xin Jian* by WANG Changling:

Example (2)
芙蓉楼 送 辛渐
fú róng lóu sòng xīn jiàn
Hibiscus-tower see off Xin Jian

王昌龄
wáng chāng líng
WANG Changling

寒 雨 连 江 夜 入 吴，
hán yǔ lián jiāng yè rù wú,
cold rain mingle river night enter Wu,

平明 送 客 楚 山 孤。
píng míng sòng kè chǔ shān gū.
daybreak see off guest Chu mountain lonely.

洛阳 亲 友 如 相问，
luò yáng qīn yǒu rú xiàng wèn,
Luoyang relative friend if ask,

一 片 冰 心 在 玉 壶。
yí piàn bīng xīn zài yù hú.
one piece ice heart be in jade jar.

This is a very popular Tang poem. As a discourse, it is undoubtedly coherent, with semantic relations existing between different units of meaning in the poem. However, according to Halliday and Hasan's (1976) definition of cohesion, no phenomenon of cohesion is seen in the poem. In other words, there is no grammatical or lexical device that realizes cohesion.

There are several English translations of this poem. The analysis in this chapter involves four translations by Jie Tao (see Wu 1997: 119), Dalian Wang (1997: 23), Changsheng Wan and Xianzhong Wang (2000: 37) and Yuanchong Xu (2000b: 83). The four translations are both cohesive and coherent. Among them, cohesive devices are most evident in Tao's translation:

Example (3) Jie Tao's translation
Seeing Xin Jian off at Hibiscus Pavilion
Along the river that merged with a cold rain,
We entered the Wu city late at night.
Early at daybreak I bid you farewell,
With only the lone Chu Mountain in sight.

If my kinsfolk in Luoyang should feel concerned,
Please tell them for my part,
Like a piece of ice in a crystal vessel,
Fore'er aloof and pure remains my heart.

Each line of the original poem is realized by one clause, while Tao's translation is realized by five clauses. The most obvious cohesive device in this translation is personal reference, with "we" in the first clause functioning as the starting point of the cohesive chain (see Figure 7.1).

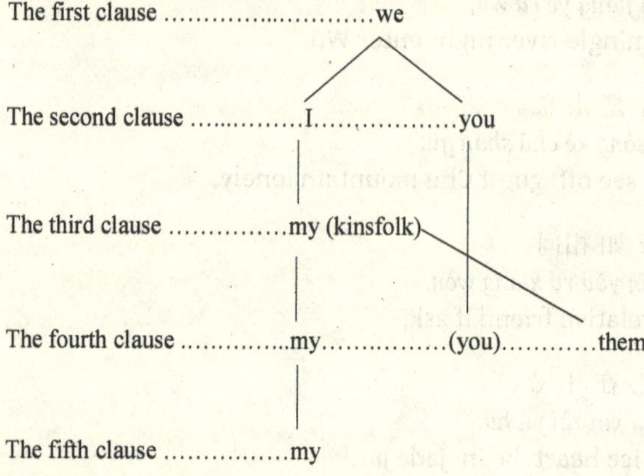

Figure 7.1. Reference relations in Tao's translation

From Figure 7.1, we find that "we" in the first clause refers to the speaker and the hearer (i.e. "I" and "you" in the second clause); "my" in the third clause is elicited from "I" in the second clause; in the fourth clause, "my" is also elicited from "I" in the second clause, and the omitted "you" is elicited from "you" in the second clause; "them" in the fourth clause and "my kinsfolk" in the third clause have also built a referential relation; "my" in the fifth clause and the two instances of "my" in the third and fourth clauses are both elicited from "I" in the second clause. Our analysis shows that personal reference is the most evident cohesive device in Tao's translation.

One aspect of studies on cohesion in translation involves equivalence. In terms of the equivalence in form, there is no corresponding element for the fourth clause in Tao's translation – "Please tell them for my part" – which is added by the translator. Therefore, the four lines (four clauses) in the original have been rendered as five clauses in the translation. Such a strategy of adding projecting clauses is also seen in another two translations, by Wang and by Wan and Wang.

Example (4) Wang's translation
In Luoyang should my folks and friends ask after me,
Tell them a heart's in jade pot, pure as it can be.
Example (5) Wan and Wang's translation
Oh, Friend, when folks in Luoyang inquires, let it be said,
My heart is as bright as crystal ice in the jar of jade.

In Wang's translation, we find "tell them", which is the same as Tao's translation and is a rather colloquial choice; in Wan and Wang's translation, "let it be said" is applied, which is both formal and elegant. Different from the other three translations, Xu's translation adds no projecting clause to introduce what is written in the fourth line of the original.

Example (6) Xu's translation
If my friends in the North should ask if I'm all right,
My heart is free of stain as ice in crystal vase.

In contrast, Xu's translation is more elegant and implicit. It leaves more space for readers to imagine, giving them a chance to recreate the poem. In this perspective, Xu's translation is better than the other three.

7.4 Analysis of logico-semantic type

In this section, we mainly discuss the logico-semantic relation in the original poem and the translations. We will first analyse WANG Changling's original, which consists of two clause complexes, with the first clause complex consisting of the former two lines and the second clause consisting of the latter two lines.

In the first clause complex – "寒雨连江夜入吴" (*hán yǔ lián jiāng yè rù wú*; cold rain mingle river night enter Wu) and "平明送客楚山孤" (*píng míng sòng kè chǔ shān gū*; daybreak see off guest Chu mountain lonely) – the tactic relation between the two clauses is parataxis and the logico-semantic relation is expansion: extension, with the second line of the poem being an addition to the first line. In other words, in terms of the expression of meaning, the second line closely follows the first line and serves as a continuation of the first line. In terms of temporal sequence, the action in the first line takes place first and then leads to the process in the second line. Therefore, the first line is the initiating clause and the second line is the continuing clause.

For the second clause complex – "洛阳亲友如相问" (*luò yáng qīn yǒu rú xiàng wèn*; Luoyang relative friend if ask) and "一片冰心在玉壶" (*yí piàn bīng xīn zài yù hú*; one piece ice heart be in jade jar) – the tactic relation is that of hypotaxis and the logico-semantic relation is expansion: enhancement, with the secondary clause in the third line providing a circumstance to the dominating clause in the fourth line. In other words, in terms of the expression of meaning, the third line provides an assumed condition to the fourth line. As the tactic relation between these two lines is hypotaxis, in terms of syntax the sequence (i.e. position) of the two clauses will not essentially impact the expression of meaning.

Moreover, in a syntactic perspective, the fourth line of the original poem is a projected clause, with the element that introduces the projected clause at the beginning of this line (i.e. the projecting clause) being omitted. As previously discussed, translations by Tao, Wang, and Wan and Wang have all added back such an element.

In terms of the logico-semantic relation in Tao's translation, the tactic and logico-semantic relation between the first and second clauses in the translation is parataxis and expansion: extension, which is the same as that between the first and the second line in the original. The third and fourth lines in the original are rendered as three clauses, because the translator adds a clause (i.e. "Please tell them for my part") to more clearly indicate the meaning in the translation. In the perspective of syntactic relation, the fifth clause in the translation is a projected clause led by the fourth clause, and the last three clauses in the translation have formed a clause complex (see Table 7.1 for the relations between these clauses).

Table 7.1. Relation between the last three clauses in Tao's translation

<table>
<tr><td rowspan="2">If my kinsfolk in Luoyang should feel concerned</td><td>Please tell them for my part</td><td>Like a piece of ice in a crystal vessel,
Fore'er aloof and pure remains my heart</td></tr>
<tr><td>projecting clause</td><td>projected clause</td></tr>
<tr><td>secondary clause</td><td colspan="2">primary clause</td></tr>
</table>

With the addition of "Please tell them for my part", the relationship between the last three clauses is stated clearly. However, given that poetry is a special genre, the explicitation of relationship will somehow reduce the reader's space for imagination and recreation, hence impacting the conveyance of artistic conception. In this respect, Xu's translation (see Example 6) is better than Tao's.

7.5 Analysis of theme and information focus

According to Halliday (1994), THEME is a textual system that mainly serves to the analysis of the starting point of a clause or clause complex and its relationship with the rest of the clause (or clause complex). Scholars on functional discourse analysis have explored the role of thematic structure in discourse and summarized the commonly used patterns of thematic progression (see Bloor & Bloor 1995: 89–94; Huang 1988: 80–85; Zhu & Yan 2001: 96–115).

In the perspective of functional discourse analysis, the beginning and ending positions, both at the level of sentence and at the level of discourse, deserve our attention. For a clause, its beginning part is the departure of message and its ending is the focus of information. For a discourse, the beginning part can be the abstract, topic sentence or topic, and the ending part can be the conclusion or resolution. In terms of thematic structure, the beginning of a clause is referred to as the Theme, which often conveys given information, while the remaining part of a clause is the Rheme, which is the location for the information focus. The beginning part of a discourse points out the main idea, major point or central issues of the discourse, with a purpose of leading readers into the discourse; the ending part of a discourse then provides a summary of the previous contents, a conclusion, or points out the moral or teaching of a discourse as seen in a fable.

Martin (1992: 437) holds that besides applying Halliday's notion of theme to the analysis of clause (or clause complex), we can also use hyper-Theme to refer to the beginning of a paragraph and macro-Theme to refer to units that are larger than hyper-Theme (e.g. a group of sentences or a paragraph) (see Figure 7.2).

macro-Theme:	discourse →
hyper-Theme:	paragraph →
Theme:	clause, clause complex

Figure 7.2. Three kinds of Theme

Based on certain theoretical foundations and analytical procedures, Martin's (1992) approach to theme analysis can be examined further. However, it has certainly provided a theoretical basis and analytical method for discourse analysis at the clause rank. Due to the limited space here and the goal of this chapter, we will not provide more discussion on Martin's approach, but will simply apply his notions to the analysis of WANG Changling's *Fu Rong Lou Song Xin Jian* and its English translations.

7.6 Theme analysis of *Fu Rong Lou Song Xin Jian*

The title of the original, "芙蓉楼 送 辛渐" (*fú róng lóu sòng xīn jiàn*; Hibiscus-tower see off Xin Jian), has pointed out the main idea of the poem. As the starting point and point of departure, the title can be regarded as the macro-Theme of the poem. Based on this macro-Theme, readers can speculate about the macro-Rheme of the poem, which will be related to the scene (e.g. time, place and persons) and utterance (e.g. words said when bidding farewell) when seeing somebody off.

In the main body of the poem, the first line describes the background (i.e. situation) of the event, lays the groundwork for the subsequent description of the event and can thus be regarded as the hyper-Theme, which serves as the starting point of narration in the following three lines (i.e. hyper-Rheme).

All clauses in the original can be divided into Themes and Rhemes. Except for the first clause of the main body – "寒雨连江夜入吴" (*hán yŭ lián jiāng yè rù wú*; cold rain mingle river night enter Wu) – which can be analyzed in different ways, analysis of the other clauses is relatively simple (see Table 7.2).

Table 7.2. Analysis of Theme in *Fu Rong Lou Song Xin Jian*

Theme	**Rheme**
芙蓉楼 (*fú róng lóu*; Hibiscus-tower)	送 辛渐 (*sòng xīn jiàn*; see off Xin Jian)
寒 雨 连 江 (*hán yŭ lián jiāng*; cold rain mingle river)	夜 入 吴 (*yè rù wú*; night enter Wu)
平明 (*píng míng*; daybreak)	送 客 楚 山 孤 (*sòng kè chŭ shān gū*; see off guest Chu mountain lonely)
洛阳 亲 友 (*luò yáng qīn yŏu*; Luoyang relative friend)	如 相问 (*rú xiàng wèn*; if ask)
一片 冰 心 (*yí piàn bīng xīn*; one piece ice heart)	在 玉 壶 (*zài yù hú*; be in jade jar.)

The analysis of the three types of Theme shows that the starting point of message in each clause is the Theme, the starting point of the main body of the text is the hyper-Theme and the starting point of the whole poem is the macro-Theme (or title of the poem). Such an analysis is very similar to Labov's (1972) description of narrative structure (see Huang 1988: 142–52), according to which macro-Theme is similar to abstract and hyper-Theme to orientation.

Based on our observation, several Tang poems share similar or identical thematic structure by containing the three types of Themes as WANG Changling's *Fu Rong Lou Song Xin Jian.* Some examples include DU Mu's (杜牧) *Qing Ming* (清明), WANG Wei's (王维) *Song Yuan Er Shi An Xi* (送元二使安西), LI Bai's (李白) *Ke Zhong Zuo* (客中作), and CUI Daorong's (崔道融) *Xi Ju Ji Shi* (溪居即事). The method of thematic analysis adopted to analyse *Fu Rong Lou Song Xin Jian* can also be applied to these poems.

7.7 Theme analysis of the English translations

In this section, we will follow Martin's (1992) three types of thematic structure to analyse the English translations of *Fu Rong Lou Song Xin Jian.* The translation by Jie Tao can be found in Example (3).

Like the original poem, the title of Tao's translation (i.e. "Seeing Xin Jian off at Hibiscus Pavilion") brings out the topic of the poem. It is the starting point of the poem and is hence the macro-Theme. From the macro-Theme, readers can predict certain words related to the poem. Tao's translation and the original are the same in this respect.

In terms of grammar, the first and the second lines of the main body of Tao's translation form one clause, which begins the event described in the poem and lays the groundwork for subsequent description. In this respect, the translation is the same as the first line of the original. Therefore, we can consider this clause in the translation as the hyper-Theme.

The four lines in the original are changed to eight lines in the translation. Further, we note that thematic analysis of a poem is different from that of a novel or other text types. Even when dealing with the translations of the same poem, the Theme choices can be different. Following our method, Tao's translation can be analysed in the following way (Themes underlined for emphasis):

> *Along the river that merged with a cold rain,* [Theme 1]
> We entered the Wu city late at night [Rheme 1].
> *Early at daybreak* [Theme 2] I bid you farewell,
> With only the lone Chu Mountain in sight [Rheme 2].
> *If my kinsfolk in Luoyang should feel concerned,* [Theme 3]
> Please tell them for my part [Rheme 3],
> *Like a piece of ice in a crystal vessel,* [Theme 4]
> Fore'er aloof and pure remains my heart [Rheme 4].

Based on the above analysis, the Theme in the first clause is realized by "along the river that merged with a cold rain", a prepositional phrase that functions as a circumstance of Location. In the second clause, the Theme is realized by "early at daybreak", which is also a prepositional phrase that functions as a circumstance of Time.

As previously discussed, the last three clauses in Tao's translation formulate a clause complex, and the subordinating clause "If my kinsfolk in Luoyang should feel concerned" here functions as the Theme of the clause complex. However, we may wonder whether the corresponding Rheme is realized by one clause or two clauses. If the three clauses appear in text types such as novels and conversations, the last two clauses will be regarded as Rheme. However, in this translation we have treated the last clause independently in terms of thematic structure. In this way, two thematic structures are found in the last three clauses. Among the two, the first Theme is realized by the subordinating clause beginning with "if" and the corresponding Rheme is "Please tell them for my part". Within the second thematic structure (i.e. the final clause), the Theme is realized by a prepositional phrase "Like a piece of ice in a crystal vessel", with the remaining part being the Rheme. We analyse in such a way because if we treat the last three clauses as one thematic structure, the Rheme will be redundant; moreover, the last line of the original poem will be rendered as part of the complicated Rheme and will not be treated properly.

7.8 Analysis of information

Our thematic analysis of WANG Changling's poem and its English translations is based on the conveyance of meaning, while we have not yet dealt with the analysis of information focus. This section is expected to touch upon this topic.

In terms of information focus of the clauses in the original poem, "吴" (*wú*; Wu) in the first line, "孤" (*gū*; lonely) in the second line, "问" (*wèn*; ask) in the third line, and "玉 壶" (*yù hú*; jade jar) in the fourth line are the focuses of the content, hence they can be regarded as the information focuses of the clauses. The information focus of the whole poem is seen in the last line (i.e. "一 片 冰 心 在 玉 壶" [*yí piàn bīng xīn zài yù hú*; one piece ice heart be in jade jar]). By comparing his heart with the bright and crystal ice in the jar of jade, the poet suggests that "he will hold a crystal icy heart from a pure and clear jar of jade to comfort his friend, and compared with any word he said, this will imply a deeper love to his friends and relatives in Luoyang" (Xiaoyin Ge, see Xiao et al. 1983: 132, our translation).

By analysing the information focus in the English translations, we find that certain components of a clause are placed at the end out of consideration of "the beauty in sound", such as end rhyme, instead of considerations of information focus. In addition, as poetry is special in form, the order of words can be reversed, certain words can be omitted and grammatical rules can be ignored. All these practices are related to the pursuit of "beauty in sound".

Tao's translation follows the end rhyme of aabb ("night"–"sight", "part"–"heart"). To achieve the effect of "beauty in sound", inversion is applied to the poem, with the positions of subject in the last clause (i.e. "my heart") and complement (i.e. "aloof and pure") being reversed. (We can compare Tao's translation with "My heart remains aloof and pure forever'.) Such a practice is seen in various English translations of ancient Chinese poems. In Tao's translation, the overall information centre is the last two lines – "Like a piece of ice in a crystal vessel, / Fore'er aloof and pure remains my heart." The information focus of the clauses in the translation can be determined by two ways of analysis, whereas these methods may not be widely accepted since too many perspectives will be involved in the analysis. Due to the limited space in this chapter, we will not discuss these issues here in detail.

In Wan and Wang's translation, the end rhyme is also aabb ("Wu"–"Chu", "said"–"jade"), which is the same as Tao's translation. The information focus of the whole poem is its last line – "My heart is as bright as crystal ice in the jar of jade" – and the information focuses in the different lines can all be found at the end of each line (highlighted in italics):

Amid the nightly haze of cold rains and streams I came to *Wu*,
And saw my friend in dawn leave the lonely mountain of *Chu*.
Oh, Friend, when folks in Luoyang inquires, let it be *said*,
My heart is as bright as crystal ice in the jar of *jade*.

By comparing the information focuses in the translations with those in the original, we find that Wan and Wang's translation is relatively closer to the original in this respect (see Table 7.3).

Table 7.3. Information focuses in the original and Wan and Wang's translation

Line	Information focuses in the original	Information focuses in Wan and Wang's translation
Line 1	"吴" (*wú*; Wu)	"Wu"
Line 2	"孤" (*gū*; lonely)	"Chu"
Line 3	"问" (*wèn*; ask)	"said"
Line 4	"玉 壶" (*yù hú*; jade jar)	"jade"

Thus, Wan and Wang's translation is similar to the original both in terms of end rhyme and information focus. We can say that this is a translation equivalent to the original in both form and meaning.

7.9 Conclusion

This chapter has compared WANG Changling's *Fu Rong Lou Song Xin Jian* with its English translations in terms of cohesion, logico-semantic relation, thematic structure and information focus. The analysis shows that, in terms of cohesion, the original in Chinese and its English translations vary significantly. No cohesive device is applied in the original, while the cohesive device of personal reference is seen throughout the whole translated poems. Such variation is not only found in the poems analysed in this chapter but can also generally be observed in all analyses of data involving Chinese source text and English target texts. Regarding such variations, scholars in comparative linguistics and translation studies in China thus suggest that Chinese is a meaning-oriented language and English is a form-oriented language (see Lian 1993: 163–73; Liu 1994: 163–78; Wu 1994: 152–62; Xiao 2001: 53–54).

The analysis in this chapter has also revealed that, in the perspectives of logico-semantic relation, thematic structure and information focus, WANG Changling's original poem is very similar to its English translations. The main reason is that, since the source text is a special type of discourse (i.e. a poem of four lines, with each line containing seven characters), translating such a poem has various restrictions – for example, the order of different lines cannot be reversed, the number of syllables has to be consistent and the choice of beauty in sound (such as end rhyme) can be considered. Therefore, translators can only recreate their works within a very limited space.

Chapter 8
Formal equivalence in translation

8.1 Introduction

Written by MA Zhiyuan (马致远), *Tian Jing Sha Qiu Si* (天净沙·秋思) is a masterpiece of short lyrics from the Yuan Dynasty as well as a popular and widely chanted work throughout history. The author of the lyric breaks the boundary of grammar and constructs images only through nouns, thus providing readers with much space for imagination. As a result, different translators understand the lyric differently and produce different English translations. In the literature, there are already seminal analyses and discussions on the English translations. In this chapter, we begin with a linguistic analysis of MA Zhiyuan's *Tian Jing Sha Qiu Si* and its three English translations before comparing our analysis, with the purpose of exploring the significance of formal equivalence in poetry and lyric translation.

8.2 On formal equivalence

Based on Systemic Functional Linguistics (SFL), Catford (1965) suggests the notion of translation equivalence.[1] He also holds that the central issue in translation practice is searching for equivalence, and the equivalent relation can be built on any intersection in terms of levels (e.g. grammar, lexis, phonology and graphology) and ranks (e.g. grammatical structure, sentence, phrase, word and morpheme). Catford's theory is in fact an account of formal equivalence.

According to Nida (1964), two forms of translation equivalence exist: equivalence in form (formal equivalence) and equivalence in content. As characterized by Nida and Taber (1969: 201), formal equivalence means that "the features of the form of the source text have been mechanically reproduced in the receptor language". By proposing his famous theory of dynamic equivalence, Nida also suggests that the primary goal of translation is to translate meaning: translation "consists in reproducing in the receptor language the closest natural equivalent of the source-language message, first in terms of meaning and secondly in terms of style" (Nida 1964: 12) and "the response of the receptor is essentially like that of the original receptors" (Nida & Taber 1964: 200). Nida's notion of highlighting meaning and placing form in the secondary place is often misunderstood. Some scholars think that only content needs to be translated, while form can be ignored, thereby labelling different sorts of free translation as dynamic equivalence.

In a later book titled *From One Language to Another: Functional Equivalence in Bible Translating* (de Waard & Nida 1986), "dynamic equivalence" is changed to "functional equivalence". As explained in the book, functional equivalence can avoid misunderstanding and highlight the communicative function of translation. A functionally equivalent translation not only requires equivalence in information content, but also attempts to achieve as much equivalence in form as possible. The authors suggest that form also indicates meaning, and change in form will lead to change in meaning. Five conditions in the change of form are then proposed: (1) literal translation will lead to errors in meaning, (2) introduction of foreign word will result in emptiness in semantics (i.e. semantic zero), (3) formal correspondence will result in serious ambiguity in meaning, (4) formal correspondence will give rise to ambiguity not seen in the original meaning and (5) formal correspondence will violate the standards in grammar and style in the target language.

The analysis in this chapter is based on the notion of formal equivalence. In functional linguistics, form is regarded as the realization of meaning (see Huang 1999). When applying different forms, the meanings indicated will be different, hence the information conveyed to target readers will also be different. Therefore, formal equivalence can be considered as a standard to measure the appropriateness of a translation.

8.3 Analysis of the original of *Tian Jing Sha Qiu Si*

The original of MA Zhiyuan's *Tian Jing Sha Qiu Si* is as follows:

天净沙·秋思
tiān jìng shā qiū sī
sky clear sand autumn thought

马致远
mǎ zhì yuǎn
MA Zhiyuan

枯 藤 老 树 昏 鸦，
kū téng lǎo shù hūn yā,
withered vine old tree dusk crow,

小 桥 流 水 人家，
xiǎo qiáo liú shuǐ rén jiā,
small bridge running water household,

古 道 西 风 瘦 马。
gǔ dào xī fēng shòu mǎ.
ancient road west wind thin horse.

夕阳 西 下，
xī yáng xī xià,
setting sun west descend,

断肠 人 在 天涯。
duàn cháng rén zài tiān yá.
heartbroken man be at skyline.

Consisting of 28 Chinese characters, this lyric is made up of two sentences. The first sentence is composed of nine nouns (nominal groups), with eight groups having the structure of Modifier + Head and the other group having only a Head:

Modifier + Head: "枯" (*kū*; withered) + "藤" (*téng*; vine), "老" (*lǎo*; old) + "树" (*shù*; tree), "昏" (*hūn*; dusk) + "鸦" (*yā*; crow), "小" (*xiǎo*; small) + "桥" (*qiáo*; bridge), "流" (*liú*; running) + "水" (*shuǐ*; water), "古" (*gǔ*; ancient) + "道" (*dào*; road), "西" (*xī*; west) + "风" (*fēng*; wind), "瘦" (*shòu*; thin) + "马" (*mǎ*; horse)

Head: "人家" (*rén jiā*; household)

In general, poems in Chinese (including lyrics) focus more on coordination in semantics rather than coordination in grammar. *Tian Jing Sha Qiu Si* closely follows the topic of the lyric – that is, "秋 思" (*qiū sī*; autumn thought). The first three lines are characterized with the juxtaposition of nominal groups, which include eight Chinese characters (i.e. "枯 藤" [*kū téng*; withered vine], "老 树" [*lǎo shù*; old tree], "昏 鸦" [*hūn yā*; dusk crow], "小 桥" [*xiǎo qiáo*; small bridge], "流 水" [*liú shuǐ*; running water],

"人家" [*rén jiā*; household], "古 道" [*gǔ dào*; ancient road], "西 风" [*xī fēng*; west wind] and "瘦 马" [*shòu mǎ*; thin horse]). The nine nominal groups depict the scene of an ancient Chinese village. Without using a verb, the lyric depicts a concise and lively scenery of dusk in autumn.

The nine nominal groups can be categorized into three types, with three groups falling into one type. Seen from the surface, they are not closely related; however, based on the following lines – "夕阳 西 下，断 肠 人 在 天涯" (*xī yáng xī xià, duàn cháng rén zài tiān yá*; setting sun west descend, heartbroken man be at skyline) – we find that all sceneries help to describe the homesickness of a miserable wandering traveler. The final sentence is composed of two clauses: the first clause (i.e. "夕阳 西 下" [*xī yáng xī xià*; setting sun west descend]) depicts the scenery, as the previous nine images do; the second clause then points out the state (i.e. "在 天涯" [*zài tiān yá*; be at skyline]) of the participant (i.e. "断肠 人" [*duàn cháng rén*; heartbroken man]) among the complicated array of scenery. In the perspective of functional semantic analysis, things are normally realized by nominal groups, while circumstances are realized by clauses. Our analysis also confirms this theoretical observation.

8.4 Xianliang Weng's translation

In his English translation, Xianliang Weng renders the ancient lyric into prose by interpreting its meaning. His strategy is similar to that of Arthur Waley (1938) in targeting the conveyance of meaning (the similarity also lies in the likeliness in spirit). Translators using this strategy suggest rhyming should give way to meaning, as a translation mainly expresses the artistic conception rather than focusing on the rhyme scheme of the original poem. According to Weng (1982; see also Yang & Liu 1994: 47, our translation):

> when translating Chinese poems into English, we should retain the true qualities of the poems. First and foremost, we should identify the true qualities, which are not in the ornate phraseology, allusion, or form, but in the image and the enhancement of its artistic effect. All we need to do is to reproduce the image of the original instead of imitating the art and diction in the original.

In Weng's translation of *Tian Jing Sha Qiu Si*, he puts his ideas into practice (see Weng 1985: 101–02; see also Gu 1993):

> **Autumn**
> Crows hovering over rugged trees wreathed with rotten vine – the day is about done. Yonder is a tiny bridge over a sparkling stream, and on the far bank, a pretty little village. But the traveler has to go on down this ancient road, the west wind moaning, his bony horse groaning, trudging towards the sinking sun, farther and farther away from home.

Weng's translation consists of three sentences, with the first sentence expressing the meaning of "枯藤老树昏鸦" (*kū téng lǎo shù hūn yā*; withered vine old tree dusk crow), the second sentence dealing with "小桥流水人家" (*xiǎo qiáo liú shuǐ rén jiā*; small bridge running water household) and the third sentence being based on "古道西风瘦马。夕阳西下，断肠人在天涯" (*gǔ dào xī fēng shòu mǎ. xī yáng xī xià, duàn cháng rén zài tiān yá*; ancient road west wind thin horse. setting sun west descend, heartbroken man be at skyline). Yanling Gu (1993: 12, our translation) comments on this translation as follows:

> By translating a lyric into a prose, he [Xianliang Weng] does not rigidly adhere to the correspondence of words, neither does he focus on the length and order of sentences. The advantage of his practices lies in that readers of his translation can easily experience the image in the poem, as if they are on the scene in person. However, if we weigh his translation word by word, we will somehow find the inappropriateness.

We will not judge the validity of Gu's comment, but we agree with him in that inappropriateness can be found in Weng's translation after careful examination. In our following discussion, we will provide a linguistic analysis of Weng's translation.

In the original, "枯藤" (*kū téng*; withered vine), "老树" (*lǎo shù*; old tree), and "昏鸦" (*hūn yā*; dusk crow) are three paralleled and juxtaposed nominal groups, whereas in Weng's translation their relationships become those of modifier and modified. On the other hand, "things" in the original have become "situations". (In terms of the realization of form, nominal groups are changed to clauses.) Then, a back translation of the first sentence in Weng's translation will be "乌鸦在盘绕着枯藤的老树上盘旋——一天快过去了" (*wū yā zài pán rào zhe kū téng de lǎo shù shang pán xuán – yì tiān kuài guò qu le*; crow be at wreath VPART rotten vine DE old tree on hover – one day almost pass ASP), which bears little resemblance to the original in terms of meaning. Regarding syntax, the sentence is composed of two clauses. In the first clause, the auxiliary verb "are" is omitted and a material process is found, indicating that crows are hovering over a certain place.

In "over rugged trees wreathed with rotten vine", which indicates the location, we find a nominal group having the structure of modifier plus modified; specifically, the head of the nominal group ("trees") has an adjective as its premodifier ("rugged") and a non-finite clause as its postmodifier ("wreathed with rotten vine"), with the nominal group that indicates the meaning of "枯 藤" (*kū téng*; withered vine) functioning as one constituent of the postmodifier. In addition, the second clause "the day is about done" is added by the translator based on his understanding of the artistic conception of the original.

Moreover, in the original, "小 桥" (*xiǎo qiáo*; small bridge), "流 水" (*liú shuǐ*; running water), and "人家" (*rén jiā*; household) are three paralleled and juxtaposed groups, which are rendered as a sentence – that is, "Yonder is a tiny bridge over a sparkling stream, and on the far bank, a pretty little village." We can provide a back translation of this sentence: "那边闪闪发光的小溪上有一座小桥，在远处的河岸边有个小村庄" (*nà biān shǎn shǎn fā guāng de xiǎo xī shang yǒu yí zuò xiǎo qiáo, zài yuǎn chù de hé àn biān yǒu ge xiǎo cūn zhuāng*; yonder sparkling DE stream on have one MEAS tiny bridge, be at far place DE river bank side have MEAS small village). In this translation, "小 桥" (*xiǎo qiáo*; small bridge) and "流 水" (*liú shuǐ*; running water) also involve the relationship of modifier plus modified in terms of structure. On the other hand, "人家" (*rén jiā*; household) is translated as an elliptical clause, in which the translator has added "on the far bank".

"古道西风瘦马。夕阳西下，断肠人在天涯" (*gǔ dào xī fēng shòu mǎ. xī yáng xī xià, duàn cháng rén zài tiān yá*; ancient road west wind thin horse. setting sun west descend, heartbroken man be at skyline) in the original is translated as one sentence – that is, "But the traveler has to go on down this ancient road, the west wind moaning, his bony horse groaning, trudging towards the sinking sun, farther and farther away from home." This sentence consists of four clauses, among which three are elliptical. In the original, only "夕阳 西 下" (*xī yáng xī xià*; setting sun west descend) may contain a process, while other clauses all serve to indicate things or states, whereas in Weng's translation, four clauses are used to indicate four actions. Besides, the relationship between "瘦 马" (*shòu mǎ*; thin horse) and "断肠 人" (*duàn cháng rén*; heartbroken man) is changed from implicit in the original to explicit in the translation; the static view of the scenery in the original is also changed to a dynamic scene in the translation.

By comparing the original and the translation, we can make the following observations. First, the original is static, while the translation is dynamic. Second, the original mainly consists of things, while the translation is composed of situations – that is, the original is mostly realized by nominal groups, while the translation is mostly realized by clauses. Third, in the translation there are certain words or clauses whose equivalents cannot be found in the original, such as "hovering over", "wreathed with", "the day is about done", "yonder is", "over", "and on the far bank", "but", "has to go on down", "this", "moaning", "his groaning", "trudging towards" and "farther and farther", which are all added by the translator. Fourth, some descriptions in the original are not translated – for example, "断肠 人" (*duàn cháng rén*; heartbroken man) is rendered as "the traveler", which obviously cannot reveal the character's identity and his homesickness. In general, Weng's translated poem has reflected his views on translation: "We only need to reproduce the image in the original, rather than to imitate its composition"; in this way, we can "totally abandon the word order and syntax in the original". By "abandoning the form and retaining the spirit, we can thus preserve the true quality of the original" (Weng 1982 our translation; see Yang & Liu 1994: 47–50).

8.5 Wayne Schlepp's translation

Selected from *Anthology of English Translations of Ancient Chinese Poems and Lyrics* (Wen 1989: 331), Wayne Schlepp's translation is very different from Weng's in terms of style:

Tune to "Sand and Sky" — Autumn Thoughts
by MA Zhiyuan
Dry vine, old tree, crows at dusk,
Low bridge, stream running, cottages,
Ancient road, west wind, lean nag,
The sun westering
And one with breaking heart at the sky's edge.

In Schlepp's translation, we find that the nine nominal groups in the original are rendered as nine nominal groups in English. In the original, only "人家" (*rén jiā*; household) is not modified by other constituents, and the same grammatical structure is applied in the translation. By comparison, such equivalence in form has become evident (see Table 8.1).

Table 8.1. Equivalence in form in *Tian Jing Sha Qiu Si* and Schlepp's translation

Original	Translation		
	Premodifier	Head	Postmodifier
枯 藤 (*kū téng*; withered vine)	dry	vine	
老 树 (*lǎo shù*; old tree)	old	tree	
昏 鸦 (*hūn yā*; dusk crow)		crows	at dusk
小 桥 (*xiǎo qiáo*; small bridge)	low	bridge	
流 水 (*liú shuǐ*; running water)		stream	running
人家 (*rén jiā*; household)		cottages	
古 道 (*gǔ dào*; ancient road)	ancient	road	
西 风 (*xī fēng*; west wind)	west	wind	
瘦 马 (*shòu mǎ*; thin horse)	lean	nag	

"夕阳 西 下，断肠 人 在 天涯" (*xī yáng xī xià, duàn cháng rén zài tiān yá*; setting sun west descend, heartbroken man be at skyline) is translated as a structure without a verb: "The sun westering / And one with breaking heart at the sky's edge." In terms of grammar, the two structures can be regarded as nominal groups, and it is also possible to regard them as elliptical sentences.

Regarding Schlepp's style of translation, Wen (1989: 332 our translation) comments as follows: "By translating word for word, the translator applies nouns and their modifiers, which together compose a dynamic picture in an interrelated and loose manner. Also, the translator purposely applies neither finite predicate nor English sentence form throughout the whole lyric, thereby expressing the feelings in the original and contributing to one style of translation."

Throughout Schlepp's translation, three non-finite verbs (i.e. present participles) are found, with two functioning as postmodifiers (i.e. "stream running" and "The sun westering") and one as the premodifier of "heart" (i.e. "breaking"). Although the three verbs indicate dynamic meanings, they merely serve as modifiers rather than heads in nominal groups and the dynamic meanings only play their roles within the groups. No unit larger than group is involved, hence the meanings of the groups are still static.

In his translation, Schlepp makes his choice and organizes language to indicate static "things". As a result, the whole lyric is composed by 11 sceneries, which form a dynamic picture in an interrelated and loose manner. In this respect, we can say that Schlepp's translation is relatively close to the original and is equivalent to the original in form.

8.6 Zuxin Ding and Burton Raffel's translation

Zuxin Ding and Burton Raffel (see Gu 1993: 13) provide a translation of *Tian Jing Sha Qiu Si* that is different from those by Weng and Schlepp:

> ***Tune: Tian Jing Sha***
> *by MA Zhiyuan*
> Withered vines hanging on old branches,
> Returning crows croaking at dusk.
> A few houses hidden past a narrow bridge,
> And below the bridge quiet creek running.
> Down a worn path, in the west wind,
> A lean horse comes plodding.
> The sun dips down in the west,
> And the lovesick traveler is still at the end of the world.

In Ding and Raffel's translation, the method of translating the beginning nine nominal groups lies between those adopted by Weng and Schlepp. We find "枯 藤" (*kū téng*; withered vine) and "老 树" (*lǎo shù*; old tree) not being translated as juxtaposed and parallel units, but as "Withered vines hanging on old branches", and "昏 鸦" (*hūn yā*; dusk crow) being rendered as "Returning crows croaking at dusk". In this way, the two "things" in the original become two "situations" in the translation. Moreover, "小 桥 流 水 人家" (*xiǎo qiáo liú shuǐ rén jiā*; small bridge running water household) is rendered as "A few houses hidden past a narrow bridge, And below the bridge quiet creek running", with the three "things" in the original becoming two "situations" in the translation. Further, "古 道 西 风 瘦 马" (*gǔ dào xī fēng shòu mǎ*; ancient road west wind thin horse) is translated as "Down a worn path, in the west wind, A lean horse comes plodding"; similarly, the three "things" have become one "situation". We also find "夕阳 西 下" (*xī yáng xī xià*; setting sun west descend) and "断肠 人 在 天涯" (*duàn cháng rén zài tiān yá*; heartbroken man be at skyline) being rendered as two "situations".

By comparing Ding and Raffel's translation with Weng's, we can observe that they are identical in changing "things" to "situations": First, the original is static, while the two translations are dynamic. Second, the original is mostly composed of "things", while the two translations are composed of "situations". Third, words indicating actions or states not found in the original are added in the two translations, such as "hanging", "returning", "croaking", "hidden", "comes" and "plodding"; in this respect, Ding and Raffel's translation is the same as Weng's translation, and contrasts sharply with Schlepp's translation. However, Ding and Raffel's translation also differs significantly from Weng's translation: Ding and Raffel adopt the form of poetry to translate poetry, while Weng renders a poem into a prose; in terms of the recreation of artistic conception, translations by Ding and Raffel as well as by Weng also adopt different forms of realization.

8.7 Conclusion

This chapter has analysed and compared MA Zhiyuan's *Tian Jing Sha Qiu Si* with its English translations in a linguistic perspective. According to our analysis, in terms of formal equivalence, Schlepp's translation, compared with the other two translations, is more faithful to the original and is better at rendering the artistic conception of the original, thus leaving readers more space for imagination and allowing for more interpretations. By following the notions in functional linguistics, form is regarded as the realization of meaning. Therefore, in translating a well-known lyric such as *Tian Jing Sha Qiu Si*, we should try to maintain the equivalence in both form and meaning. It is exactly for this reason that we prefer Schlepp's translation over the other two. Of course, we should note that formal equivalence, as merely one standard of assessing translation quality, may not be suitable to assess other translations.

Note

1. *Translators' note:* Catford (1965) is regarded as the first scholar that comprehensively applies Halliday's (1961) scale-&-category theory (i.e. an early stage in the development of SFL) to translation (see e.g. Matthiessen et al. 2022: Ch. 8; Wang & Ma 2021: Ch. 1).

Chapter 9

Translating dynamic and static meaning

9.1 Introduction

In this chapter, we examine *Jiang Xue* (江雪) by LIU Zongyuan (柳宗元) and its English translations in two perspectives: (1) static and dynamic and (2) the relationship between form and meaning. These two perspectives serve as a basis for our analysis and are oriented towards the research focus in this chapter. We will first interpret the original of *Jiang Xue* and then examine its English translations; finally, we will analyse and discuss the poem and its translations in terms of dynamic and static nature as well as form and meaning.

9.2 Interpreting *Jiang Xue*

The original poem of *Jiang Xue* is as follows:

江 雪
jiāng xuě
river snow

柳宗元
liǔ zōng yuan
LIU Zongyuan

千 山 鸟 飞 绝，
qiān shān niǎo fēi jué,
thousand mountain bird fly die out,

万 径 人 踪 灭。
wàn jìng rén zōng miè.
ten thousand path man footprint wipe out

孤 舟 蓑 笠 翁，
gū zhōu suō lì wēng,
lonely boat bamboo cape bamboo hat old man,

独钓寒江雪。
dú diào hán jiāng xuě.
alone fish cold river snow.

The following paragraph is Xiaoru Wu's (1983: 932, our translation; see Xiao et al. 1983) interpretation of *Jiang Xue*:

> the poet brings us to a secluded and frigid place with merely twenty Chinese characters. A picture is presented before the readers: a little boat floats on the river in the snow and an old fisherman fishes alone in the middle of the river. The poet depicts the purity and quietness between heaven and earth ... and the description is extremely simple, including merely a small boat and an old fisherman fishing in the middle of the river in the heavy snow. However, to highlight the major object being described, the poet uses half of his poem to depict the background, making the background boundless and as wide as possible. We find that the wider the background is, the more prominent the major object being described will be. At first, the poet uses "千 山" (*qiān shān*; thousand mountain) and "万 径" (*wàn jìng*; ten thousand path) to contrast with "孤 舟" (*gū zhōu*; lonely boat) and "独 钓" (*dú diào*; alone fish) in the following two lines ... Furthermore, birds flying in the sky and footprints on the paths are extremely common; whereas the poet places the common scenes after "千 山" (*qiān shān*; thousand mountain) and "万 径" (*wàn jìng*; ten thousand path) and adds "绝" (*jué*; die out) and "灭" (*miè*; wipe out), thus changing the most common routines to an extreme and unusual tranquil scenery. As a result, since the remaining two lines of static description are placed under the secluded and quiet background, they become exquisitely elegant and are brought to life.

In Haiou Zhang's (2000: 300–01, our translation) view, "*Jiang Xue* is a static poem"; "the poet sets off a contrast: the grandness of the mountains and the paths is contrasted with the tininess of the lonely old fisherman; the quietus of birds and men is contrasted with the liveliness of the fishing activity; the tranquility of the scenery is contrasted with the emotional turmoil of the character".

Two points in Wu's discussion above deserve special attention. First, the beginning two lines depict two unusually tranquil sceneries; second, contrasted with this is the vivid presentation in the last two lines, which brings the whole picture to life. The interpretations by Zhang (2000) and Wu (1983) are congruent in that both reveal a contrast between "dynamic" and "static": the stillness presented by the disappearance of birds and humans, and the tranquil picture, are contrasted with the liveliness of fishing and the emotion of the fisherman.

9.3 Eleven English translations of *Jiang Xue*

As one of LIU Zongyuan's masterpieces, *Jiang Xue* has several English translations. We have collected 11 of them and categorized them into two groups for comparison:

Group 1 (including seven translations)

Example (1) Witter Bynner's translation (see Wen 1989: 162)
River Snow
A hundred mountains and no bird,
A thousand paths without a footprint;
A little boat, a bamboo cloak,
An old man fishing in the cold river-snow.

Example (2) Xianliang Weng's (1985: 51) translation
Snow
No sign of birds in the mountains; nor of men along the trails; nor any craft on the river but a little boat, with an old man in rustic hat and cape dangling a line in the frigid waters – a solitary figure veiled in silent snow.

Example (3) Shouyi Wang and John Knoepfle's (1989: 45) translation
snow on the river
no singing of birds in the mountain ranges
no footprints of men on a thousand trails
there is only one boat on the water
with an old man in a straw rain cape
who stands on deck and fishes by himself
where the snow falls on the cold river

Example (4) Dayu Sun's (1997: 423) translation
Snowing on the River
Not a bird o'er the hundreds of peaks,
Not a man on the thousands of trails.
An old angler alone in a boat,
With his rod and line, in raining outfit,
Is fishing on the river midst th' snowdrift.

Example (5) Yuanchong Xu's translation (see Xu, Lu & Wu 1988: 305)
Fishing in the Snow
From hill to hill no bird in flight;
From path to path no man in sight.
A straw-cloak'd man in a boat, lo!
Fishing on river clad in snow.

Example (6) Yuanchong Xu's (2000b: 457) translation
Fishing in Snow
From hill to hill no bird in flight;
From path to path no man in sight.
A lonely fisherman afloat
Is fishing snow in lonely boat.

Example (7) John C.H. Wu's translation (see Zhu 2000: 10)
River Snow
Myriad mountains – not a bird flying.
Endless roads – not a trace of men.
Only an old fisherman in a lonely boat,
Angling silently in the river covered with snow.

One common feature of the seven translations in Group 1 is that the first and second lines of the original are not rendered as clauses but as nominal groups.

Group 2 (including four translations)

Example (8) Burton Watson's translation (see Wen 1989: 163)
River Snow
From a thousand hills, bird flights have vanished;
on ten thousand paths, human traces wiped out:
lone boat, an old man in straw cape and hat,
fishing alone in the cold river snow.

Example (9) Dalian Wang's (1997: 127) translation
River Snowfall
Amidst all mountains, birds no longer fly;
On all roads, no more travelers pass by.
Straw hat and cloak, old man's in boat, head low,
Fishing alone on river cold with snow.

Example (10) Soame Jenyns' translation (see Zhu 2000: 10)
Snow on the River
On a thousand hills all birds life is cut off,
On ten thousand paths there is no trace of human footsteps;
In a lonely boat the old man with the bamboo hat and cape
Sits by himself fishing the river in the winter snow.

Example (11) Juntao Wu's (1997: 645) translation
The Snowbound River
O'er mountains and mountains no bird is on the wing;
On thousand lines of the pathways there's no footprint.

In a lone boat on the snowbound river, an old man,
In palm-bark cape and straw hat, drops his angle string.

The four translations in Groups 2 all translate the first and second lines in the original as clauses. However, variations are also found among them. For example, Juntao Wu's translation is the same as translations by Burton Watson (Example [8]) and Dalian Wang (Example [9]) in adopting clauses to translate the first and second lines in the original, whereas the three translations differ in terms of the static and dynamic meanings. Although in Jenyns' translation and the other three translations (Examples [8], [9] and [11]), the first and second lines in the original are rendered as clauses, their choices of verb are different, as discussed in the following section.

9.4 Discussion

In Section 9.3, we categorized the English translations of *Jiang Xue* into two types. In this section, we will discuss the translations in the perspective of static meaning and explore the relationship between form and meaning based on our analysis.

In *Jiang Xue*, three scenarios are presented in total, with two scenarios indicated by the first two lines and one scenario indicated by the last two lines. Following Xiaoru Wu's (1983: 932, our translation) explanation, the first and second lines have presented two "extremely secluded and silent" scenarios, while the last two lines indicate a "lively", "active" and "invigorate" scenario. In other words, the first two scenarios indicate static meaning and the third scenario indicates dynamic meaning. In terms of the realization of form and meaning, significant variations are found between the first and second groups of translations.

9.4.1 Dynamic and static

All translations in the first group use nominal groups to translate the first and second lines of the original. In terms of congruence, nominal group often indicates a certain entity (e.g. a person, thing or place) or an abstract concept, and clause often indicates a situation. In most cases, nominal groups are adopted to indicate complex entities (e.g. "the Chinese students of English" and "English as a foreign language") or complex abstract concepts (e.g. "the distinction between the terrorists who committed those acts and those who harboured them"). In general, noun and nominal group on the one hand often indicate static entities (e.g. "John", "the man", "South China Agricultural University" and "English as an international language"), whereas certain nominal groups can also be used to indicate dynamic situations (e.g. "their arrival" and "the singing of those beautiful birds"). On the other hand, clause indicates a situation and is often not used to indicate an entity – for instance, in the case of "what I need" in "What I need is this", "need" is adopted to indicate a nominalized situation. The situation indicated by clause can express both static meaning and dynamic meaning, depending on the experiential meaning indicated by the process (i.e. verb) in the clause. A nominal group, whether it indicates entity or situation, often expresses static meaning.

In the first group of translations (see Examples [1] to [7]), when translating the first and second lines of the original, nominal groups are used in most cases to indicate static meaning. For the second group of the translations (see Examples [8] to [11]), clauses are chosen to translate the situations in the original. Also, in the second group, some clauses indicate dynamic meaning and some indicate static meaning. Specifically, the following three translations (except for "On ten thousand paths there is no trace of human footsteps", translated by Jenyns) all indicate dynamic meaning:

Example (12) Burton Watson's translation
From a thousand hills, bird flights have vanished;
on ten thousand paths, human traces wiped out:

Example (13) Dalian Wang's translation
Amidst all mountains, birds no longer fly;
On all roads, no more travelers pass by.

Example (14) Soame Jenyns' translation
On a thousand hills all birds life is cut off;
On ten thousand paths there is no trace of human footsteps.

In Juntao Wu's translation, two clauses are used to render the first two lines in the original, and relational and existential processes are used to indicate static meanings, hence the two clauses have indicated static situations:

Example (15) Juntao Wu's translation
O'er mountains and mountains no bird is on the wind;
On thousand lines of the pathways there's no footprint.

In accordance with the above analysis, for static meanings, two nominal groups are adopted in Examples (1) to (7), while clauses are applied in Example (11). As for dynamic situations, only clauses are used in Examples (8) to (10).

For the translation of the third and fourth lines in the original, the 11 English translations can also be categorized into two groups: in the first group, the third scenario in the poem is translated as a static one; in the second group, the scenario is translated as a dynamic one.

In translations by Witter Bynner and Xiangliang Weng, the third scenario is translated as a static one:

Example (16) Witter Bynner's translation
A little boat, a bamboo cloak,
An old man fishing in the cold river-snow.

Example (17) Xiangliang Weng's translation
nor any craft on the river but a little boat, with an old man in rustic hat and cape dangling a line in the frigid waters – a solitary figure veiled in silent snow.

The other nine translations all render the third scenario as a dynamic one, among which two translations – those by Shouren Wang and John Knoepfle, and by Jun Wu – have purposely used verbs indicating the flowing movement:

Example (18) Shouren Wang and John Knoepfle's translation
there is only one boat on the water
with an old man in a straw rain cape
who stands on deck and fishes by himself
where the snow falls on the cold river

The sentence has a complex structure, which embeds two finite clauses. In its first layer, the existential clause indicates static meaning, the relative clause that indicates modificatory meaning includes two verbs (i.e. "stands" and "fishes"), and the clause indicating circumstantial meaning (i.e. "where the snow falls on the cold river") includes the verb "fall" that construes the flowing movement. Although the clause at the highest layer indicates static meaning, the two clauses it included have applied three verbs indicating movement, which are all found towards the end of the sentence, providing the impression that the whole sentence indicates dynamic meaning.

Another translation that obviously indicates flowing movement is provided by Juntao Wu:

Example (19) Juntao Wu's translation
In a lone boat on the snowbound river, an old man,
In palm-bark cape and straw hat, drops his angle string.

Most translations choose the structure of "an old man (is) fishing", which involves no obvious flowing movement, whereas in Wu's translation, the verb "drop" has highlighted such movement.

9.4.2 Form and meaning

As pointed out previously, the two translations by Witter Bynner and Xianliang Weng both render the third scenario in the poem as a static one. This is because, although verbs including "fishing" and "dangling" are used in the two translations, they function as postmodifiers syntactically, hence they are found in nominal groups and cannot indicate dynamic situations as clauses. One can compare the two examples:

Example (20)
The old man is fishing in the cold river-snow

Example (21)
The old man fishing in the cold river-snow

In terms of form, Example (20) is a clause that indicates a situation, whereas Example (21) is a nominal group that indicates an entity. On this basis, Witter Bynner's translation of the third scenario is composed of three nominal groups, as shown in Example (16a):

Example (16a)
a + little + boat (determiner + premodifier + head)
a + bamboo + cloak (determiner + premodifier + head)
an + old + man + fishing in the cold river-snow (determiner + premodifier + head + postmodifier)

These three nominal groups are related paratactically. In Xianliang Weng's translation, the third scenario in the original is also translated as three nominal groups:

Example (17a)
(nor) any craft on the river
(but) a little boat, with an old man in rustic hat and cape dangling in the frigid waters
– a solitary figure veiled in silent snow

Among the three nominal groups, the first and the third groups have both indicated meanings that are not seen in the original and are added by the translator based on his understanding of the artistic conception. The first nominal group serves to highlight and foreground the artistic conception expressed in "孤" (*gū*; lonely) and "独" (*dú*; alone), while the third nominal group deals with the translator's evaluation.

The translations by Bynner and Xianliang Weng both use nominal groups to indicate meaning, thus they convey identical or similar meanings as well as artistic conceptions. In their translations, in which no clause is seen throughout, the translators have depicted a completely static picture of "a lonely fisherman in the cold river" (Wen 1989: 162).

As pointed out in Section 9.4.1, although Juntao Wu adopts the same method as Burton Watson and Dalian Wang in using clauses to translate the first two lines in the original, Juntao Wu has indicated a dynamic meaning different from the other two translations. This is because verbs indicating motion are chosen in translations by Burton Watson and Dalian Wang – "vanish" and "wipe out" in Burton Watson's translation, "fly" and "pass by" in Dalian Wang's translation – whereas in Juntao Wu's translation, two instances of "be" that respectively indicating relational and existential meanings are found, thereby expressing static meanings in the translation.

Like the translation by Shouyi Wang and John Knoepfle, the goal of Weng's translation is to achieve the "likeness in spirit", with a focus on paraphrasing. The two translations are similar in adding interpretations to the original. As discussed previously, "nor any craft on the river (but)" and "a solitary figure" in Weng's translation are added by the translator, while in Wang and Knoepfle's translation, the translators have added "who stands on deck" and "where snow falls". Both translations are successful in terms of their artistic conceptions. However, translating and paraphrasing are two kinds of activities. If a translator is allowed to paraphrase as much as they like, how should we define the standard of "faithfulness" in translation?

9.4.3 "Fishing fish" or "fishing snow"

In the last line of the original – "独 钓 寒 江 雪" (*dú diào hán jiāng xuě*; alone fish cold river snow) – "寒 江 雪" (*hán jiāng xuě*; cold river snow) is normally regarded as the circumstance (which indicates location) along with the process "钓" (*diào*; fish); therefore, it is translated as complements (or objects) of prepositions such as "on". However, as noted by Chunshen Zhu (2000: 6, our translation), "in this ending line of the poem, what follows the verb '钓' [*diào*; fish] is the nominal group '寒 江 雪' [*hán jiāng xuě*; cold river snow], which structurally functions like an object". Such a collocation, which is similar to a verb–object construction, can be interpreted in different ways. In the 11 English translations of the poem, "钓" (*diào*; fish) is rendered in the following ways:

1. In seven translations (including those by Bynner 1989; Sun 1997; Wang 1997; Wang & Knoepfle 1989; Watson 1989; Wu 1972; and Xu 1988), "钓" (*diào*; fish) is rendered as an intransitive verb. Except for Wu's translation, in which the verb "angle" is used, the other translations all choose the verb "fish" to indicate the meaning of "钓" (*diào*; fish).
2. In two translations (including those by Jenyns [1944] and Xu [2000b]), "钓" (*diào*; fish) is translated as a transitive verb. In Jenyns" translation, "江" (*jiāng*; river) is the complement of "fishing", as seen in "Sits by himself fishing in the river in the winter snow." According to the translator's notes to this line, he also wonders whether the fisherman is "fishing for winter snow". In Xu's (2000b) translation, "雪" (*xuě*; snow) is the complement of "fishing", as seen in "Is fishing snow in lonely boat".
3. In two translations, verbs such as "fish" and "angle" are not directly selected to render "钓" (*diào*; fish): Weng's (1985) translation is "dangling a line in the frigid waters", while Wu's (1997) is "drops his angle string". Although expressed in an implicit way, the meaning of "钓" (*diào*; fish) can still clearly be identified.

9.4.4 Translating the contrast

As previously stated, following Xiaoru Wu (1983) and Haiou Zhang (2000), the first two lines and the latter two lines in *Jiang Xue* have formed a contrast between "static" and "dynamic". Such a multi-layered and multi-angle comparison is reflected in various ways. When conducting discourse analysis of the translations, we can find examples in language use to illustrate their point.

Based on our analysis, most English translations make use of nominal groups or clauses that indicate states to render the scenario of silence and seclusion depicted in the first and second lines of the original; meanwhile, clauses (also verbs) expressing dynamic meaning are used to indicate the dynamic state in the third and fourth lines of the original. Such a choice of linguistic form serves the purpose of highlighting the contrast. In other words, specific forms have realized specific meanings.

In Bynner's translation (Wen 1989), five images are presented to readers: (1) a mountain with no bird, (2) a path with no footprint, (3) a small boat, (4) a bamboo cape and (5) an old man fishing in the river in snow. If we assume that contrast can be seen in Bynner's translation, it will then be the contrast between things (including men). Such a contrast is different from those in translations by Sun (1997: 423) and Xu (2000b: 457), who convey such contrast on the level of situation. Based on Wu's (1983) notion of contrast, the translations by Sun and Xu are better at conveying the contrast between "static" and "dynamic". Further, it can be pointed out that our assessment of the translations is based on the use of linguistic structure rather than on the things and situations being referred to. In this way, if we focus on the things and situations *per se*, contrasts between "static" and "dynamic" can also be observed among things (including men); in this respect, Bynner's translation is certainly as good as translations by Sun or Xu.

9.5 Conclusion

Our discussion in this chapter reveal that the static or dynamic meaning of the original can be rendered equivalently in the translations. However, when assessing the quality of translations, can we regard "formal equivalence" as one standard? We have the following suggestions: form is the realization of meaning; when a certain form is selected by a translator, a certain meaning has in fact already been selected along with the choice of form.

In Chapter 8, we compared several translations of MA Zhiyuan's *Tian Jing Sha Qiu Si* in the perspective of formal equivalence and provided a preliminary evaluation of the translations based on such a perspective. Our conclusion may not be accepted by everyone, but our evaluation is indeed based on the discourse analysis of the translations, rather than based on subjective impression or experience. In this sense, our comparison in this chapter is similar to that in Chapter 8.

Chapter 10

Proper nouns and their English translations

10.1 Introduction

In some previous chapters (e.g. Chapter 2), we touched upon the English translation of proper nouns in ancient Chinese poems. In this chapter, we will explore this topic further. First, we will define common noun in simple terms, before briefly analysing four Chinese poems; finally, we will classify, analyse and discuss the English translations of proper nouns.

10.2 A brief introduction to proper nouns

In terms of word class, there are open classes such as nouns, verbs, adjectives and adverbs. In terms of the structure of noun, a single noun is referred to as a noun, and a noun combined with a modifier is then a nominal group. In the perspective of specific and general reference, nouns can be classified into proper noun and common noun. When number is involved, nouns can then be differentiated as countable and uncountable. We will not discuss these issues here, as more detailed discussions in books on grammar are available (e.g. Zhang 1997; Huang & Xiao 1996, 1999).

The fundamental distinction between proper noun and common noun is that the former indicates specific reference, while the latter indicates general reference. A proper noun refers to a certain and specific person, object, time and place, such as "Shakespeare", "Catherine", "the Rockies", "January", "Sunday", "London" and "the United Nations". In written language, the first letter of a proper noun must be capitalized, and its article should also sometimes be capitalized – for example, "*The Scholars*" [儒林外史], a book written by WU Jingzi [吴敬梓] and translated by Xianyi Yang and Gladys Yang. The article "the" must be capitalized here. in some cases, the article "the" does not have to be capitalized – for example, "the" in "the United States" should not be capitalized as long as it does not appear at the beginning of a sentence.

10.3 Data in this chapter

Ancient Chinese poems and lyrics involve a large number of proper nouns. One reason is that a poet will often describe and narrate specific situations (including a certain person, thing, time and place) in their poem. In this chapter, we will select four poems from the Tang Dynasty and their translations (see Appendix 1) as our data for analysis.

(1) 枫 桥 夜 泊
fēng qiáo yè bó
maple bridge night anchor

张继
zhāng jì
ZHANG Ji

月 落 乌 啼 霜 满 天，
yuè luò wū tí shuāng mǎn tiān,
moon set crow cry frost fill sky,

江 枫 渔 火 对 愁 眠。
jiāng fēng yú huǒ duì chóu mián.
river maple fishing fire to sorrow sleep.

姑苏 城 外 寒山 寺，
gū sū chéng wài hán shān sì,
Gusu (Suzhou) city outside cold-hill temple,

夜半 钟 声 到 客船。
yè bàn zhōng shēng dào kè chuán.
midnight (night-half) bell sound reach boat.

(2) 芙蓉楼 送 辛渐
fú róng lóu sòng xīn jiàn
Hibiscus-tower see off Xin Jian

王昌龄
wáng chāng líng
WANG Changling

寒雨连江夜入吴，
hán yǔ lián jiāng yè rù wú,
cold rain mingle river night enter Wu,

平明送客楚山孤。
píng míng sòng kè chǔ shān gū.
daybreak see off guest Chu-mountain lonely.

洛阳亲友如相问，
luò yáng qīn yǒu rú xiāng wèn,
Luoyang relative friend if ask,

一片冰心在玉壶。
yí piàn bīng xīn zài yù hú.
one piece ice heart be in jade jar.

(3) 黄鹤楼送孟浩然之广陵
huáng hè lóu sòng mèng hào rán zhī guǎng líng
yellow-crane-tower see off Meng Haoran to Guangling

李白
lǐ bái
LI Bai

故人西辞黄鹤楼，
gù rén xī cí huáng hè lóu,
old friend west leave yellow-crane-tower

烟花三月下扬州。
yān huā sān yuè xià yáng zhōu.
misty flower third month go to Yangzhou.

孤帆远影碧空尽，
gū fān yuǎn yǐng bì kōng jìn,
lonely sail distant shadow azure sky end,

惟见长江天际流。
wéi jiàn cháng jiāng tiān jì liú.
only see Yangtze River sky end flow.

(4) 泊秦淮
bó qín huái
moor Qinhuai River

杜牧
dù mù
DU Mu

烟笼寒水月笼沙，
yān lǒng hán shuǐ yuè lǒng shā,
mist veil cold water moon veil sand,

夜泊秦淮近酒家。
yè bó qín huái jìn jiǔ jiā.
night moor Qinhuai River near wineshop

商女不知亡国恨，
shāng nǚ bù zhī wáng guó hèn,
singsong-girl not know subjugate nation hatred,

隔江犹唱《后庭 花》。
gé jiāng yóu chàng hòu tíng huā.
across river still sing backyard flower.

The selection of these four poems does not mean other poems are not suitable for our analysis. The four poems were selected simply due to the author's preference. Poems can either be selected randomly or carefully chosen to achieve certain purposes.

10.4 Analysis

In our analysis, we will investigate the English translations of proper nouns in ancient Chinese poems based on the following four possibilities: (1) proper nouns in the Chinese original being translated as equivalent proper nouns in English, (2) proper nouns in the Chinese original being translated as common nouns in English, (3) proper nouns in the Chinese original being translated as inequivalent proper nouns in English and (4) proper nouns in the Chinese original being left untranslated.

10.4.1 Proper nouns in the Chinese original translated as equivalent proper nouns in English

Based on the data in this chapter, most proper nouns in the Chinese original are translated as proper nouns in English. For instance, "姑苏城外寒山寺" (*gū sū chéng wài hán shān sì*; Gusu/Suzhou city outside cold-hill temple) in ZHANG Ji's poem is translated as follows:

Tinggan Cai's translation (see Wen 1989: 125)
Outside the Suzhou wall, from Hanshan Temple's bell

Dalian Wang's (1997: 95) translation
Outside Gusu Cold-Hill Temple's in sight

Yuanchong Xu's translation (see Xu, Lu & Wu 1988: 224)
Beyond the Gusu walls the Temple of Cold Hill

In the original, there are two proper nouns, "姑苏" (*gū sū*; Gusu/Suzhou) and "寒山 寺" (*hán shān sì*; cold-hill temple). In all the three translations cited above, proper nouns are applied – for example, "Suzhou" and "Gusu", "Hanshan Temple", "Cold-Hill Temple" and "Temple of Cold Hill". We also note that "姑苏" (*gū sū*; Gusu/Suzhou) is another name for "苏州" (*sū zhōu*; Suzhou), so both transliterations (i.e. "Suzhou" and "Gusu") are suitable.

In the title of "芙蓉楼 送 辛渐" (*fú róng lóu sòng xīn jiàn*; Hibiscus-tower see off Xin Jian) by WANG Changling, we find two proper nouns, which are all rendered as proper nouns in the four translations:

Dalian Wang's (1997: 23) translation
Bidding Farewell to Xin Jian at Lotus Pavilion

Jie Tao's translation (see Wu 1997: 119)
Seeing Xin Jian off at Hibiscus Pavilion

Changsheng Wan and Jianzhong Wang's (2000: 37) translation
Send-off to Xin Jian at Hibiscus Tower

Yuanchong Xu's (2000b: 83) translation
Farewell to Xin Jian at Lotus Tower

For "辛渐" (*xīn jiàn*; Xin Jian), which is the name of a person, pinyin is applied in all four translations. However, for "芙蓉楼" (*fú róng lóu*; Hibiscus-tower), the four different translations are found, including "Lotus Pavilion", "Hibiscus Pavilion", "Hibiscus Tower" and "Lotus Tower".

We have collected ten translations of *Huang He Lou Song Meng Hao Ran Zhi Guang Ling* (黄鹤楼送孟浩然之广陵) written by LI Bai (李白), including translations by Changsheng Wan and Xianzhong Wang (2000), Di Tu and An Tu (see Wu 1997: 193), Xianyi Yang and Gladys Yang (2001a), Dalian Wang (1997), Witter Bynner and Kanghu Jiang (see Wen 1989: 83), Yuanchong Xu (see Xu, Lu & Wu 1988: 224), Yuanchong Xu (2000b), Dayu Sun (1997), Shouyi Wang and John Knoepfle (1989: 21) and Bingxing Zhang (2001: 41). In eight of the translations, the same strategy of applying pinyin is adopted in translating "孟浩然" (*mèng hào rán*; Meng Haoran). However, differences are found in the translations of other proper nouns. For example, in five translations, "广陵" (*guǎng líng*; Guangling) in the title is not rendered, whereas in three translations it is rendered by following two different strategies.

1. "广陵" (*guǎng líng*; Guangling) is translated as "Guangling". Tu and Tu's (see Wu 1997: 193) translation: Seeing Meng Haoran off to Guangling; Sun's (1997: 223) translation: Seeing Meng Haoran off to Guangling on the Yellow Crane Tower.
2. "广陵" (*guǎng líng*; Guangling) is translated as "Yangzhou". Bynner and Jiang's translation (see Wen 1989: 83): A Farewell to Meng Haoran on His Way to Yangzhou.

Moreover, it can be noted that "黄鹤楼" (*huáng hè lóu*; yellow-crane-tower) is rendered as a proper noun in eight of the translations, in which different choices are made:

1. Yellow Crane Tower: Tu and Tu's translation, Yang and Yang's translation, Wang's 1997 translation, Sun's 1997 translation, Xu's 1989 translation, Xu's 2000 translation
2. Tower of Yellow Crane: Wan and Wang's 2000 translation
3. Yellow Crane Terrace: Bynner and Jiang's translation (see Wen 1989)
4. Crane Tower: Wang's 1997 translation.

Among the four above-mentioned types of translation, types (1) and (2) vary in terms of the position of the modifier, with a premodifier being used in type (1) and a postmodifier being found in type (2). Type (3) is different from types (1) and (2) in the choice of "Terrace" or "Tower". For type (4), "黄" (*huáng*; yellow) is not translated: in Wang's (1997) translation, "黄鹤楼" (*huáng hè lóu*; yellow-crane-tower) is translated as "Yellow Crane Tower" in the title and as "Crane Tower" in the main body of the poem.

In "泊 秦淮" (*bó qín huái*; moor Qinhuai River) by DU Mu, although "秦淮" (*qín huái*; Qinhuai River) (i.e. Qinhuai River in Nanjing) is rendered as a proper noun in the translations, different choices are made:

1. Qinhuai River: Luo's translation (see Wu 1997: 639); Wang's (1997: 141) translation; Yang and Yang's (2001a: 270) translation
2. River Qinhuai: Xu's translation (see Xu, Lu & Wu 1988: 317); Xu's (2000b: 524) translation
3. Qinhuai Canal: Wang's (1997: 141) translation.

Based on our analysis, we find that when proper nouns in the original are translated as proper nouns in the English translations, two possibilities are involved. First, the English translations are directly rendered from the original – for example, translating "姑苏" (*gū sū*; Gusu/Suzhou) as "Gusu" (see Wang 1997: 95; Xu 1988: 224) and "广陵" (*guǎng líng*; Guangling) as "Guangling" (Tu and Tu's translation – see Sun 1997: 223; Wu 1997: 193); this method is contrasted with translating "姑苏" (*gū sū*; Gusu/Suzhou) as "Suzhou" (Cai's translation – see Wen 1989: 125) and "广陵" (*guǎng líng*; Guangling) as "Yangzhou" (Bynner & Jiang– see Wen 1989: 83), with the latter approach being to some extent explanatory. Second, when providing explanations for a certain thing, different translators will understand differently and hence make different choices – for instance, rendering "寒山 寺" (*hán shān sì*; cold-hill temple) as "Hanshan Temple" (in Cai's translation) combines both the sound and meaning in the original, whereas "Cold-Hill Temple" (in Wang's translation) and "the Temple of Cold Hill" (in Xu's translation) are translations based on meaning; in another example, "楼" (*lóu*; tower) in "芙蓉 楼" (*fú róng lóu*; Hibiscus-tower) and "黄鹤楼" (*huáng hè lóu*; yellow-crane-tower) are rendered in three different ways, namely as "pavilion", "tower" and "terrace".

Proper nouns in the original are not always translated as proper nouns. However, no matter in which form they are translated, the expression of meaning and conveyance of artistic conception are of crucial importance. The ideal case would be to achieve the beauty in meaning, in form and in sound, as suggested by Yuanchong Xu.

10.4.2 Proper nouns in the Chinese original translated as common nouns in English

In the four Chinese poems and their translations, which serve as data in this chapter, instances of translating proper nouns as common nouns can be found. We can first examine the translation of "烟 花 三 月" (*yān huā sān yuè*; misty flower third month) from the second line of *Huang He Lou Song Meng Hao Ran Zhi Guang Ling* – that is, "烟 花 三 月 下 扬州" (*yān huā sān yuè xià yáng zhōu*; misty flower third month go to Yangzhou). Based on the ten translations we collected, only four of them render " 烟 花 三 月" (*yān huā sān yuè*; misty flower third month) as a common noun, while in the other six translations, "故人 西 辞 黄鹤楼，烟 花 三 月 下 扬州" (*gù rén xī cí huáng hè lóu, yān huā sān yuè xià yáng zhōu*; old friend west leave yellow-crane-tower, misty flower third month go to Yangzhou) is rendered in the following ways:

Wan and Wang's translation
From Tower of Yellow Crane my friend is going away to
Yangzhou in the mouth of glowing blooms and dimming willows.

Tu and Tu's translation
My friend leaves Yellow Crane Tower towered in the west,
Going to Yangzhou in the third moon when blooms are vying their best.

Yang and Yang's translation
At Yellow Crane Tower in the west
In the mist and flowers of spring
He goes down to Yangzhou;

Bynner and Jiang's translation
You have left me behind, old friend, at the Yellow Crane Terrace,
On your way to visit Yangzhou in the misty mouth of flowers;

Xu's (1988) translation
My friend has left the west where towers Yellow Crane
For River Town when willow-down and flowers reign.

Xu's (2000b) translation
My friend has left the west where the Yellow Crane towers
For River Town veiled in green willows and red flowers.

One common feature of the six translations is that the translators adopt the third lunar month to render "烟 花 三 月" (*yān huā sān yuè*; misty flower third month), as seen in "in the month of glowing blooms and dimming willows" (Wan and Wang's [2000: 169] translation), "in the mist and flowers of spring" (Yang and Yang's [2001a: 69] translation), "in the misty month of flowers" (Bynner and Jiang's [Wen 1989: 83] translation), and "in the third moon when blooms are vying their best" (Tu and Tu's [1997: 193] translation). In these four translations, season or month is mentioned, which is not only equivalent to the original in structure, but also conveys the meaning in the original.

Also, Xu's two translations deserve our attention. In Xu's (1988) translation, "烟 花 三 月" (*yān huā sān yuè*; misty flower third month) is translated as "when willow-down and flowers reign". In terms of structure, this translation is inequivalent to the original, as the original is a group and the equivalent form in English should be a group rather than a clause. However, in terms of syntactic function, the source text and the target text are equivalent, both serving as the circumstance indicating the time of going to Yangzhou. In the other translation by Xu (2000b), however, we can hardly find an equivalence to "烟 花 三 月"

(*yān huā sān yuè*; misty flower third month). In the first two lines of this translation (i.e. "My friend has left the west where the Yellow Crane towers / For River Town veiled in green willows and red flowers."), "veiled in green willows and red flowers" functions as the postmodifier of "River Town". In the perspectives of structure and function as well as artistic conception, this translation does not seem as good as the other five translations.

In our data (i.e. the four poems of the Tang Dynasty), the following six proper nouns are included:

1. *Feng Qiao Ye Bo*: "枫 桥" (*fēng qiáo*; maple bridge), "姑苏" (*gū sū*; Gusu/Suzhou) and "寒山 寺" (*hán shān sì*; cold-hill temple)
2. *Fu Rong Lou Song Xin Jian*: "芙蓉楼" (*fú róng lóu*; Hibiscus-tower), "辛渐" (*xīn jiàn*; Xin Jian), "吴" (*wú*; Wu), "楚山" (*chǔ shān*; Chu-mountain) and "洛阳" (*luò yáng*; Luoyang)
3. *Huang He Lou Song Meng Hao Ran Zhi Guang Ling*: "黄鹤楼" (*huáng hè lóu*; yellow-crane-tower) (applied twice), "孟浩然" (*mèng hào rán*; Meng Haoran), "广陵" (*guǎng líng*; Guangling), "三 月" (*sān yuè*; third month), "扬州" (*yáng zhōu*; Yangzhou), and "长江" (*cháng jiāng*; Yangtze River);
4. *Bo Qin Huai*: "秦淮" (*qín huái*; Qinhuai River) (applied twice) and " 后庭 花" (*hòu tíng huā*; backyard flower).

We will now discuss how these proper nouns are rendered in the English translations of the four poems.

Feng Qiao Ye Bo

We have collected four English translations of this poem, including translations by Tinggan Cai (see Wen 1989: 125), Dalian Wang (1997: 95), Yuanchong Xu (see Xu, Lu & Wu 1988: 224) and Yuanchong Xu (2000b: 329). Table 10.1 tabulates how the three proper nouns are translated.

Table 10.1. English translations of the three proper nouns in *Feng Qiao Ye Bo*

Proper noun / Translator	枫 桥 (*fēng qiáo*; maple bridge)	姑苏 (*gū sū*; Gusu/ Suzhou)	寒山 寺 (*hán shān sì*; cold-hill temple)
Tinggan Cai	Maple Bridge	Suzhou	Hanshan Temple
Dalian Wang	Maple Bridge	Gusu	Cold-Hill Temple
Yuanchong Xu 1988	Maple Bridge	Gusu	Temple of Cold Hill
Yuanchong Xu 2000b	Maple Bridge	—	Temple of Cold Hill

As shown in Table 10.1, there is only one instance in which no proper noun (i.e. "city") is adopted to render a proper noun. To explore this issue further, we can compare the third and fourth lines in Xu's two translations:

Xu's (1988) translation (see Xu, Lu & Wu 1988)
Beyond the Gusu walls the Temple of Cold Hill
Rings bells which reach my boat, breaking the midnight still.

Xu's (2000b) translation
Beyond the city wall, from Temple of Cold Hill
Bells break the ship-borne roamer's dream and midnight still.

When translating the third line in the original, the two translations differ in the middle part of the line. "Gusu walls", a plural noun in Xu's 1988 translation, is changed to "city wall" – a singular noun – in Xu's 2000b translation. Other changes include those from "Gusu" to "city" and from "walls" to "wall". In addition, "the Temple of Cold Hill" in Xu (1988) is changed to "Temple of Cold Hill" in Xu (2000b). (The definite article "the" is purposely omitted, perhaps to keep the number of syllables in this line equivalent to those in other lines.)

By carrying out a syntactic analysis of the third and fourth lines, we find that the subject is changed from "the Temple of Cold Hill" in Xu (1988) to "bells" in the fourth line of Xu (2000), whereas "Temple of Cold Hill" here becomes the complement (or object) of "from" – a preposition in a prepositional phrase (or an adverbial). However, this syntactic change is not closely related to the choice of translating "姑苏" (*gū sū*; Gusu/Suzhou) as "Gusu" or "city". In our view, changing "wall" in Xu (2000b) to replace "walls" in Xu (1988) is a perfection in the translation, whereas it may not be appropriate to replace "city" with "Gusu". We assume that "city" in Xu (2000b) represents one way of "simplifying" his translation (e.g. Xu 1990a) (see further discussion in Section 10.5).

Fu Rong Lou Song Xin Jian

In the five English translations we have collected, by Dalian Wang (1997: 23), Jie Tao (see Wu 1997: 119), Changsheng Wan and Xianzhong Wang (2000: 37), Yuanchong Xu (2000a: 85) and Yuanchong Xu (2000b: 83), two strategies are adopted to render the proper nouns. First, all proper nouns are translated as proper nouns, as seen in translations by Wang, Tao, and Wan and Wang. Second, some proper nouns are translated as proper nouns, while others are rendered as common nouns or inequivalent proper nouns, or left untranslated, as seen in Xu's (2000a, 2000b) translation.

Table 10.2. English translations of the five proper nouns in *Fu Rong Lou Song Xin Jian*

Proper noun / Translator	芙蓉楼 (*fú róng lóu*; Hibiscus-tower)	辛渐 (*xīn jiàn*; Xin Jian)	吴 (*wú*; Wu)	楚山 (*chǔ shān*; Chu-mountain)	洛阳 (*luò yáng*; Luoyang)
Dalian Wang	Lotus Pavilion	Xin Jian	Wu	Mount Chu	Luoyang
Jie Tao	Hibiscus Pavilion	Xin Jian	The Wu city	Chu Mountain	Luoyang
Changsheng Wan and Xianzhong Wang	Hibiscus Tower	Xin Jian	Wu	the (lonely) Mountain of Chu	Luoyang
Yuanchong Xu (2000a)	Lotus Tower	Xin Jian	–	Southern Hills	the North
Yuanchong Xu (2000b)	Lotus Tower	Xin Jian	–	Southern Hills	the North

As shown in Table 10.2, the first three translations all adopt proper nouns to render the proper nouns in the original, whereas the latter two translations adopt a different method. In fact, the only difference between Xu's (2000a, 2000b) two translations lies in their first lines. It can be estimated that Xu (2000b: 83) is a revised version of Xu (2000a):

> ***Farewell to Xin Jian at Lotus Tower***
> A cold rain mingled with East Stream invades the night;
> At dawn you leave the Southern hills lonely in haze.
> If my friends in the North should ask if I'm all right,
> My heart is free of stain as ice in crystal vase.

In Xu's (2000a) translation, the first line – which is a clause – is changed to a nominal group – "A cold rain mingled with Eastern Stream at night". Despite the differences between Xu (2000a) and Xu (2000b), their similarities are not related to the discussion in this chapter, so we will only focus on Xu (2000b).

In Xu (2000b), "吴" (*wú*; Wu) is not translated, which is perhaps based on Xu's (e.g. 1990a) method of "reduction" in translation;

"楚山" (*chǔ shān*; Chu-mountain) is translated as "Southern hills", and "洛阳" (*luò yáng*; Luoyang) as "the North", both perhaps involving the method of "word replacement". In this translation, direction is emphasized. By adding "East (Eastern)", the translator renders "楚山" (*chǔ shān*; Chu-mountain) as "Southern hills" and "洛阳" (*luò yáng*; Luoyang) as "the North" to highlight the directions involved. The limitation of this translation is that it cannot convey the associative meaning in the original and has abstracted the concrete content. Its advantage lies in "the conversion of the poet's personal experience to experience in general" (Zhu 1990: 49, our translation), thereby empowering readers to experience, imagine and recreate the poem. Xu (2002: 2, our translation) has commented on his method as follows: "Although this method cannot convey the original appeal achieved through association, it is more meaningful than the previous translation[1] and has created new meanings."

Huang He Lou Song Meng Hao Ran Zhi Guang Ling

Six proper nouns are found in the original, with "黄鹤楼" (*huáng hè lóu*; yellow-crane-tower) being used twice. As previously stated, the proper noun "三 月" (*sān yuè*; third month) in "烟 花 三 月" (*yān huā sān yuè*; misty flower third month) is not rendered as a proper noun. We also note that "长江" (*cháng jiāng*; Yangtze River) is not rendered as a proper noun in all translations:

Tu and Tu's translation: "the Yangtze River"
Wang's translation: "River"
Xu's (1988, 2000b) translations: "(the endless) River"
Sun's translation: "the Long River".

Although these five translations differ from each other, they are similar in selecting a proper noun to render a proper noun. In the other three translations, "长江" (*cháng jiāng*; Yangtze River) is respectively rendered as "a mighty river" (Wan and Wang's translation), "the great river" (Yang and Yang's translation) and "the river" (Bynner and Jiang's translation, see Wen 1989). Whether to adopt a proper noun or not depends on the translators' interpretation of the original. Since "长江" (*cháng jiāng*; Yangtze River) refers specifically to "扬子江" (*yáng zǐ jiāng*; Yangtze River) in the poem, it is most appropriate to choose "Yangtze River"; even if other choices are made, proper nouns will still be better than common nouns.

Bo Qin Huai

As previously discussed, only two proper nouns are found in *Bo Qin Huai*, namely "秦淮" (*qín huái*; Qinhuai River) and "后庭 花" (*hòu tíng huā*; backyard flower), with "秦淮" (*qín huái*; Qinhuai River) – the current Qinhuai River in Nanjing – being used twice in the poem. Such method of abbreviation is frequently seen in ancient poems. For instance, the fourth poem of *Ben Wang Dao Zhong Wu Shou* (奔亡道中五首) by LI Bai involves two abbreviations in "函谷 如 玉关" (*hán gǔ rú yù guān*; Hangu Pass be like Yumen Pass), namely "函谷" (*hán gǔ*; Hangu Pass) for "函谷关" (*hán gǔ guān*; Hangu Pass) and "玉关" (*yù guān*; Yumen Pass) for "玉门关" (*yù mén guān*; Yumen Pass) (see Guo 2002: 72). Abbreviation is applied mainly due to the restriction of word number in regulated verses.

Among the five translations analysed, Luo's translation adopts a common noun – "the river" – to render "秦淮" (*qín huái*; Qinhuai River) in the second line of the original; further, in Xu's (1988) translation, "后庭 花" (*hòu tíng huā*; backyard flower) is not rendered as a common noun. We will first analyse Luo's translation (see Wu 1997: 639).

Berthed at Qinhuai River
Over the river so cold is the mist
and over the sand the moonlit so bright,
I moor my boat by the river,
a wineshop is near, at night.
The singing girls in the merchant's ship
no sense of the conquered's spite,
Sing still Blooms in Backyard, a love song,
from the other side of the river, out of sight.

In the original, "秦淮" (*qín huái*; Qinhuai River) is found both in the title and the second line. In Luo's translation, the instance of "秦淮" (*qín huái*; Qinhuai River) from the title is rendered as "Qinhuai River", while "the River" is found twice in the main body, with the first instance in the first line being added by the translator and the second instance in the third line being a translation of "秦淮" (*qín huái*; Qinhuai River). Since a proper noun is applied in the title, no other proper noun but "the river", which includes a definite article, is adopted in the main body to connect to the "Qinhuai River" in the title through lexical cohesion.

Similar instances of applying a proper noun in the title without repeating it in the main body can also be found in translations of other poems. For example, in Changsheng Wan and Xianzhong Wang's (2000: 166) translation of DU Mu's *Qing Ming*, the two translators avoid repetition of proper nouns by adopting this method:

The Tomb-visiting Day
The ceaseless drizzles drips all the dismal day,
So broken-hearted fares the traveler on the way.
When asked where could be found a tavern bower,
A cowboy points to yonder village of the apricot flower.

In the title of the original poem, "清明" (*qīng míng*; Qingming) is first translated as a proper noun, whereas the same "清明" (*qīng míng*; Qingming) in the first line is rendered as "all the dismal day" – a common nominal group. Such a method is contrasted with other approaches adopted in the other translations of this poem.

In the original of *Bo Qin Huai*, "后庭 花" (*hòu tíng huā*; backyard flower) refers to "玉 树 后庭 花" (*yù shù hòu tíng huā*; jade tree backyard flower), which is said to be a song composed by CHEN Shubao (陈叔宝), the last (profligate) emperor of the Chen Dynasty. In Xu's (1988: 317) translation, the title of the song is not rendered as a proper noun, with some explanations being provided:

Mooring on River Qinhuai
Cold water veiled in mist and shores steeped in moonlight,
I moor on River Qinhuai near wineshops at night,
Where songgirls knowing not the grief of conquered land
Are singing songs composed by a captive ruler's hand.

Two points need to be noted in Xu's translation. First, "后庭 花" (*hòu tíng huā*; backyard flower) is rendered as "songs composed by a captive ruler's hand", rather than as a proper noun, to highlight the composer of the song. Secondly, "歌" (*gē*; song) is rendered as "songs" in plural form. These two strategies deserve further attention. It is obvious that Xu's (2000b: 524) other translation is much better than the 1998 translation:

Moored on River Qinhuai
Cold water and sand bars veiled in misty moonlight,
I moor on River Qinhuai near wineshops at night.
The songstress knows not the grief of the captive king,
By riverside she sings his song of Parting Spring.

In this translation, "后庭 花" (*hòu tíng huā*; backyard flower) in the original is rendered as a proper noun – that is, "Parting Spring" – and "歌" (*gē*; song) is rendered as "song" in singular form. This translation is therefore better than the 1998 translation both in form and meaning.

10.4.3 Proper nouns in the Chinese original translated as inequivalent proper nouns in English

Based on our analysis, we find that in some translations, although proper nouns are adopted to translate proper nouns in the original, certain variations can be identified between the inequivalent choices in the source and the target texts.

As discussed previously, in the translations of *Feng Qiao Ye Bo*, "姑苏" (*gū sū*; Gusu/Suzhou) is translated as "Gusu" or "Suzhou" and "寒山" (*hán shān*; cold-hill) as "Cold Hill" or "Hanshan"; in the translations of *Huang He Lou Song Meng Hao Ran Zhi Guang Ling*, "广陵" (*guǎng líng*; Guangling) is translated either as "Guangling" according to its sound or as "Yangzhou" according to its referential meaning. Despite the differences in the translations, these choices do not vary significantly in meaning.

Further, Xu's method of translating proper nouns deserves our special attention. In addition to "simplification", he adopts other strategies. In his two translations of *Huang He Lou Song Meng Hao Ran Zhi Guang Ling*, "扬州" (*yáng zhōu*; Yangzhou) is rendered as "River town", as shown in the first two lines of both translations:

Xu's (1988) translation
My friend has left the west where towers Yellow Crane
For River Town when willow-down and flowers reign.

Xu's (2000b) translation
My friend has left the west where the Yellow Crane towers
For River Town veiled in green willows and red flowers.

In terms of graphology, Xu regards "River Town" as a proper noun, which does not, however, indicate the referential meaning as "Yangzhou" does. In other words, "River Town" is not as specific as "Yangzhou" and readers may not understand its referential meaning.

As discussed previously, Xu provides two translations of DU Mu's *Bo Qin Huai*. In his 1988 translation, "后庭 花" (*hòu tíng huā*; backyard flower) is not rendered as a proper noun; in his 2000 translation, "Parting Spring", which is a proper noun, is applied (Xu 200b). Following

Qijun Zhao (see Xiao et al. 1983: 1087) and Haiou Zhang's (2000: 367) interpretations, we know that "后庭 花" (*hòu tíng huā*; backyard flower) refers to a song titled "玉 树 后庭 花" (*yù shù hòu tíng huā*; jade tree backyard flower). Hence, "Parting Spring" in Xu's translation is less appropriate than "Blooms in Backyard" (Luo's translation), "Backyard Flowers" (Yang and Yang's translation) and "Back Court Flower" (Wang's translation).

In Wang's (1997: 141) translation of *Bo Qin Huai*, "秦淮" (*qín huái*; Qinhuai River) is rendered as "Qinhuai River" and "Qinhuai Canal" respectively. Although both choices are proper nouns, the different words may mislead readers, who will regard them as two different rivers; thus, applying one proper noun would be more appropriate here. However, while translating "广陵" (*guǎng líng*; Guangling) and "扬州" (*yáng zhōu*; Yangzhou) in LI Bai's *Huang He Lou Song Meng Hao Ran Zhi Guang Ling*, some translators render both names as "Yangzhou", while some render them as "Guangling" and "Yangzhou" respectively. In our opinion, to better express the meaning in the original, we can adopt two different proper nouns to differentiate them, but the best approach is that adopted by Sun (1997: 553), who has added a note to state that "广陵" (*guǎng líng*; Guangling) is the other name of "扬州" (*yáng zhōu*; Yangzhou).

As discussed previously, when translating "(烟 花) 三 月" (*[yān huā] sān yuè*; [misty flower] third month) in LI Bai's *Huang He Lou Song Meng Hao Ran Zhi Guang Ling*, some translators use common nouns while others use proper nouns. Among the translations in which proper nouns are used, one interesting phenomenon deserves our attention.

When translating "三 月" (*sān yuè*; third month), Wang chooses "May" (from "in misty, flowery May"), Sun selects "April" (from "in this flowery April"), and Wang and Knoepfle adopt "March" (In Wang and Knoepfle's translation, no capitalized letter is seen, but we still regard "march" as a proper noun), and similarly Zhang (2001: 41) also applies "March" (as seen in "it was just March of the lovely spring full of flower"). Obviously, all these translations adopt proper nouns to render proper nouns, but different meanings are indicated. In the original, "三 月" (*sān yuè*; third month) means the third lunar month, which should be April according to the solar calendar; hence, it is an accurate choice for Sun (1997: 554) to render it as "April" and to provide further explanations.

10.4.4 Proper nouns in the Chinese original untranslated in the English translations

Based on our discussions, while translating *Fu Rong Lou Song Xin Jian*, Xu (2000a, 2000b) has omitted "吴" (*wú*; Wu) in "寒雨连江夜入吴" (*hán yǔ lián jiāng yè rù wú*; cold rain mingle river night enter Wu). In his 2000b translation, this line is translated as "A cold rain mingled with East Stream invades the night", whereas in his 2000a translation, the clause in the original is rendered as a structure with a postmodifier – "A cold rain mingled with Eastern Stream at night". We wonder why "入吴" (*rù wú*; enter Wu) is omitted in Xu's two translations, but such a choice is contrasted sharply with the other translations:

> *Wang's translation*
> Cold rains reigning the stream last eve, I got in Wu
>
> *Tao's translation*
> Along the river that merged with a cold rain,
> we entered the Wu city late at night.
>
> *Wan and Wang's translation*
> Amid the nightly haze of cold rains and streams I came to Wu

In these three translations, "夜入吴" (*yè rù wú*; night enter Wu) means that somebody – I or we – has arrived in Wu at night. In the perspective of experiential meaning, the three translations above are more appropriate than Xu's translation.

Based on our observation, Xu tends to "simplify" proper nouns in his translations, as he regards his method of "simplification" as one way of creating new meanings and as a reflection of his "creative method of translation" (Xu 2002: 2 our translation). From his two translations of DU Mu's *Qian Huai*, we find that "simplification" is applied more obviously in his latter translation:

遣怀
qiǎn huái
express thought

杜牧
dù mù
DU Mu

落魄江湖载酒行，
luò pò jiāng hú zǎi jiǔ xíng,
down and out river lake carry wine roam,
楚腰纤细掌中轻。
chǔ yāo xiān xì zhǎng zhōng qīng.
Chu waist slim palm in light.

十年一觉扬州梦，
shí nián yí jiào yáng zhōu mèng,
ten year one sleep Yangzhou dream,
赢得青楼薄倖名。
yíng dé qīng lóu báo xìng míng.
obtain VPART brothel unfaithful name.

Xu's 1988 translation (see Xu, Lu & Wu 1988: 321)
A Confession
Luckless, I roved the lakes and rivers with my wine
And spent my life with slender Southern girls so fine.
Having dreamed ten years in Yangzhou, I woke a rover
Who earned in mansions green the name of fickle lover.

Xu's (2000b: 529) translation
A Confession
I roved the rivers, indulged in pleasure and wine
With slender Southern girls who'd dance on palms of mine
Having dreamed happy dreams ten years, I woke a rover
Who earned in mansions green the name of fickle lover.

From these two translations, we find "Luckless, I roved the lakes and rivers with my wine" and "Having dreamed ten years in Yangzhou, I woke a rover" in Xu's translation in 1988, whereas these two lines are changed to "I roved the rivers, indulged in pleasure and wine" and "Having dreamed happy dreams ten years, I woke a rover" in his translation in 2000b. The choices such as "indulged in pleasure" and "having dreamed happy dreams" both illustrate his "simplification" method. With the application of this method, the proper noun "扬州" (*yáng zhōu*; Yangzhou) in the original is not explicitly translated. In the other three translations we collected (i.e. translations by Zhiye Luo [see Wu 1997: 645], Dalian Wang [1997: 151] and Shi Zong [1999: 215]), literal translations of the proper noun "扬州" (*yáng zhōu*; Yangzhou) are found. For instance, the following translation is rendered by Dalian Wang (1997: 151):

A Regret
Lacking success in life, I used to roam and drink around
With some sweet, slender southern maidens here and there I found.
My ten years life in Yangzhou is a dream of but one night;
I've only earned a name of faithless swain at brothel site.

There are various examples of adopting the "simplification" method to render proper nouns as common nouns in Xu's translation. To further illustrate Xu's preference for common nouns to replace proper nouns in his translation, we will examine two more translations of *Jin Ling Jiu Si Liu Bie* (金陵酒肆留别) by LI Bai.

金陵 酒肆 留别
jīn líng jiǔ sì liú bié
Jinling tavern parting

李白
lǐ bái
LI Bai

风吹柳花满店香，
fēng chuī liǔ huā mǎn diàn xiāng,
wind blow willow flower whole shop fragrant,

吴姬压酒劝客尝，
wú jī yā jiǔ quàn kè cháng,
Wu woman squeeze wine bid guest taste,

金陵子弟来相送，
jīn líng zǐ dì lái xiāng sòng,
Jinling junior come see off,

欲行不行各尽觞。
yù xíng bù xíng gè jìn shāng.
plan go not go all great extent wine cup.

请君试问东流水。
qǐng jūn shì wèn dōng liú shuǐ.
please you try ask east flow water.

别意与之谁短长？
bié yì yǔ zhī shuí duǎn cháng?
part thought and it who short long?

Three proper nouns are found in the original, including "金陵" (*jīn líng*; Jinling), "吴" (*wú*; Wu) ("吴姬" [*wú jī*; Wu woman] refers to women from Wu and here indicates a maid in the tavern) and "金陵" (*jīn líng*; Jinling). Two translations of this poem are as follows:

Yuanchong Xu's (2000b: 136) translation
Parting at a Tavern in Jinling
The tavern's sweetened when wind blows in willow-down;
A southern maiden urges guests to taste her wine.
My dear young friends have come to see me leave the town;
They who stay drink their cups and I who leave drink mine.
O ask the river flowing to the east, I pray,
Whether its parting grief or mine will longer stay!

In Xu's (2000b) translation, among the three proper names in the original, only the one in the title is translated, with one proper name (i.e. "吴" [*wú*; Wu]) being simplified and the other being omitted.

The following translation is rendered by Di Tu and An Tu (see Wu 1997: 203):

Parting at an Inn in Jinling
The inn is so sweet with the willow catkins in the wind aflying.
The maid from Wu bids us the flavour of the vintage trying.
Here come my young friends from Jinling to see me off.
I drink my fill and to their hearts' content they quaff.
O my friend, please ask this river eastward going,
Is my grief of parting longer than its ceaseless flowing?

In Tu and Tu's translation, the three proper nouns in the original are all rendered as proper nouns (i.e. "Jinling", "Wu" and "Jinling"). Such a method of literal translation is sharply contrasted with the "simplifying" method hailed by Yuanchong Xu. Based on our observation, most translators of ancient Chinese poems tend to render the proper nouns in the original as proper nouns by way of literal translation.

Following our discussion on the translation of proper nouns in LI Bai's *Huang He Lou Song Meng Hao Ran Zhi Guang Ling*, we will now investigate the strategies used in translating the title of this poem. Among the ten translations we collected, only Dayu Sun (1997: 223) provides a complete translation of the title: "Seeing Meng Haoran off to Guangling on the Yellow Crane Tower".

For seven of the translations, each has omitted one proper noun. Some translators have chosen to omit "黄鹤楼" (*huáng hè lóu*; yellow-crane-tower), including Tu and Tu ("Seeing Meng Haoran off to Guangling") as well as Bynner and Jiang ("A Farewell to Meng Haoran on

His Way to Yangzhou"). Some translators have omitted "广陵" (*guǎng líng*; Guangling), including Wan and Wang ("Seeing off Meng Haoran at Tower of Yellow Crane", Yang and Yang ("Seeing Meng Haoran off from Yellow Crane Tower"), Wang ("A Farewell Song to Meng Haoran at Yellow Crane Tower") and Xu (1998, 2000b) ("Seeing Meng Haoran off at Yellow Crane Tower").

LI Bai's original title, "黄鹤楼 送 孟浩然 之 广陵" (*huáng hè lóu sòng mèng hào rán zhī guǎng líng*; yellow-crane-tower see off Meng Haoran to Guangling) is very informative and includes a relatively complex structure. Sun's translation is equivalent to the original in terms of both the conveyance of message and the equivalence of structure. Therefore, we suggest that Sun's translation is more accurate compared with other translations that omit either "黄鹤楼" (*huáng hè lóu*; yellow-crane-tower) or "广陵" (*guǎng líng*; Guangling).

10.5 Discussion

Our analysis in this chapter is related to the translators' interpretation of the original and their translation strategies. Two possibilities are involved: first, a translator may not purposely render a proper noun by way of literal translation; and second, the translators' interpretations of the original may vary from one another.

10.5.1 Free translation and literal translation

In "On the English Translation of *300 Tang and Song Lyrics*", Xu (2002) clearly points out that the method of translating proper nouns in the original as common nouns is one way of applying his "creative method of translation" (see e.g. Xu 1990a). He also illustrates how this "creative method of translation" can fully exploit the advantages of the target language. We will now compare Xu's (2002) two translations of *Chang Xiang Si* (长相思) by BAI Juyi (白居易). Due to the limited space and the focus of our discussion, we will only cite the first half of the poem (see also Appendix 1 for translations by Yuanchong Xu [1990b] and Jinghao Gong [1999: 5]):

长相思
cháng xiāng sī
everlasting longing

白居易
bái jū yì
BAI Juyi

汴水 流，
biàn shuǐ liú,
Bian River flow,
泗水 流，
sì shuǐ liú,
Si River flow,

流 到 瓜州 古 渡头。
liú dào guā zhōu gǔ dù tóu.
flow to Guazhou (melon-shoal) ancient ferry.

吴山 点 点 愁。
wú shān diǎn diǎn chóu.
Wu-mountain dot dot woe.

(1) Xu's (1986: 13) translation
See the Bian River flow
And the Si River flow!
By Ancient Ferry, mingling waves, they go;
The Southern hills reflect my woe.

(2) Xu's (2002) translation
See Northern River flow
And Western River flow!
By Melon Islet, mingling waves, they go.
The Southern hills dotted with woe.

Between the two renditions, the first one is a previous translation (see Xu 1986: 13), while the second is a more recent translation. Xu (2002: 2, our translation) comments on his previous translation as follows:

> My translation of "汴水 流，泗水 流," (*biàn shuǐ liú, sì shuǐ liú*; Bian River flow, Si River flow) is basically literal or based on the resemblance in form. However, "汴水" (*biàn shuǐ*; Bian River) and "泗水" (*sì shuǐ*; Si River) in the original are associated with history and geography, thus increasing the aesthetic beauty of the poem and adding implied meanings. That is to say, its content plays a vital role than its form, whereas a translation resembling to the original in form cannot achieve all these effects.

Due to his dissatisfaction with the literal strategy or the resemblance in form in his previous translation, in his more recent translation he changes to "a free method of translation to take the advantages of the target language and to adopt the best means of expression in the target language" (Xu 2002: 2, our translation). Moreover, Xu (2002: 2, our translation) makes the following observation on his more recent translation:

> In my recent translation, proper nouns such as "汴水" (*biàn shuǐ*; Bian River), "泗水" (*sì shuǐ*; Si River), and "吴山" (*wú shān*; Wu-mountain) are translated as commons nouns, i.e. "Northern River", "Western River", and "Southern hills" by adopting the method of "simplification". Although the lasting appeal achieved by associating the original cannot be conveyed, my recent translation has delivered more meanings than my previous translation and it has even created new meanings.

Xu's comments on his two strategies of translation are acceptable and both translations have advantages and disadvantages. According to Xu (2002: 2, our translation),

> when translating "流 到 瓜州 古 渡头" (*liú dào guā zhōu gǔ dù tóu*; flow to Guazhou [melon-shoal] ancient ferry), I apply "Ancient Ferry" in my previous translation and "Melon Islet" in my recent translation. The change involves both gains and losses. If I applied both "Melon Islet" and "Ancient Ferry", the translation would be too long; if I omitted "mingling waves", there would be more losses, which would outweigh the gains. After consideration, I believe "Melon Islet" offers a more concrete image than "Ancient Ferry", hence I have changed it to "Melon Islet".

In our opinion, if Xu's translation is not strictly following the metrical pattern and rhyme scheme, there will be no such dilemma.

When translating proper nouns in the original, Xu adopts the method of free translation to take the advantage of the target language, thereby creating new meanings. His notion is reflected in his various translations of Tang and Song poems as well as other ancient proses, where similar examples can be found (see e.g. Xu 1986, 1988, 1990b, 1996, 2000a, 2000b, 2003a, 2003b, 2003c). We will now compare *Cai Sang Zi* (采桑子), a poem composed during the Song Dynasty by LÜ Benzhong (吕本中), and its two translations to investigate the strategies of translating proper nouns.

采桑子
cǎi sāng zǐ
pick mulberry

吕本中
lǚ běn zhōng
LÜ Benzhong

恨君不似江楼月，
hèn jūn bú sì jiāng lóu yuè,
grieve you not be like river tower moon,

南北东西。
nán běi dōng xī.
south north east west

南北东西，
nán běi dōng xī.
south north east west

只有相随无别离。
zhǐ yǒu xiāng suí wú bié lí.
only-have companion no separation.

恨君却似江楼月，
hèn jūn què sì jiāng lóu yuè,
grieve you yet be like river tower moon,

暂满还亏。
zàn mǎn huán kuī.
brief wax then wane.

暂满还亏，
zàn mǎn huán kuī,
brief wax then wane.

待得团圆是几时？
dài dé tuán yuán shì jǐ shí.
wait VPART union be what time?

The following translation is by Robert Kotewell and Norman Smith (see Wen 1989: 280):

To "Picking Mulberries"
I grieve that my love is not like the moon over the riverside tower:
South and North, East and West,

South and North, East and West,
Only constant companionship and no separation.

I grieve that my love is all too like the moon over the riverside tower:
A brief waxing, and then a waning,
A brief waxing, and then a waning,
I wait for the full circle of union – but how short-lived!

In Kotewell and Smith's translation, "南 北 东 西" (*nán běi dōng xī*; south north east west) is rendered as proper nouns – "South and North, East and West" – whereas in Xu's (1996: 335) translation, the proper noun is "simplified" and is drawn away from the original by translating a nominal group that indicates directions into "shining all night" – a group with a present participle. By adopting the method of "free translation", "shining all night" semantically serves to provide an example to "the full moon bright" in the preceding line. (In terms of grammatical structure, "shining all night" here modifies "the full moon bright".)

Xu's (1996: 335) translation
I regret you could not be like the full moon bright,
Shining all night,
Shining all night,
It is ever in view and never out of sight.

In the other two English translations we collected (i.e. Gong 1999: 137–38; Qiu 2003: 159), both translators render "南 北 东 西" (*nán běi dōng xī*; south north east west) in the original as corresponding nominal groups. Like Kotewell and Smith, Gong (1999: 137) translates "南 北 东 西" (*nán běi dōng xī*; south north east west) as a proper noun – "North, South, East, West" – with the order of "South" and "North" being reversed. On the other hand, in Qiu's (2003: 159) translation, the translator renders this proper noun as common nouns (i.e. "east, west, north, and south") (see Appendix 1 for the two translations).

As both an outstanding practitioner of translating ancient Chinese poems and a creator of theories on poetry translation (see Guo et al. 1999: 443), Yuanchong Xu highlights the translator's psychological experience during translation and his suggestion deserves our attention. In addition, his method of "creative translation" is unique and has its own theoretical basis and practical value. In many of his translations, proper nouns in the originals are rendered as common nouns by way of "simplification", which represents a practice of his method of "creative translation".

10.5.2 Determining the proper nouns

China is a kingdom of poetry. Through poems, poets express their ambitions based on their thoughts. Naturally, their poems have unavoidably involved various names for places and persons. Such a feature has been especially prominent in ancient poems (see Guo 2002). However, as China is a vast territory, many places share the same name. For example, in DU Mu's *Qing Ming* (清明) (i.e. "清明 时节 雨 纷纷，路 上 行人 欲 断 魂。借 问 酒家 何 处 有，牧 童 遥 指 杏 花 村。" (*qīng míng shí jié yǔ fēn fēn, lù shàng xíng rén yù duàn hún. jiè wèn jiǔ jiā hé chù yǒu, mù tóng yáo zhǐ xìng huā cūn.*; Qingming season rain succession, road on pedestrian will lose soul. may ask tavern what place have, herd child far point apricot flower village), where can we find "杏 花 村" (*xìng huā cūn*; apricot flower village) in China? It can be found in Guichi County, Anhui Province, where liquor named "Apricot Flower Village" is made and where DU Mu once worked as an official. It can also be found in Fenyang, Shanxi Province – a place famous for "*fenjiu*" (a kind of spirit distilled in Fenyang) and where DU Mu had visited. (The facts about which "杏 花 村" [*xìng huā cūn*; apricot flower village] DU Mu had visited needs further verification by historians.) Furthermore, following Ruchang Zhou (see Xiao et al. 1983: 1102, our translation), "'杏 花 村' (*xìng huā cūn*; apricot flower village) may not necessarily be a real village or a tavern"; instead, it could be "a village amid apricot flowers" (Chen & Huang 2000: 76; Li & Zhang 2001: 239, our translation) or "a village where apricot flowers bloom" (Sanqin Press, 2000: 108, our translation). According to Li and Zhang (2001: 239, our translation), "杏 花 村" (*xìng huā cūn*; apricot flower village) found in places such as Fenyang, Shanxi "could have been named after DU Mu's poem by the later generations".

Given that it is difficult to determine whether or not some nouns in the original are proper nouns, the problem arises of choosing proper nouns in translation. Among the six English translations of *Qing Ming*, "杏 花 村" (*xìng huā cūn*; apricot flower village) is rendered as proper nouns in three of them; while it is rendered as common nouns in the other three translations (cf. Chapter 2). The translations of the fourth line in the original (i.e. "牧 童 遥 指 杏 花 村" [*mù tóng yáo zhǐ xìng huā cūn*; herd child far point apricot flower village]) can be found as follows:

Translating "杏 花 村" (xìng huā cūn; apricot flower village) as proper nouns
Juntao Wu's translation: He points at Apricot Bloom Village faraway

Tinggan Cai's translation: And there the herdboy's fingers Almond-Town suggest
Dayu Sun's translation: The shepherd boy the Apricot Bloom Vill / doth point to afar and say

Translating "杏花村" (xìng huā cūn; apricot flower village) as common nouns
Xianyi Yang and Gladys Yang's translation: He points at a distant hamlet nestling amidst apricot blossoms
Changsheng Wan and Xianzhong Wang's translation: A cowboy points to yonder village of the apricot flower
Yuanchong Xu's (2000b) translation: A cowherd points to a cot 'mid apricot flowers.

As discussed in "The Inspiration of Functional Linguistic Analysis on Translation Studies" (Huang 2002a), based on the references we collected, scholars in the literary circles in China commonly hold that "杏花村" (*xìng huā cūn*; apricot flower village) in *Qing Ming* is not a real name, but rather refers to villages where apricot flowers come into bloom in general. Therefore, it may not be appropriate to render "杏花村" (*xìng huā cūn*; apricot flower village) in this poem as common nouns.

10.6 Conclusion

Based on the analysis of four Tang poems and their English translations, this chapter explores the translation of proper nouns. Specifically, four possibilities are dealt with in this chapter. First, proper nouns in the original are translated as equivalent proper nouns into English. Second, proper nouns in the original are translated as common nouns into English. Third, proper nouns in the original are translated as inequivalent proper nouns. Finally, proper nouns in the original are not translated.

According to our discussion in this chapter, when proper nouns in the original are rendered as common nouns, Xu's (e.g. 1990a) method of "word replacement" will be applied. In fact, we have already touched on the issue of literal translation and free translation, which is associated with debates on the principle of translation between scholars advocating resemblance in form and those advocating resemblance in spirit in China.

After I finished my first draft of this chapter, a friend of mine, who was then a visiting scholar in the United Kingdom, heard that I was studying the English translations of LI Bai's *Huang He Lou Song Meng Hao Ran Zhi Guang Ling* and kindly found several English translations from Minglong Pei's website of "China the Beautiful" (www.chinapage.com) for me. These translations exhibit various phenomena of language use and deserve further analysis. Some of the uses can even serve as starting points for new discussions. I originally planned to include these English translations in this chapter, but eventually had to abandon them due to space considerations.

For studies on the English translation of proper noun in ancient Chinese poems and lyrics, we can also refer to the discussions in Gu (2003: 90–123).

Note

1. In the previous translation, Xu translated the proper nouns equivalently.

Chapter 11

Quoting-reporting in English translations

11.1 Introduction

In this chapter, we investigate the issue of quoting-reporting in English translations of Tang poems in a linguistic perspective. We first briefly explore the theoretical concept of quoting-reporting by drawing insights from translating this specific language form. We also differentiate quoting, reporting, direct speech, and indirect speech in simple terms. Then we analyse the instances of quoting-reporting in some English translations of Tang poems. Finally, we discuss the problems we find in the analysis and make some comments.

11.2 Problematizing quoting-reporting

In linguistic research, quoting-reporting is a topic worthy of further exploration. In this section, we briefly analyse and differentiate some basic terms in order to analyse some examples from the English translations of ancient Chinese poems.

11.2.1 Quoting and reporting

In a linguistic perspective, quoting means to apply another's wording, with the purpose of relating the meaning conveyed by others (see Halliday 1994; Thompson 1996). Quoting not only applies another person's words but also maintains the meaning. Reporting, on the other hand, refers to relating another person's meaning by applying little or no original linguistic forms. For instance, suppose Catherine had said to me, "I enjoy talking to you." I could quote or report this speech act by at least using the following five linguistic forms:

Example (1): Catherine said (to me), "I enjoy talking to you."
Example (2): Catherine said (to me) that she enjoyed talking to me.
Example (3): Catherine said (to me) that she liked talking to me.

> Example (4): Catherine said (to me) that she liked having conversations with me.
> Example (5): Catherine said (to me) that she liked my conversation with her.

Among the five examples above, only Example (1) is quoting, while the other four are all reporting. Example (2) changes "I" in the original wording to "she", "enjoy" to "enjoyed" and "you" to "me"; while in Example (5), none of the words is said by Catherine in her original words. Therefore, in Example (1), "I enjoyed talking to you" is identical with the original words both in terms of wording and meaning. Differences can be seen among Examples (2) to (5): Examples (2) and (3) include words that are obviously identical to or that correspond with the original, whereas Examples (4) and (5) share no similarity with the original.

Many linguists regard the instance of quoting-reporting in Example (1) as direct speech and the quoting-reporting in Examples (2) to (5) as indirect speech. Such a distinction is based on the use of quotation marks in the sentence. Regarding this issue, Zhang (1997: 1262, our translation) observes:

> There are in general two ways of quoting other's words: one is direct speech, which serves to quote the exact original words and to place them inside the quotation mark; the other way is indirect speech or reported speech, which serves to report the other's words, with the reported speech not being placed in the quotation mark.

This opinion concurs with that of Quirk et al. (1985: 1021), who discuss direct speech as follows: "Direct speech purports to give the exact words that someone (who may be the reporter) utters or has uttered in speech or in writing." Quirk et al. (1985) and Zhang (1997: 1262) share the same view on direct speech by regarding it as "[quoting] the exact original words".

Similar to the practice of applying punctuation marks (e.g. full stop, question mark, exclamation mark) to determine whether certain sentence structures are sentences, the application of quotation marks in the differentiation of direct speech and indirect speech has so far been widely accepted, particularly in the analysis of written language.

11.2.2 Quoting-reporting in translation

If we regard quoting the exact original words as the standard of differentiating direct speech and indirect speech, direct speech will not be involved in translation, as translation is conducted through code switching from code A to code B to reproduce the message conveyed by code A, and the basis of such code switching is the change of linguistic form. Therefore, we can treat all quoting and reporting in translation as reporting.

Under the heading of "reporting", we can differentiate direct speech and indirect speech based on the use of quotation marks. However, our use of direct speech here is different from direct speech examined in works on grammar (e.g. Zhang 1997: 1262). In a translated work, for both direct speech and indirect speech, no exact original words are quoted, as the original words (in the original language) and the quoted words (in the target language) are expressed through different codes.

Based on this notion, we can characterize quoting-reporting in language use with the system network shown in Figure 11.1.

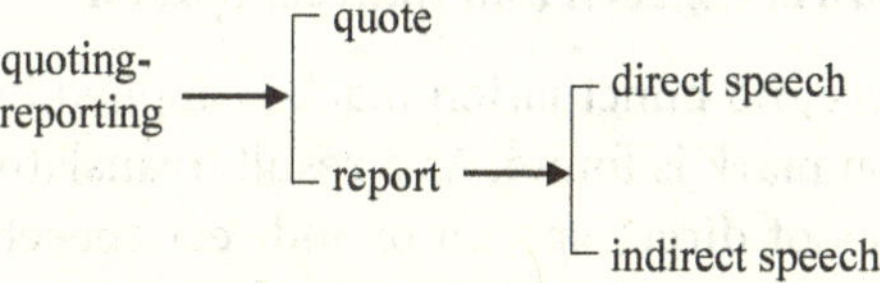

Figure 11.1. Categories of quoting-reporting

The standard of differentiating quoting from reporting is to identify whether the exact original words are quoted in the structure. To differentiate direct speech from indirect speech, on the other hand, the standard is to find whether a quotation mark is applied in the structure.

In the following discussion, the instances of quoting-reporting involved will also be indirect speech, as our examples are all quoted from translations. For the convenience of discussion, we will first differentiate "reporting clause" (i.e. the aforementioned "projecting clause") from "reported clause" (i.e. the aforementioned "projected clause") (see Chapter 3). Among the two, "reported clause" means that the contents (or situations) have already been said by others before reporting, while "reporting clause" is a structure adopted to report what has already been said by others. In Example (1), "Catherine said (to me)" is a reporting clause, and "I enjoy talking to you" is a reported clause. In the reporting clause – "Catherine said (to me)" – the verb "said" is known as a "reporting verb".

11.3 Analysis of the English translations of Chinese poems

Before we explore English translations of Tang poems, we need to point out that no punctuation mark was applied at the time when Tang poems were written, hence there will naturally be no quotation mark in the original poems. However, in the English translations, the translators have treated certain "words" skilfully based on their own understandings by rendering these words either as direct speech or as indirect speech. As Chinese poems cannot be interpreted in a fixed way, there can be various interpretations of a poem or even of one poetic line; moreover, as the translators' cultural attainment and language proficiency vary, the translations of certain poetic lines by different translators also vary.

11.3.1 Choice of direct speech and indirect speech

As discussed above, no punctuation mark is applied in ancient poems, thus no quotation mark is found. As a result, translators have to make their own choices of direct speech or indirect speech based on their interpretations, styles and techniques of translation. We can first examine the English translations of the beginning two lines in *Xun Yin Zhe Bu Yu* (寻隐者不遇) by JIA Dao (贾岛) (i.e. "松 下 问 童子 / 言 师 采 药 去" [*sōng xià wèn tóng zǐ / yán shī cǎi yào qù*; pine under ask boy / say master gather herb go]):

Example (6) Juntao Wu's (1997: 621) translation
"Where is your Master?" under pines I ask a lad;
"He's gathering medicinal herbs," so he says,

The translator here chooses direct speech, hence rendering the possible implied question in the original (e.g. "你的 师父 在 家 吗？" [*nǐ de shī fu zài jiā ma*; your master be at home MOD; Is your master at home?] or "你的 师父 去 哪儿 了？" [*nǐ de shī fu qù nǎ er le*; your master go where ASP; Where has your master been?]) as a quotation and treating it as a direct speech. Wu's method is different from the other six translations we collected: Yuanchong Xu (1988: 308), Dalian Wang (1997: 129), Dayu Sun (1997: 427), Changsheng Wan and Xianzhong Wang (2000: 160), Bynner (see Wen 1989: 166) and Watson (see Wen 1989: 167).

The following example is Bynner's translation of the first line of *Xun Yin Zhe Bu Yu*:

Example (7) Bynner's translation (Wen 1989: 166)
When I questioned your pupil, under a pine tree,

Regarding the translation of "松 下 问 童子" (*sōng xià wèn tóng zǐ*; pine under ask boy), Example (7) is more appropriate than Example (6), as Example (7) is more implied and thus much closer to the original. The original is brief and implicit, giving more space for imagination and recreation to readers; Example (7) has basically achieved this goal, while Example (6) is relatively too blunt and straightforward, and fails to give readers the space of imagination and recreation.

When translating the third line of *Qing Ming* (清明) by DU Mu (杜牧) – "借 问 酒家 何 处 有" (*jiè wèn jiǔ jiā hé chù yǒu*; may ask tavern what place have) – Juntao Wu also applies direct speech, leading to a different translation compared with the other five translations we collected: Tinggan Cai (see Wen 1989: 174), Dayu Sun 1997: 435, Xianyi Yang and Gladys Yang (2001a: 266), Changsheng Wan and Xianzhong Wang (2000: 166) and Yuanchong Xu (2000b: 537); see also Huang (2002b). We can compare the following two examples:

Example (8) Juntao Wu's (1997: 621) translation
"Is there a public house somewhere, cowboy?"
He points at Apricot Bloom Village faraway.

Example (9) Xianyi Yang and Gladys Yang's (2001a: 266) translation
When I ask a shepherd boy where I can find a tavern.
He points at a distant hamlet nestling amidst apricot blooms.

When translating "借 问 酒家 何 处 有" (*jiè wèn jiǔ jiā hé chù yǒu*; may ask tavern what place), the choices of direct speech and indirect speech both have their own unique features, whereas indirect speech may be a better choice, as it leaves readers the space of imagination and recreation. Further, it can be pointed out that the use of "cowboy" in Wu's translation seems to be inappropriate (see Huang 2002b, 2002c).

In the English translations of *Song Bie* (送别) by WANG Wei (王维) ("下 马 饮 君 酒 / 问 君 何 所 之 / 君 言 不 得 意 / 归 卧 南 山 陲 / 但 去 莫 复 问 / 白 云 无 尽 时" [*xià mǎ yǐn jūn jiǔ / wèn jūn hé suǒ zhī / jūn yán bù dé yì / guī wò nán shān chuí / dàn qù mò fù wèn / bái yún wú jìn shí*; dismount horse drink your wine / ask you which place go to / you say not achieve ambition / return lie south mountain foot / just go not again ask / white cloud no end time]), the instance of quoting-reporting is rendered differently. We will begin with the following translation:

Example (10): Herbert A. Giles's translation (see Lü 1980: 148)
Goodbye to Meng Hao-jan
Dismounted o'er wine we had said our last say;
Then I whisper, "Dear friend, tell me whither away."
"Alas!" he replied, "I am sick of life's ills
"And I long for repose on the slumbering hills.
"But oh seek not to pierce where my footsteps may stray.
"The white clouds will soothe me for ever and ay."

From Example (10), we find that except for the first line "Dismounted o'er wine we had said our last say" and the reporting clause "Then I whisper" in the second line, the remaining parts are all reported by a direct speech. We can compare Example (10) with Example (11).

Example (11) W.J. Fletcher's translation (see Lü 1980: 148)
So farewell, and if for ever, still for ever fare ye well.
Quitting my horse, a cup with you I drank.
And drinking, asked you whither you were bound.
Your hopes unprospered, said you, turned you round.
You went. I asked no more. The white Clouds pass,
And never yet have any limit found.

In Fletcher's translation, only the second and third lines contain the quoted-reported parts, which are all in the form of indirect speech. In Xianyi Yang and Gladys Yang's (2001a: 28) translation, a similar approach is adopted, hence we will not discuss their translation here in detail.

Translators in China have adopted different approaches to translate WANG Wei's *Song Bie*. For instance, Yuanchong Xu (2000b: 87) renders "问 君 何 所 之" (*wèn jūn hé suǒ zhī*; ask you which place go to) as an indirect speech and the remaining four lines as direct speech; on the other hand, Dayu Sun (1997: 139) renders all sentences as indirect speech. Whether to apply direct speech or indirect speech in translation depends on the translator's understanding of artistic conception and the mastery of skills in expression.

11.3.2 Scope of quoting-reporting

By comparing Examples (10) and (11), we can find that the two translators have interpreted the original differently. In Giles's translation, the second, third, fourth, fifth and sixth lines in the original are all rendered as direct speech, while in Fletcher's translation, indirect speech is only used when translating the second and third lines in the original. For Fletcher, the fourth and fifth lines in the original are not said by "君" (*jūn*; you) in the poem. Based on our comparison here, Examples (10) and (11) have defined different scopes of quoting-reporting.

There are several English translations of *Xun Yin Zhe Bu Yu* by JIA Dao (i.e. "松下问童子 / 言师采药去 / 只在此山中 / 云深不知处" [*sōng xià wèn tóng zǐ / yán shī cǎi yào qù / zhǐ zài cǐ shān zhōng / yún shēn bù zhī chù*; pine under ask boy / say master gather herb go / only be in this mountain in / cloud deep not know place]"). Yuanchong Xu has provided the following two translations successively:

Example (12) Yuanchong Xu's (1988: 308) translation
I ask your lad 'neath a pine-tree.
"My master's gone for herbs," says he,
"Amid the hill I know not where,
For clouds have veiled them here and there."

Example (13) Yuanchong Xu's (2000b: 479) translation:
I ask your lad 'neath a pine tree.
"My master's gone for herbs," says he,
You hide amid the mountains proud,
I know not where deep in the cloud.

In Example (12), the third and fourth lines in the original are regarded as words said by "the boy", hence they are rendered as direct speech. However, in Example (13), the third and fourth lines in the original are not said by "the boy" but by the narrator (i.e. the poet) to the hermit after the unsuccessful visit. Within a short period of time, the same translator has interpreted the same poem in two different ways. This also suggests that Chinese poems cannot be interpreted in a fixed way.

11.3.3 Use of quoting/reporting verb

When quoting/reporting others' words, we will usually point out the source of the quoting-reporting, namely the sender of the message. The subject of the quoting-reporting clause is the sender of the message, and the quoting/reporting verb is the means of sending the message. In some quoting-reporting clauses, there are also other elements (adverbials) indicating circumstantial meaning, such as time, place, and manner. In this way, the first line in Example (6) can be analysed as follows (see Table 11.1).

Table 11.1. Analysis of "'Where is your Master?'under pines I ask a lad"

"Where is your Master?"	under pines	I	ask	a lad
projected/reported clause	locative adverbial	subject	verb	complement
	projecting/reporting clause			

Quoting/reporting verbs, which not only indicate the semantic relations between projected/reported clauses and projecting/reporting clauses, but also in most cases signal the means of sending information, are of vital importance in projected-reported clauses. For instance, in Example (1), "said" indicates the meaning of "giving information", namely the subject – "Catherine" is sending the content to another person; in Example (6), "ask" indicates "seeking information", as the subject – "I" wishes (or demands) another person to provide some information. In the second line of Example (10) – "Then I whisper, 'Dear friend, tell me whither away'." – the quoting/reporting verb "whisper" indicates both the behavior and the manner of talking; although the following quoted/reported clause is also adopted to seek information, it is realized as an imperative in terms of form. By comparing this usage with the corresponding part in the second line of Example (11) – namely "(I) asked you whither you were bound" – we can then observe the differences: "asked" merely indicates the behavior of talking, while the meaning of "talking in a low voice" in "whisper" is excluded.

In translations, four possibilities exist in terms of the selection and application of quoting/reporting verb (see Table 11.2).

Table 11.2. Four possibilities in the selection and application of quoting/reporting verb in English translations

source language ◄——►	target language
use	use
non-use	non-use
use	non-use
non-use	use

The four possibilities can be discussed as follows:

1. use ↔ use

When quoting/reporting verbs are applied in both the source text and the target text, "formal equivalence" will be attained. In Example (6), equivalence is achieved between the second line of the original and its translation.

> Source text: 言 师 采 药 去 (*yán shī cǎi yào qù*; say master gather herb go)
> Wu's translation: "He's gathering medicinal herbs," so he says.

In Wan and Wang's (2000: 160) translation (i.e. "And he answers that his master is gone out into the mountains to gather herbs for medicine"), equivalence is also attained in form. However, in Wu's (1997: 621) translation, direct speech is applied; in Wan and Wang's (2000: 160) translation, indirect speech is applied. Also, in the original, the speaker is not explicitly stated, whereas in the English translations the subjects have to be added by following the conventions in English.

2. non-use ↔ non-use

Equivalence in form can also be achieved when no quoting/reporting verb is used in both the source text and the target text. For instance, in *Fu Rong Lou Song Xin Jian* (芙蓉楼送辛渐) by WANG Changling (王昌龄) (i.e. "寒 雨 连 江 夜 入 吴 / 平 明 送 客 楚山 孤 / 洛阳 亲 友 如 相问 / 一 片 冰 心 在 玉 壶" [*hán yǔ lián jiāng yè rù wú / píng míng sòng kè chǔ shān gū / luò yáng qīn yǒu rú xiāng wèn / yí piàn bīng xīn zài yù hú*; cold rain mingle river night enter Wu / daybreak see off guest Chu-mountain lonely / Luoyang relative friend if ask / one piece ice heart be in jade jar]), the third and fourth clauses are quotations, which are the narrator's (i.e. the poet's) own words, but no quoted-reported clause is seen in the original. Similarly, in Yuanchong Xu's (2000b: 83) translation, no quoted-reported clause is found.

> *Example (14)*
> ***Farewell to Xin Jian at Lotus Tower***
> A cold rain mingled with East Stream invades the night;
> At dawn you leave the Southern hills lonely in haze.
> If my friends in the North should ask if I'm all right,
> My heart is free of stain as ice in crystal vase.

There are several English translations of this poem. In the other three translations, however, quoted-reported clauses are applied: see Examples (16), (17) and (18).

3. *use ↔ non-use*

When quoted-reported verbs are found in the original rather than in the translation, non-equivalence in form will be seen between the source text and the target text. For example, in Xianyi Yang and Gladys Yang's (2001a: 266) translation of "借 问 酒家 何 处 有" (*jiè wèn jiǔ jiā hé chù* yǒu; may ask tavern what place have) by DU Mu (see Example [9]), the quoted-reported clause "借 问" (*jiè wèn*; may ask) is rendered to achieve the equivalence in form. However, some translators would render only the question and leave readers to look for the questioner based on context. As seen in Juntao Wu's translation, such a method has been adopted: see Example (8). By applying direct speech (i.e. "Is there a public house somewhere, cowboy?"), the clause in the source text is translated, and readers are thus requested to look for the questioner in the previous clause. Although no quoted-reported clause is seen in Wu's translation, the meaning in the original is conveyed and readers will have no difficulty reading his translation.

However, in some translations the quoted/reported clause in the original is not rendered, thus the questioner is difficult to be determined. Example (15) is Yuanchong Xu's (2000b: 537) translation of *Qing Ming* by DU Mu.

Example (15)

The Mourning Day

A drizzling rain falls like tears on the Mourning Day;
The mourner's heart is going to break on his way.
Where can a wineshop be found to drown his sad hours?
A cowherd points to a cot 'mid apricot flowers.

From Xu's translation, only two persons have appeared: "the mourner" and "a cowherd". Based on common sense, the speaker should be "the mourner" and the hearer should be "a cowherd". However, as shown in the interrogative in the third line (i.e. "Where can a wineshop be found to drown his sad hours?"), the use of "his" clearly indicates that the questioner cannot be "the mourner" in the last clause (i.e. "The mourner's heart is going to break on his way.") because "his" in "his sad hours" actually refers to "the mourner's". We wonder why the translator has selected "his" rather than "my". Had we changed "his" to "my", the questioner should then be "the mourner". Of course, "Where can a wineshop be found to drown his sad hours?" can also be regarded as voice-over spoken by the narrator.

4. non-use ↔ use

As previously discussed, the third and fourth lines in *Fu Rong Lou Song Xin Jian* by WANG Changling (i.e. "洛阳亲友如相问 / 一片冰心在玉壶" [*luò yáng qīn yǒu rú xiāng wèn / yí piàn bīng xīn zài yù hú*; Luoyang relative friend if ask / one piece ice heart be in jade jar]) are the quoted-reported speech. Since the narrator is quoting his own words, no quoted-reported clause is seen in the poem. However, among the translations we collected, except for Xu's (2000b: 83) translation, the other translations – those by Dalian Wang (1999: 23), Jie Tao (see Wu 1997: 119) and Changsheng Wan and Xianzhong Wang (2000: 37) – have all added quoted-reported clauses. The translations of these quoted-reported clauses are as follows:

Example (16) Dalian Wang's (1997: 23) translation
In Luoyang should my folks and friends ask after me,
Tell them a heart's in jade pot, pure as it can be.

Example (17) Jie Tao's translation (see Wu 1997: 119)
If my kinsfolk in Luoyang should feel concerned,
Please tell them for my part,
Like a piece of ice in a crystal vessel,
Fore'er aloof and pure remains my heart.

Example (18) Changsheng Wan and Xianzhong Wang's (2000: 37) translation
Oh, Friend, when folks in Luoyang inquires, let it be said,
My heart is as bright as crystal ice in the jar of jade.

In Example (16), "tell them" in the second line is the quoting-reporting clause, and the remaining part is the quoted-reported clause. In Example (17), "Please tell them for my part" in the second line is the quoting-reporting clause. In Example (18), "let it be said" is the quoting-reporting clause. In contrast, quoting-reporting clauses are applied in translations rather than in the original. Hence, in terms of the use of quoting-reporting clause in the translations, Examples (16), (17) and (18) are no better than Example (14) because, when quoting-reporting clauses are applied in translations, the brevity and implicitness will disappear and there will then be no space of imagination and recreation for readers.

11.4 Discussion

The above analysis shows that quoting is not seen in translation because the translation process involves the transfer of one code to another and the target language cannot quote the linguistic form in the source language. In this respect, the instances of quoting-reporting in translations are all instances of reporting. In terms of the realization of form, the parts signalled by quotation marks are direct speech, while the parts without quotation marks are indirect speech. Based on our classification, quoting is not equivalent to direct speech and reporting is not equivalent to indirect speech.

As there are no punctuation marks in ancient Chinese poems, quotation marks will naturally not be found. In the collections of poems published nowadays, the quotation marks are in fact added by people from later generations. However, the quoted-reported speeches are seldom marked out by quotation marks. If form is the realization of meaning, the non-use of quotation mark thus indicates that the quoted-reported speech is indirect speech.

When translating quoted-reported speech manifested by indirect speech, we hold that indirect speech should be applied, as is requested by "formal equivalence". If we adopt direct speech to translate indirect speech in the original, which is brief and implicit, the translation may in most cases be made explicit, thus failing to give more space for imagination and recreation to readers. For instance, by translating "松下问童子" (*sōng xià wèn tóng zǐ*; pine under ask boy) as "'Where is your Master?' under pines I ask a lad", as in Example (6), the translation has evidently destroyed the artistic conception in the original. In contrast, JIA Dao's original poem "has incorporated the questions in the answers" (in Xiqian Shen, see Xiao et al. 1983: 968, our translation), whereas in Example (6), the translator has clearly pointed out the possible implicit question, producing a translation far from the original in terms of both form and meaning. In another example, when "借问酒家何处有" (*jiè wèn jiǔ jiā hé chù yǒu*; may ask tavern what place have) is rendered as a direct speech, as seen in "Is there a public house somewhere, cowboy?" in Example (8), the translation may not be as appropriate as a translation with an indirect speech; moreover, the translation in Example (8) has omitted the quoting-reporting clause, so is not equivalent to the original.

When translating quoting-reporting speech, the choice of quoting-reporting verb is also very important. For example, in the second line of Example (10) (i.e. "Then I whisper, 'Dear friend, tell me whither away.'"), "whisper" seems to be redundant when adopted to render "问" (*wèn*; ask) in "问 君 何 所 之" (*wèn jūn hé suǒ zhī*; ask you which place go to), because "whisper" not only expresses the meaning of "说" (*shuō*; talk), but also indicates the manner of talking in a low voice.

11.5 Conclusion

This chapter explores the issue of quoting-reporting in English translations of Tang poems. We hold that it is necessary to differentiate quoting from reporting as well as direct speech from indirect speech.

As shown in our discussion, translation is a special activity of shifting between languages, thus the act of quoting the original intactly will never happen in translation. This is because translation involves the change of code A to code B to recreate the information conveyed in code A. Since the basic activity of translation lies in code switching, after translating the source text into the target text, the original words have never been quoted. Further, in this chapter, we propose the system network of quoting-reporting and classify quoting-reporting as quoting and reporting and then categorize reporting as direct speech and indirect speech.

After comparing the use of quoting-reporting in source texts (i.e. ancient Chinese poems) and target texts, we summarize four possibilities, among which two belong to formal equivalence and the other two belong to non-equivalence. By comparing the translations, we suggest that when translating quoting-reporting in Tang poems, translators should first take "formal equivalence" into consideration and meanwhile try to avoid using direct speech. Also, by analysing some examples of non-equivalence in form, we find that translators will leave little space for imagination and recreation for readers if providing too much explanation or making the implicit meaning too explicit, thereby impacting the transmission of artistic conception in the original poem.

Chapter 12

Translating person into English

12.1 Introduction

This chapter explores the issue of person in English translations of ancient Chinese poems. Our focus is on how the issue of person in the original poems is dealt with in the translations. We will first briefly review person and personal pronouns before analysing some English translations of ancient poems in terms of person. Finally, we will analyse and compare some ancient poems and their English translations in terms of the selection of personal pronouns and the expression of meaning.

12.2 Person and personal pronouns

In terms of language use, person can be categorized into three types: (1) first person, which indicates the speaker; (2) second person, which indicates the hearer; and (3) third person, which relates to the third-party in the interaction. The change of person also involves the change in the process of interaction. For instance, when Wang is present, Zhang asks Li, "你忙吗？" (*nǐ máng ma*; you busy MOD; Are you busy?), Zhang is the first person, Li is the second person, and Wang is the third person. If Wang interposes by saying "她比你忙。" (*tā bǐ nǐ máng*; she than you busy; She's busier than you.), Wang is then the first person, Zhang is the second person, and Li is the third person.

Every language has its grammatical system of indicating different persons. In English, the personal pronoun is the major (but not the only) way of indicating person. For instance, "I", "we", "me", "us" and so on indicate first person; "you" indicates second person; "he", "she", "it", "they", "him", "her", "them" and so on indicate third person. In terms of the referential meaning of personal pronouns, they can be distinguished according to unmarked use and marked use: unmarked use refers to the ordinary, conventional and established usage; while marked use refers to the special, particular, exceptional or unconventional usage. For example, when "we" is adopted to refer to more than one people including the speaker, as seen in "Catherine and I are classmates. We study Applied Linguistics in Edinburgh", "we" is used in the unmarked way; when "we" does not include the speaker, as seen in "How are we feeling today?" said by a nurse to a patient, "we" is used in the marked way (see also Huang 1999: 41–47).

Among the English personal pronouns, in addition to the distinction between first, second and third person, there are also distinctions in number and case. Figure 12.1 shows the system network of personal pronouns in English (see also Fawcett 1988; Hu, Zhu & Zhang 1989: 50).

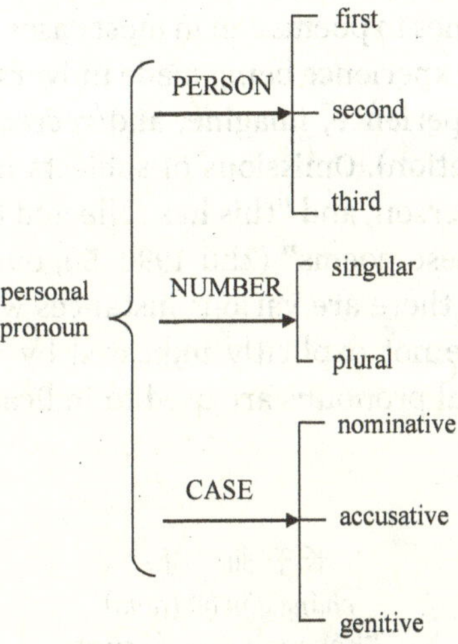

Figure 12.1 System of personal pronoun in English

As shown in the system network, when choosing a personal pronoun, we need to consider not only "person", but also "number" and "case". For instance, "I" is the choice of first-person singular, "we" first-person plural, "he" and "she" third-person singular and "they" third-person plural. These are all choices of nominative case. In terms of person and number, "me", "I" and "my" are all choices of first-person singular, whereas "I" is of nominative case, "me" accusative case and "my" genitive case. Other pronouns also have such a distinction. We will not discuss all of them here.

The marked use of personal pronouns is different from their original meaning. For example, when "we" is used to indicate a listener in singular, as seen in "How are we feeling today?" said by a nurse to a patient, "we" is different from its original use of first-person plural. Here also lies the difference between usage and use.

The system of personal pronoun in Chinese is roughly the same as that of English. They are similar or identical in various respects. As the focus of this chapter is not the comparison of personal pronoun systems between the two languages, we will not pursue this topic here in detail (see also Zhang & Chen 1981; Shikai Zhao 1999).

12.3 Use of personal pronouns in the original

In ancient Chinese poems, subjects in various lines tend to be omitted. In this way, "the scenes in poems can in most cases be popularized, with the poets' personal experience being made universal and readers being moved inside to experience, imagine, and recreate the poems" (Zhu 1990: 50, our translation). Omissions of subjects in ancient poems are often omissions of person, and "this has reflected the succinctness and implicitness of Chinese poems" (Zhu 1990: 50, our translation). Based on our observation, there are various instances when persons are not clearly stated or are not explicitly indicated by words. Of course, in some poems personal pronouns are used to indicate person, as seen in Example (1).

Example (1)

长干曲（唐）
cháng gān qǔ (tang)
Changgan song (Tang)

崔颢
cuī hào
CUI Hao

（其一）"君家何处住？
(qí yī) "jūn jiā hé chù zhù?
(one) "your home which place live?

妾住在横塘。"
qiè zhù zài héng tang."
I live be at sideward pond."

停船暂借问，
tíng chuán zàn jiè wèn,
stop boat moment may ask,

或恐是同乡。
huò kǒng shì tóng xiāng.
also perhaps be same village.

（其二）“家临九江水，
(qí èr) "jiā lín jiǔ jiāng shuǐ,
(two) "home be close to Jiujiang (nine-river) water,

来去九江侧。
lái qù jiǔ jiāng cè.
come go Jiujiang (nine-river) side.

同是长干人，
tóng shì cháng gān rén,
same be Changgan people,

生小不相识。”
shēng xiǎo bù xiāng shí."
born little not each other know."

Written by CUI Hao (崔颢), *Chang Gan Qu* (长干曲) consists of two parts. The first part is the question from a woman to a man and the second part is the man's reply. We have collected four English translations, by Burton Watson (see Wen 1989: 76), Yuanchong Xu (see Xu, Lu & Wu 1988: 139), Juntao Wu (1997: 283) and Yuanchong Xu (2000b: 205). The translations are identical in translating "君" (*jūn*; you) and "妾" (*qiè*; I) in the first two lines as "you" and "I":

Example (2): Burton Watson's translation
Tell me, where is your home?
I live at Sloping Banks myself –

Example (3) Yuanchong Xu's (1988) translation
"Tell me where you are from!
On riverbank's my home.

Example (4) Juntao Wu's translation
"Where do you live? Tell me, man, if you like;
And I, a girl, live at the Sideward Dyke.

Example (5) Yuanchong Xu's (2000b) translation
Where are you coming from?
On the shore I've my home.

In these four translations, the translators apply personal pronouns (e.g. "I", "me", "my", "you" and "your"), imperative clauses and interrogative clauses to render the persons in the original. As "其一" (*qí yī*; one) is the question from one person and "其二" (*qí èr*; two) is the answer from another person, only two persons (i.e. first person and second person) are involved in the interaction.

In the first part of the original, the subjects in the third and fourth lines are omitted and no personal pronoun is applied. In these two lines, the four translations vary from one another:

Example (6): Burton Watson's translation
Stop the boat, let me ask a minute –
who knows but maybe we're from the same town!

Example (7) Yuanchong Xu's (1998) translation
Let us stop rowing down!
Maybe we're from same town?

Example (8) Juntao Wu's translation
I ask briefly with my boat slowing down,
Because I think we were from the same town.

Example (9) Yuanchong Xu's (2000b) translation
Will you rest on your oar?
Are we from the same shore?

While translating the third line in the original, different approaches are adopted in the four translations:

Burton Watson's translation
The woman offers suggestion. The man stops the boat. The woman asks the question.

Yuanchong Xu's (1988) translation
The woman suggests that the two of them stop the boat.

Juntao Wu's translation
The woman stops the boat and asks the question.

Yuanchong Xu's (2000b) translation
The woman offers suggestion. The man stops the boat.

For the two translations by Yuanchong Xu, their similarity lies in the fact that "暂 借 问" (*zàn jiè wèn*; moment may ask) in the original is not translated. Their difference, on the other hand, is that in one translation the woman makes the suggestion and the two persons stop the boat, while in the other translation the woman makes the suggestion and the man stops the boat. In Burton Watson's translation, the woman wants the man to stop the boat. In Juntao Wu's translation, it is the woman who stops the boat. We can see that since the personal pronoun is not clearly stated, different translators can have different interpretations. In terms of experiential meaning, the translations by Burton Watson and Juntao Wu are more appropriate.

For the fourth line in the original, although the subject is omitted, only two persons are involved in the interaction and the implicit person is obviously "we" (i.e. "you and I"). As a result, the personal pronoun "we" is applied in the four translations.

In *Song Bie* (送别) by WANG Wei (王维) in the Tang Dynasty (i.e. "下马饮君酒 / 问君何所之 / 君言不得意 / 归卧南山陲 / 但去莫复问 / 白云无尽时" [*xià mǎ yǐn jūn jiǔ / wèn jūn hé suǒ zhī / jūn yán bù dé yì / guī wò nán shān chuí / dàn qù mò fù wèn / bái yún wú jìn shí*; dismount horse drink your wine / ask you which place go to / you say not achieve ambition / return lie south mountain foot / just go not again ask / white cloud no end time]), the personal pronoun indicating person is "君" (*jūn*; you), and it is rendered differently in the translations. For instance, in terms of "下马饮君酒" (*xià mǎ yǐn jūn jiǔ*; dismount horse drink your wine), at least the following four different interpretations are involved:

Example (10): (I dismount from the horse and I drink your wine.)
Xianyi Yang & Gladys Yang's (2001a: 28) translation
I dismount from my horse and drink your wine.

Example (11) (I dismount from the horse and you drink my wine.)
Witter Bynner's translation (see Lü 1980: 148)
I dismount from my horse and I offer you wine.

Example (12) (We dismount from the horses and we drink wine together.)
H.A. Giles's translation (see Lü 1980: 148)
Dismounted, o'er wine we had said our last say.

Example (13) (I dismount from the horse and I drink wine with you together.)
W.J. Fletcher's translation (see Lü 1980: 148)
Quitting my horse, a cup with you I drank.

Yuanchong Xu's (2000b: 87) translation
Dismounted, I drink with you.

Based on our discussions above, we find that the same line is understood differently by different translators, hence is rendered differently. This also proves that Chinese poems cannot be interpreted in a fixed way.

12.4 No personal pronouns in the original

In terms of the choice of person, most ancient Chinese poems are ambiguous or uncertain. Such a feature has reflected the brevity and implicitness of ancient Chinese poems and "has given the space of imagination and recreation to readers" (Zhu 1990: 50, our translation). On the one hand, this kind of uncertainty provides the space of recreation in translation; one the other hand, people may find that ancient Chinese poems are translated in a random manner.

In the translation of poems without any personal pronoun, one method is to add certain personal pronouns based on the translator's interpretation of the original. This is in most cases demanded by grammatical rules in English and is therefore a common practice. Another method is to avoid using personal pronouns by following the style of the original. This is sometimes difficult. We will first examine *Feng Qiao Ye Bo* (枫 桥 夜 泊) by ZHANG Ji (张继) in the Tang Dynasty.

Example (14)

枫 桥 夜 泊
fēng qiáo yè bó
maple bridge night anchor

张继
zhāng jì
ZHANG Ji

月 落 乌 啼 霜 满 天，
yuè luò wū tí shuāng mǎn tiān,
moon set crow cry frost fill sky,

江 枫 渔 火 对 愁 眠。
jiāng fēng yú huǒ duì chóu mián.
river maple fishing fire to sorrow sleep.

姑苏 城 外 寒山 寺，
gū sū chéng wài hán shān sì,
Gusu (Suzhou) city outside cold-hill temple,

夜半钟声到客船。
yè bàn zhōng shēng dào kè chuán.
midnight bell sound reach boat.

Our collected English translations of this poem can be categorized into two types: (1) translations that explicitly describe "my" experience and (2) translations that describe the experience of an uncertain traveler. The translations that explicitly describe "my" experience include those by Dalian Wang (1997: 95) and Tinggan Cai (see Wen 1989: 125). The following example is translated by Dalian Wang.

Example (15)
A Night Mooring by Maple Bridge
Moon's down, crows cry and frosts fill all the sky;
By maples and boat light, I sleepless lie.
Outside Gusu Cold-Hill Temple's in sight;
Its ringing bells reach my boat at midnight.

In Dalian Wang's translation, the translator places "I" in the poem and explicitly points out the uncertain personal relation.

Yuanchong Xu has provided two translations of the poem: see Example (14). In his first-published translation (see Xu, Lu & Wu 1988: 224), a first-person pronoun – "my" – is applied in the fourth line (i.e. "Rings bells which reach my boat, breaking the midnight still."), whereas in his second translation (Xu 2000b: 329), no personal pronoun is used, as shown in Example (16).

Example (16)
Mooring by Maple Bridge at Night
At moonset cry the crows, streaking the frosty sky;
Dimly lit fishing boats 'neath maples sadly lie.
Beyond the city wall, from Temple of Cold Hill.
Bells break the ship-borne roamer's dream and midnight still.

By comparing Examples (15) and (16), we find that Example (15) describes the poet's personal experience, while Example (16) describes an uncertain experience. In terms of conveying the artistic conception in the original, Example (16) is a more appropriate translation. It is also interesting to note that in Example (15) the subject of "lie" is a person – "I", whereas in Example (16) the subject of "lie" is things, namely "fishing boats".

Based on our observation, Yuanchong Xu tends to avoid using personal pronouns in his English translations of ancient poems. We can take his translation of the first sentence in *Fu Rong Lou Song Xin Jian* by WANG Changling (i.e. "寒 雨 连 江 夜 入 吴" [*hán yǔ lián jiāng yè rù wú*; cold rain mingle river night enter Wu]) as an example. Most translators explicitly state that the poet has entered the Wu city (see Examples [17], [18] and [19]), whereas Yuanchong Xu's two translations involve different choices (see Examples [20] and [21]). We can compare the following examples.

Example (17) Dalian Wang's (1997: 23) translation
Cold rains reigning the stream last eve, I got in Wu;

Example (18) Jie Tao's translation (see Wu 1997: 119)
Along the river that merged with a cold rain, / We entered the Wu city late at night.

Example (19) Changsheng Wan and Xianzhong Wang's (2000: 37) translation
Amid the nightly haze of cold rains and streams I came to Wu,

Example (20) Yuanchong Xu's (2000b: 83) translation
A cold rain mingled with East Stream invades the night;

Example (21) Yuanchong Xu's (2000a: 85) translation
A cold rain mingled with Eastern Stream at night;

In Examples (20) and (21), "入 吴" (*rù wú*; enter Wu) in the original is not translated. In Example (20), Xu adopts the same method in translating "江 枫 渔 火 对 愁 眠" (*jiāng fēng yú huǒ duì chóu mián*; river maple fishing fire to sorrow sleep) by applying things rather than human beings as the subjects of the clauses.

Similar to Example (14), in *Lu Zhai* (鹿柴) by WANG Wei (王维) from the Tang Dynasty (i.e. "空 山 不 见 人 / 但 闻 人 语 响 / 返景 入 深 林 / 复 照 青 苔 上" [*kōng shān bú jiàn rén / dàn wén rén yǔ xiǎng / fǎn jǐng rù shēn lín / fù zhào qīng tái shàng*; empty mountain not see man / but hear man voice sound / sunlight enter deep wood / again shine green moss on]), the persons are not explicitly pointed out either. Some translators (e.g. Example [22]) specify the person, while some (e.g. Example [23]) do not apply personal pronouns by following the style in the original (see Wen 1989: 69–70 for these two kinds of translations).

Example (22) Chen and Bullock's translation
The Deer Enclosure
On the lonely mountain
I met no one,
I hear only the echo
of human voices.
At an angle the sun's rays
enter the depth of the wood,
And shine
upon the green moss.

Example (23) Burton Watson's translation:
Deer Fence
Empty hills, no one in sight,
only the sound of someone talking;
late sunlight enters the deep wood,
shining over the green moss again.

According to Wen (1989: 70, our translation), Example (23) is a better translation:

> In addition to the third and fourth lines, which conform to the original meaning, the first and second lines are also very well rendered because Chinese sentences mostly do not need subjects and are thus more flexible. If a translator is uncertain about the use of first person and manages to adopt "I" as the subject, the sentence will become sluggish.

In fact, the style in Example (23) is consistent with that in Example (16) since they both do not explicitly point out the speaker and do not restrict the constant experience and situation in the poem to those that are individual and unlimited to a certain time or space (see also Yip 1992: 247).

12.5 Choice of personal pronouns and the expression of meaning

As discussed above, if the information of person in the original is uncertain, it will be necessary to add some words indicating person in the translation. In this way, the multiple meanings in the original poem have become one meaning. Example (24) is a poem titled *Wu Ti* (无题) by LI Shangyin (李商隐) in the Tang Dynasty:

Example (24)

无题
wú tí
no title

（唐）李商隐
(tang) lǐ shāng yǐn
(Tang Dynasty) LI Shangyin

相见时难别亦难，
xiāng jiàn shí nán bié yì nán,
meet time difficult part also difficult,

东风无力百花残。
dōng fēng wú lì bǎi huā cán.
east wind no force hundred flower wither.

春蚕到死丝方尽，
chūn cán dào sǐ sī fāng jìn,
spring silkworm until death thread just end,

蜡炬成灰泪始干。
là jù chéng huī lèi shǐ gān.
candle become ash tear just dry.

晓镜但愁云鬓改，
xiǎo jìng dàn chóu yún bìn gǎi,
morning mirror only worry cloud-like hair change,

夜吟应觉月光寒。
yè yín yīng jué yuè guāng hán.
night hum should feel moonlight chill.

蓬山此去无多路，
péng shān cǐ qù wú duō lù,
Penglai mountain here go not have much distance,

青鸟殷勤为探看。
qīng niǎo yīn qín wèi tàn kàn.
green bird (messenger) attentively for visit see.

This is a very popular love poem. Its author, LI Shangyin, has provided neither any background nor any relevant information, thus the poem has been interpreted differently (see Wen 1989: 186). When analysing the English translation in terms of person, the fifth and sixth lines (i.e. "晓镜但愁云鬓改 / 夜吟应觉月光寒" [*xiǎo jìng dàn chóu yún bìn gǎi / yè yín yīng jué yuè guāng hán*; morning mirror only worry cloud-like hair change / night hum should feel moonlight chill]) are relevant here. Examples (25) to (29) are five translations of the two lines:

Example (25) Yuanchong Xu's translation (see Xu, Lu & Wu 1988: 347)
At dawn she'd be afraid to see mirrored hair gray; / At night she would feel cold while I croon by moonlight.

Example (26) Yuanchong Xu's (2000b: 565) translation
At dawn I'm grieved to think your mirrored hair turns grey; / At night you would feel cold while I croon by moonlight.

Example (27) Bingheng Zeng's translation (see Wu 1997: 677, 679)
In the morning mirror you grieve at your dishevelled hair; / In the moonlight, humming poems, you stan in the cold air.

Example (28) Changsheng Wan and Xianzhong Wang's (2000: 178) translation
She'll fear to see in the morning glass some hairs white, / And feel, as I read aloud at night, the chilly moonlight.

Example (29) Tingchen Zhang and Bruce M. Wilson's (1994: 221) translation
Before the mirror, you will fret to find those cloudlike tresses changing. / Making rhymes at night, you'll find the moonlight has grown chill.

In "晓镜但愁云鬓改" (*xiǎo jìng dàn chóu yún bìn gǎi*; morning mirror only worry cloud-like hair change), who is worrying? Whose cloud-like hair is changing? In "夜吟应觉月光寒" (*yè yín yīng jué yuè guāng hán*; night hum should feel moonlight chill), who is humming a verse? Who is feeling the chill of moonlight? Among the five translations in Examples (25) to (29), we find different understandings by the translators, as shown in Table 12.1.

Table 12.1. Participants and processes in the fifth and sixth lines of *Wu Ti*

Participant (who) / **Process**	she	you	I
"愁" (*chou*; worry)	(25) (28)	(27) (29)	(26)
"云鬓改" (*yún bìn gǎi*; cloud-like hair change)	(25) (28)	(26) (27) (29)	–
"吟" (*yín*; hum)	–	(27) (29)	(25) (26) (28)
"觉 (月光寒)" (*jué [yuè guāng hán]*; feel [moonlight chill])	(25) (28)	(26) (27) (29)	–

From Table 12.1, we find that the process of "愁" (*chóu*; worry) can be related to three types of person: "云鬓改" (*yún bìn gǎi*; cloud-like hair change) is only related to second and third person, the process of "吟" (*yín*; hum) is conducted by first or second person and "觉 (月光寒)" (*jué [yuè guāng hán]*; feel [moonlight chill]) realizes the experience of second or third person. In Examples (25) to (29), the five translations indicate the following three different meanings:

Examples (25) and (28): She is worrying about the change of her cloud-like hair. I am humming the verse. She is feeling the chill of moonlight.

Example (26): I am worrying about the change of your cloud-like hair. I am humming the verse. You are feeling the chill of moonlight.

Example (27) and (29): You are worrying about the change of your cloud-like hair. You are humming the verse. You are feeling the chill of moonlight.

In LI Shangyin's original poem, the following questions remain unclear: Who is worrying? Whose cloud-like hair is changing? Who is humming? Who is feeling the chill of moonlight? However, once the original is translated into English, the uncertainty has to be made clear.

Example (30) is also a translation of "晓镜但愁云鬓改 / 夜吟应觉月光寒" (*xiǎo jìng dàn chóu yún bìn gǎi / yè yín yīng jué yuè guāng hán*; morning mirror only worry cloud-like hair change / night hum should feel moonlight chill). However, the major difference between this example and the other five translations (Examples [25] to [29]) is that the translator attempts to imitate the grammatical structure in the original with a purpose of building up a similar artistic conception and to recreate the original in terms of both content and form.

Example (30) Innes Herdan's translation (see Ma 2000: 167)
Grief at the morning mirror –
cloud-like hair must change;
Verses hummed at night,
feeling the chill of moonlight ...

In *Xin Jia Niang Ci* (新嫁娘词) by WANG Jian (王建) in the Tang Dynasty (i.e. "三日入厨下 / 洗手作羹汤 / 未谙姑食性 / 先遣小姑尝" [*sān rì rù chú xià / xǐ shǒu zuò gēng tāng / wèi ān gū shí xìng / xiān qiǎn xiǎo gū cháng*; three day go to kitchen / wash hand make broth-soup / not know mother-in-law food habit / first dispatch sister-in-law taste]), the issue of person also deserves our attention. In the translations we collected, most – for example, translations by Burton Watson (see Wen 1989: 140), W.J. Fletcher (see Wen 1989: 141), Zhiye Luo (see Wu 1997: 523) and Yuanchong Xu (2000b: 375) – adopt the first person, and a few – for example, the translation by Dalian Wang (1997: 117) – apply the third person. While commenting on Fletcher's translation, Lü (1980: 8, our translation) finds that the original poem seems to apply the third person, while the translation adopts the first person: "It is difficult to point out the losses and gains. However, a Chinese poem can be without subject and person. When translated into English, there must be subjects and persons. This will be a frequently encountered difficulty in translating Chinese poems." Three translations of *Xin Jia Niang Ci* are presented below.

Example (31) Yuanchong Xu's (2000b: 375) translation
A Bride
Married three days, I go shy-faced
To cook a soup with hands still fair.
To meet my mother-in-law's taste,
I send to her daughter the first share.

Example (32) Burton Watson's translation (see Wen 1989: 140)
Words of the Newly-wed Wife
The third day I went into the kitchen,
Washed my hands and made the soup.
Not yet sure of my mother-in-law's tastes,
I sent some first for sister-in-law to try.

Example (33) Dalian Wang's (1997: 117) translation
A Newly Wedded Daughter-in-law
She comes to kitchen, married but three days;
Having washed hands, she makes some consommés.
Knowing her mother-in-law's taste not yet,
She let young sis have first, a clue to get.

Examples (31) and (32) both adopt the first person to narrate "my" personal experience, whereas simple present tense is used in Example (31) and simple past tense in Example (32), with the two tenses indicating different meanings. Example (33) uses the third person to narrate the experience of a bride. Since Examples (31) and (33) both adopt simple present tense, the translations and the original have converted the individual experience restricted by time and place to universal and constant experience. In this respect, compared with Example (32),

Examples (31) and (33) are better at expressing the artistic conception in the original.

According to Zhu (1990: 50, our translation), the choice of person in WANG Jian's poem is unclear, hence we can apply three persons in translation: "By applying the first person – 'I', the whole poem will narrate personal experience; by applying second person – 'you', the poem will concern with warning and advising; by applying the third person – 'she', the poem will deal with the universal experience of a bride." Among the translations we collected, although none of them applies the second person, "you", we agree with Zhu's opinion and hold that it is also possible to adopt second person to render *Xin Jia Niang Ci*.

12.6 Conclusion

As widely recognized, ancient Chinese poems are brief and implicit, with the use of person being unclear, thereby leaving the space of imagination and recreation to readers (see Zhu 1990: 50). According to Yip (1992: 29, 250, our translation), words such as "你" (*nǐ*; you), "我" (*wǒ*; I), and "他/她" (*tā*; he/she) are not applied in ancient Chinese poems:

> One feature is that readers are kept in touch with one kind of ambiguity, through which objectivity and subjectivity are simultaneously interchanging ... By avoiding inserting personal pronouns, a poet is allowed to not only universalize the situation, but also to present the subjective experience in an objective (rather than analytical) way.

The under-use or non-use of personal pronoun is one of the features of ancient Chinese poems. By exhibiting a dim beauty that spans across, rather than being restricted by, time and space, a poet can provide the space of imagination and recreation to readers. This method of converting personal experience to universal experience is a prominent feature as well as a charm of ancient Chinese poem. After these poems are translated into English, the uncertain relations are made explicit, hence leaving little space for imagination and recreation for readers, as discussed previously. Based on our observation, most translators have unavoidably added personal pronouns. On the one hand, this is restricted by the grammatical rules of English. On the other hand, this indicates that translation activity is itself an activity of interpretation. Regarding this activity, Yip (1992: 19 our translation) has the following comments:

> Following the sentence structure in ancient Chinese, the sceneries appear by themselves and put on a performance before our eyes. The performance is clear, exquisite, lively, and succinct. It is performed within a space that we can have access to from our real world. After the interpretations (including most English translations of ancient poems), however, such a performance has disappeared, and the autonomous independence and objectivity of the sceneries have been interrupted, because a redundant and protruding interpreter is giving directions and providing explanations there ...

Regarding the selection of personal pronoun in English translations of ancient Chinese poems, we hold that choice has itself indicated meaning. For instance, when a translator chooses Example (15) rather than Example (16) to interpret the original poem in Example (14), this will be the result of the translator's interpretation of the original. Similarly, although Examples (22) and (23) are both English translations of *Lu Zhai* by WANG Wei, there will certainly be a reason of making the choices in Example (22) or Example (23).

Chapter 13

Choice of tense in English translations

13.1 Introduction

Ancient Chinese poems have their own grammatical features (Zhu 1990). Written in classical Chinese, ancient poems differ from modern Chinese and English poems in their linguistic expression. This chapter investigates tense in English translations of ancient Chinese poems and provides a simple analysis of the realizations of different tenses. This chapter is based on linguistic analysis; hence, it emphasizes the use of language in translation, encompassing Wai-lim Yip's (1992: 250, 248, 262–63, our translation) notions, such as "the intellectual explanatory note", "instructional wording" and "narrative and deductive manifestation".

13.2 A brief review of tense

"Time" is a concept for all of humanity. Speakers of Chinese and English are certain about the establishment of time and hold consistent views on "past", "present" and "future". As a linguistic concept, tense is investigated in grammar and different languages have different realizations of tense. For instance, in English differences between present and past tense are seen mainly in the variation of verbs – for example, "talk" and "is" indicate present tense, and "talked" and "was" indicate past tense. On the other hand, aspect is mainly applied when indicating the state of an action realized by a verb or the way the action exists. For example, "is working" is a combination of "present tense" and "progressive aspect", commonly known as "present progressive". Regarding the issue of tense in Chinese, scholars have not reached a consensus: some agree with the notion of tense (e.g. Zhang & Chen 1981: 310–14), while some disagree (e.g. Yip 1992: 247). However, it is indisputable that English and Chinese have different ways of indicating the time and manner of an action.

When discussing ancient Chinese poems and their English translations, Wai-lim Yip (1992: 247, our translation) makes the following suggestion:

> Ancient Chinese has overcome the boundary of a specific time, because there is no tense for Chinese verbs. The past, present, and future tenses in Indo-European languages are categories artificially imposed to restrict notions of time and space. Verbs in Chinese tend to return to the "phenomenon" itself, which is not temporal, as the concept of time is imposed to the phenomenon by man. In ancient Chinese poems, words such as "今天" (*jīn tiān*; today), "明天" (*míng tiān*; tomorrow), and "昨天" (*zuó tiān*; yesterday) are seldom used to denote a specific time; however, when applied, they will have a special effect. In other words, in Chinese sentences, there is no change of tense in verbs.

We cite Yip's opinion here because it is crucial for our discussion in this chapter. He not only relates the non-existence of tense in Chinese, but also covers the linguistic expression of ancient poems.

Regardless of whether there is tense in Chinese, we definitely have to face the choice of tense when translating ancient poems into English. This issue is the key to this chapter. In our following discussion, we will further explore this issue with examples.

As two different concepts, time and tense have their own features and can never be equivalent. For instance, both simple present tense and present progressive tense can be adopted to narrate things happened in the past to "enhance the vividness and sense of reality" (Zhang 1997: 442, our translation). When discussing the usage of simple present tense, Quirk et al. (1985: 181) cite the following example:

> *Example (1)*
> I couldn't believe it! Just as we arrived, up comes Ben and slaps me on the back as if we're life-long friends. "Come on, old pal," he says. "Let me buy you a drink!" I'm telling you, I nearly fainted on the spot.

In the example above, the words in italics are all instances of using present tense to indicate actions or behaviors in the past. Such usage is commonly referred to as historical present tense or dramatic present tense.

13.3 Choice of tense

According to our observation, most English translations of ancient poems apply simple present tense. For poems that do not apply simple present tense, three possibilities exist. First, present past tense is used to describe things that have happened in the past, with the focus on the poet's personal experience at a certain time or place. This kind of simple past tense can also be changed to simple present tense. Second, a situation depicted in a certain line has obviously happened in the past, with words indicating the past being found explicitly. Thus, by following grammatical rules, only past tense can be applied. In most cases, this kind of simple past tense cannot be changed to simple present tense. Third, different tense forms are applied alternatively for the vivid depiction of past events. In this section, we will first deal with the first possibility.

Our example is *Xin Jia Niang Ci* (新嫁娘词) by WANG Jian (王建), a poet from the Tang Dynasty:

新嫁娘词
xīn jià niáng cí
newly wedded bride lyric

王建
wáng jiàn
WANG Jian

三日入厨下，
sān rì rù chú xià,
three day go to kitchen,

洗手作羹汤。
xǐ shǒu zuò gēng tang.
wash hand make broth-soup.

未谙姑食性，
wèi ān gū shí xìng,
not know mother-in-law food habit,

先遣小姑尝。
xiān qiǎn xiǎo gū cháng.
first dispatch sister-in-law taste.

In *Anthology of English Translations of Ancient Chinese Poems and Lyrics*, edited by Shu Wen (1989: 140–41), we find two English translations of the poem by Burton Watson and W.J. Fletcher respectively. The former translator applies simple past tense, while the latter adopts simple present tense:

Example (2) Burton Watson's translation
Words of the Newly-wed Wife
The third day I went into the kitchen,
Washed my hands and made the soup.
Not yet sure of my mother-in-law's tastes,
I sent some first for sister-in-law to try.

Example (3) W.J. Fletcher's translation
The Daughter-in-law
Now married three days, to the kitchen I go,
And washing my hands, a fine broth I prepare.
But what kind of taste auntie likes, I don't know.
So send to my sister-in-law the first share.

Watson adopts simple past tense to recount the things that happened in the past, focusing on personal experiences. Fletcher uses simple present tense to convert the personal and unique experience into universal and constant experience. In terms of the effects of the two tenses, it is generally believed that simple present tense is better at "presenting a misty beauty unrestricted by time and place" (Zhu 1990: 48, our translation), hence providing imaginative space to readers; in this way, personal experiences are changed to universal situations and the poet is capable of presenting his subjective experience objectively (see also Yip 1992: 247, 250).

Based on our observation, Chinese translators of ancient poems prefer to apply simple present tense. For instance, for the English translations of LI Bai's (李白) *Jing Ye Si* (静夜思), we find 13 translations by Chinese translators, including those by Xianliang Weng (1985: 19), Zhenying Zhuo (1996: 114), Di Tu and An Tu (see Wu 1997: 251), Dayu Sun (1997: 189), Zhentao Zhao (1999: 37), Dalian Wang (1997: 53), Yuanchong Xu (2000b: 141), Changsheng Wan and Xianzhong Wang (2000: 57), Bingxing Zhang (2001: 41), Xinqu Huang (2002: 229), Junping Liu (2002: 59), and Zhongjie Xu and Hongjun Ma (see Ma 2000: 192, 195, 198). In most of these translations, simple present tense is applied. However, when rendering this poem, some foreign translators have selected simple present tense – for example, Herbert Giles, Amy Lowell,

L. Cranmer-Byng and A. Cooper (see Lü 1980: 105–06; Ma 2000: 193–96), some have chosen simple past tense – for example, Witter Bynner and S. Obata (see Lü 1980: 105, Ma 2000: 193–94), while W.J. Fletcher (see Example [16] below; see also Lü 1980: 104) and Burton Watson (see Wen 1989: 77) have used a mixture of simple past tense and simple present tense.

Our discussion reveals that both simple past tense and simple present tense can be adopted to translate ancient poems, whereas different artistic conceptions are conveyed in this way. However, this does not mean English translations of all ancient poems are free to use these two or other tenses.

13.4 Restriction on tense

In some ancient poems, changes of time are implied. Based on Zhu's (1990: 48) analysis, in LI Bai's *Su Tai Lan Gu* (苏台览古) ("旧苑荒台杨柳新 / 菱歌清唱不胜春 / 只今惟有西江月 / 曾照吴王宫里人" [*jiù yuàn huāng tái yáng liǔ xīn / líng gē qīng chàng bú shèng chūn / zhǐ jīn wéi yǒu xī jiāng yuè /céng zhào wú wáng gōng lǐ rén*; old garden deserted terrace willow new / caltrap song clear chant not surpass spring / now only have west-river moon / once shine Wu-king palace in person]), the description starts with present tense and is suddenly shifted to ancient times in the last line, involving a change to past tense. In LI Bai's *Yue Zhong Lan Gu* (越中览古) ("越王勾践破吴归 / 战士还家尽锦衣 / 宫女如花满春殿 / 只今惟有鹧鸪飞" [*yuè wáng gōu jiàn pò wú guī / zhàn shì huán jiā jìn jǐn yī / gōng nǚ rú huā mǎn chūn diàn / zhǐ jīn wéi yǒu zhè gū fēi*; Yue-king Goujian destroy Wu return / warrior return home all brocade robe / palace maid be like flower fill spring court / now only have partridge fly]), the poet begins with past tense and suddenly changes to present tense in the last line. These abrupt changes of time is a technique adopted by the poet to express his feelings on the ups and downs that occur through time. For each of the two ancient poems, we have collected three translations (Wen 1989: 86; Wang 1997: 61; Xu 2000b: 171; Wen 1989: 87; Sun 1997: 241; Xu 2000b: 173), which suggest that descriptions of past and present are revealed by verbs in different tenses. The following example is a translation of LI Bai's *Su Tai Lan Gu* (translated by Burton Watson, see Wen 1989: 86):

Example (4)
At Su Terrace Viewing the Past
Old gardens, a ruined terrace, willow trees new;
caltrap gatherers, clear chant of songs, a spring unbearable;
and now there is only the west river moon
that shone once on a lady in the palace of the king of Wu.

In Example (4), the first and second lines of the original are translated as a verbless clause; if we add back the verbs, the tense will be simple present tense. In the third line, the verb in the translation (i.e. "is") is in simple present tense, while the verb in the last line (i.e. "shone") is in simple past tense. In fact, "只今" (*zhǐ jīn*; now) and "曾" (*céng*; once) in the original have already indicated the time expressed in this sentence. In another translation of this poem by Dalian Wang (1997: 61), we find different selections of time:

Example (5)
The Ruin of the Gusu Palace
In the deserted gardens willows swing;
Sweet water-nut songs fail to praise the spring.
Over West River now remains but moon
That once shone on Wu King's fair ladies boon.

In Example (5), the verbs in the first three lines (i.e. "swing", "fail", and "remains") are all in simple present tense, while the verb in the last line ("shone") is in simple past tense. The choices of tense are the same as Example (4).

Examples (6) and (7) are two English translations of LI Bai's *Yue Zhong Lan Gu*. Example (6) is rendered by Burton Watson (see Wen 1989: 87):

Example (6)
In Yue Viewing the Past
Goujian, king of Yue, came back from the broken land of Wu;
His brave men returned to their homes, all in robes of brocade.
Ladies in waiting like flowers filled his spring palace
Where now only the partridges fly.

In Watson's translation, the verbs in the first three lines (i.e. "came", "returned", and "filled") are in simple past tense, while the verb in the last line ("fly") is in simple present tense. Example (7) is rendered by Dayu Sun (1997: 241):

Example (7)

Looking Back to Olden Times in Yue

When Goujian King of Yue, had crushed his state foe Wu,
His homing warriors were dressed in brocade all.
Then beauties held captive, lush like flowers, thronged the spring court;
Now only partridges are flying and each to each call.

Compared with Example (6), the tense selections in Example (7) are relatively more complex. The verb in the first line ("had crushed") is in past perfect tense; that in the second line ("were dressed") is in simple past tense; in the third line, "thronged" is also in simple past tense; in the fourth line, the verb ("are flying") is in present progressive tense. Although different choices of tense are seen in Examples (6) and (7), they share one similarity in the application of past tense before present tense. Similarly, Yuanchong Xu (2000b: 171, 173) has provided another two translations of the two poems by LI Bai, and the choices of tense are the same as those in Examples (4) to (7), with present tense (or past tense) being applied before past tense (or present tense). Therefore, we do not discuss Xu's translation here.

In *Ti Du Cheng Nan Zhuang* (题都城南庄) by CUI Hu (崔护), a poet from the Tang Dynasty, ("去年今日此门中 / 人面桃花相映红 / 人面不知何处去 / 桃花依旧笑春风" [*qù nián jīn rì cǐ mén zhōng / rén miàn táo huā xiāng yìng hóng / rén miàn bù zhī hé chù qù / táo huā yī jiù xiào chūn fēng*; last year this day this gate in / human face peach blossom each other mirror red / human face not know which place go / peach blossom still smile spring wind]), the events narrated are also shifted from the past to present, with the first two lines discussing events in the last year and the last two lines dealing with now (or today). The four English translations we collected (see Wen 1989: 137; Wang 1997: 113; Sun 1997: 395; Xu 2000b: 463) all begin with past tense and end with present tense.

Example (8)

By the City Gate

A year ago today by
This very gate your face and
The peace blossoms mirrored each
Other. I do not know where
Your beautiful face has gone.
There are only peach blossoms
Flying in the spring wind.

Selected from *Anthology of English Translations of Ancient Chinese Poems and Lyrics*, edited and annotated by Shu Wen (1989: 137), Example (8) was originally collected in Kenneth Rexroth's *100 More Poems from the Chinese*. The choices of verb tense include simple past tense ("mirrored"), simple present tense ("do not know" and "are") and present perfect tense ("has gone"). Such usages of tense cannot be changed at will.

Example (9)
Written in a Village South of the Capital
Within this door and on this day last year,
Peach flowers and fair face both shone pink right here.
Though no one knows where fair face is today,
Peach flowers in spring wind still smile in same way.

Translated by Dalian Wang (1997: 113), Example (9) is the same as Example (8) in using past tense ("shone") to render the first and second lines of the original and present tense ("knows", "is" and "smile") to translate the third and fourth lines of the original. In translations of CUI Hu's *Ti Du Cheng Nan Zhuang* by Dayu Sun (1997: 395) and Yuanchong Xu's (2000b: 463), the same tense selections as Examples (8) and (9) are made by beginning with past tense and ending with present tense. Hence, we will not analyse these two translations here.

In *Chou Nu Er* (丑奴儿) (*Cai Sang Zi* [采桑子]), a lyric written by XIN Qiji (辛弃疾) in the Song Dynasty ("少年不识愁滋味 / 爱上层楼 / 爱上层楼 / 为赋新词强说愁 / 而今识尽愁滋味 / 欲说还休 / 欲说还休 / 却道天凉好个秋" [*shào nián bù shí chóu zī wèi / ài shàng céng lóu / ài shàng céng lóu / wèi fù xīn cí qiáng shuō chou / ér jīn shí jìn chóu zī wèi / yù shuō huán xiū / yù shuō huán xiū / què dào tiān liáng hǎo gè qiū*; young age not know sorrow taste / love climb storey tower / love climb storey tower / to compose new lyric manage talk sorrow / now know all sorrow taste / want talk but refrain / want talk but refrain / but say day cool good such autumn]), the poet begins with the past and then moves back to the present, with the first half of the lyric discussing the past and the second half dealing with the present. When the poem is rendered into English, past and present tenses are adopted, as seen in Example (10), translated by Yuanchong Xu (1986: 201).

Example (10)
Tune: "Song of Picking Mulberry"
While young, I knew no grief I could not bear,
  I'd like to go upstair.
  I'd like to go upstair
To write new verses, with a false despair.

I know what grief is now that I am old,
  I would not have it told.
  I would not have it told
But only say I'm glad that autumn's cold.

In Example (10), the first half of the poem is in past tense and the second half is in present tense. The same choices of tense are also seen in other translations (see e.g. Gong 1999: 160–61; Wen 1989: 305–06 for the translation by Robert Kotewell and Norman Smith; Yang & Yang 2001b: 231).

In addition, for poems such as *Ji Li Dan Yuan Xi* (寄李儋元锡) by WEI Yingwu (韦应物) ("去 年 花 里 逢 君 别 / 今 日 花 开 又 一 年" [*qù nián huā lǐ féng jūn bié / jīn rì huā kāi yòu yì nián*; last year flower in meet you part / this day flower blossom another one year]) and *Hui Xiang Ou Shu* (回乡偶书) by HE Zhizhang (贺知章) ("少小 离 家 老大 回 / ......" [*shào xiǎo lí jiā lǎo dà huí*; young-small leave home old-big return]), words that obviously indicate the time are applied. If these poems are rendered into English (see Appendix 1 for the English translations of these poems), it will be evident that the tense selections are restricted and the tenses in different lines cannot be exchanged or altered randomly.

As revealed by our discussion above, when translating certain ancient Chinese poems into English, we must take the selection of tense into consideration. Our primary concern is the restriction of grammar in the target language – for example, in Example (9), "last year" requires the verb to be in past tense rather than in present tense. Then we can consider choosing different forms of tense to indicate different meanings and artistic conceptions – for example, the different artistic conceptions expressed in Examples (2) and (3).

13.5 Tense in relation to quotation

In some English translations of ancient poems, we find changes in tense that may be due to the use of quotations in the poems. Our following discussions will first focus on the English translation of quotation.

For the English translations of *Fu Rong Lou Song Xin Jian* (芙蓉楼送辛渐) by WANG Changling (王昌龄) in the Tang Dynasty ("寒雨连江夜入吴 / 平明送客楚山孤 / 洛阳亲友如相问 / 一片冰心在玉壶" [*hán yǔ lián jiāng yè rù wú / píng míng sòng kè chǔ shān gū / luò yáng qīn yǒu rú xiāng wèn / yí piàn bīng xīn zài yù hú*; cold rain mingle river night enter Wu / daybreak see off guest Chu-mountain lonely / Luoyang relative friend if ask / one piece ice heart be in jade jar]), some translations begin with past tense – for example, those by Dalian Wang (1997: 23), Jie Tao (see Wu 1997: 119), Changsheng Wan and Xianzhong Wang (2000: 37) – and some begin with present tense – for example, those by Yuanchong Xu (2000a: 85; 2000b: 83). Two translations of the poem are as follows:

Example (11) Changsheng Wan and Xianzhong Wang's (2000: 37) translation
Send-off to Xin Jian at Hibiscus Tower
Amid the nightly haze of cold rains and streams I came to Wu,
And saw my friend in dawn leave the lonely mountain of Chu.
Oh, Friend, when folks in Luoyang inquire, let it be said,
My heart is as bright as crystal ice in the jar of jade.

Example (12) Yuanchong Xu's (2000b: 83) translation
Farewell to Xin Jian at Lotus Tower
A cold rain mingled with East Stream invades the night;
At dawn you leave the Southern hills lonely in haze.
If my friends in the North should ask if I'm all right,
My heart is free of stain as ice in crystal vase.

As seen in these two examples, no matter whether simple present tense (e.g. "came" and "saw") or simple past tense (e.g. "invades" and "leave") is applied when translating the first two lines, the verbs in the third and fourth lines can only be in present tense (e.g. "inquire", "let" and "is"; "should ask", "am" and "is"). This is because the third and fourth lines of the original are in fact a quotation, hence its tense is not restricted by the preceding text.

There are several English translations of *Song Bie* (送别) by WANG Wei (王维) ("下马饮君酒 / 问君何所之 / 君言不得意 / 归卧南山陲 / 但去莫复问 / 白云无尽时" [*xià mǎ yǐn jūn jiǔ / wèn jūn hé suǒ zhī / jūn yán bù dé yì / guī wò nán shān chuí / dàn qù mò fù wèn / bái yún wú jìn shí*; dismount horse drink your wine / ask you which place go to / you say not achieve ambition / return lie south mountain foot / just go not again ask / white cloud no end time]) and the instances of quoting-reporting in the poem are rendered differently (see Chapter 11), with tense selection also being involved. In the narrative part, some translators apply simple present tense – for example, Witter Bynner (see Lü 1980: 148), Yuanchong Xu (2000b: 87), Xianyi Yang and Gladys Yang (2001a: 28) – and some apply simple past tense – for example, translations by Baotong Wang (see Wu 1997: 131), Herbert Giles, and W.J. Fletcher (see Lü 1980: 148). Example (13) is rendered by Yuanchong Xu (2000b: 87):

Example (13)
At Parting
Dismounted, I drink with you
And ask what you've in view.
"I can't do what I will,
So I'll go to south hill.
Be gone, ask no more, friend,
Let cloud drift without end!"

In Example (13), the narration in the first and second lines is in simple present tense, whereas a quotation is found in the third to the sixth lines, in which the choices of tense are not restricted by the tense selections in the first two lines. Suppose we change the tense in the narrative part in the first two lines to simple present, the tense in the quoted part will not be impacted. The following Example (14) is translated by Baotong Wang (see Wu 1997: 131).

Example (14)
Farewell
Dismounting, I asked you to have a draught,
"And where to, my friend?" I inquired.
"My hopes are shattered," you bitterly laughed,
"To the southern hills. I'm retired."
Then go ahead, say no more, my dear.
The fleecy clouds have endless cheer.

In Example (14), the narration in the first line is in simple past tense, the quoting-reporting sentences in the third and fourth lines (i.e. "I inquired" and "you bitterly laughed") are also in simple past tense and the fifth and sixth lines are in simple present tense. Obviously, the last two lines of the translation are usage of quoting-reporting, which are free direct speeches and are different from the direct speeches in the second and the third lines. However, even if we changed the verb forms in the narration (in the first and second lines) and in the quoting-reporting sentences (in the second and third lines) to simple tense, the tense in the last two lines would still be different from the simple present tense in the fifth and sixth lines, with the former applying "historical present tense" and the latter being the general usage of simple present tense.

Further, it is worth noting that in Example (14), the fifth and sixth lines are said by the narrator (i.e. the poet) to the receiver of the narration. The fifth line is an imperative, serving as a suggestion from the narrator to the receiver, with the subject of "go ahead" and "say no more" being the receiver. The sixth line is the assertion of a certain situation by the narrator. However, in Example (13), as "Be gone, ask no more, friend, / Let cloud drift without end!" is a direct speech said by the receiver, the subjects of these clauses are then the narrator, rather than the receiver of narration, as found in Example (14). In other words, the fifth and sixth lines in Example (13) are the receiver's words to the poet, while the fifth and sixth lines in Example (14) are the poet's words to the receiver.

In Examples (13) and (14), the action in the fifth line has not taken place, whereas in Example (15), the past tense of the verb indicates that the action has already taken place.

Example (15) W.J. Fletcher's translation (see Lü 1980: 148)
"So farewell. And if for ever, still for ever fare ye well."
Quitting my horse, a cup with you I drank.
And drinking, asked you whither you were bound.
Your hopes unprospered, said you, turned you round.
You went. I asked no more. The white Clouds pass,
And never yet have any limit found.

It should also be noted that in Example (15), the subject of "went" in the fourth line is the recipient of the narration (i.e. "you"), while the subject of "asked no more" is the narrator – "I".

In Example (16), which is translated by Xianyi Yang and Gladys Yang (2001a: 28), the action and the speech act ("you're gone, no one will ask") are all events that are likely to happen in the future. They are different from those in Example (15), which have already happened, and those in Examples (13) and (14), which indicate the narrator's persuasion to the receiver.

Example (16) Xianyi Yang and Gladys Yang's (2001a) translation
A Farewell
I dismount from my horse and drink your wine.
I ask where you're going.
You say you are a failure.
And want to hibernate at the foot of Deep South Mountain.
Once you're gone no one will ask about you.
There are endless white clouds on the mountain.

Even if we changed the present tense in the first four lines in Example (16) to past tense, the tense in the final two lines still could not be changed because the two lines are quotations.

Quotations are also seen in *Xun Yin Zhe Bu Yu* (寻隐者不遇) by JIA Dao (贾岛) in the Tang Dynasty ("松下问童子 / 言师采药去 / 只在此山中 / 云深不知处" [*sōng xià wèn tóng zǐ / yán shī cǎi yào qù / zhǐ zài cǐ shān zhōng / yún shēn bù zhī chù*; pine under ask boy / say master gather herb go / only be in this mountain in / cloud deep not know place]). The English translation of the quotation will not be restricted by the tense in the other non-quoted lines. The following examples are two English translations of the beginning two lines of the poem.

Example (17) Yuanchong Xu's translation (see Xu, Lu & Wu 1988: 308)
I ask your lad 'neath a pine-tree.
"My master's gone for herbs," says he.

Example (18) Dalian Wang's (1997: 129) translation
Beneath pine trees I asked your lad nearby;
"My master's gone for herbs," was the reply.

In Examples (17) and (18), the verbs in the first lines are respectively in simple present tense and simple past tense. However, in the second lines in both translations, present perfect tense is applied, suggesting that the variation of verb tense in the first line does not influence the choice of tense in the second line. Furthermore, the quotations in Examples (17) and (18) are direct speech, while those in Examples (11) and (12) are free direct speech. However, in all these circumstances, the selection of verb tense is based on the expression of meaning and will not be restricted by the tense in the narrative part of the poem.

As shown in our discussion, in translations of poems with quotations, the choice of tense not only concerns the expression of meaning but is also related to the completeness or occurrence of the action. Of course, these selections in linguistic form will also influence the expression of artistic conception in poetry.

13.6 Change of tense: Vividness and reality

We have just discussed the change in tense in English translations with quotations. We will here examine the change in tense that serves to increase the vividness and sense of reality in description.

In Example (1), the starting point of narration is in simple past tense and thereafter the tense is changed to simple present (tense realizations italicized for emphasis):

> Just as we arrived, up comes Ben and slaps me on the back as if we're life-long friends. "Come on old pal," he says. "Let me buy you a drink!"

In terms of grammatical rule, it is also possible to change the italicized verbs in Example (1) to their forms in simple past tense, whereas the historical present tense will then be changed to common simple past tense. The application of historical present tense serves to vividly depict past events, thereby recreating the scene in a real and lively way.

The previous Examples (2) and (3) are two English translations of *Xin Jia Niang Ci* by WANG Jian. In Example (2), all verbs are in simple past tense, whereas in Example (3), all verbs are in simple present tense. In Zhiye Luo's translation (see Wu 1997: 523), however, the verbs are first in simple past tense, then changed to simple present tense, and finally changed back to simple past tense.

Example (19)
A Bride's Song
On the third day being a bride
I went to cook as a maid;
My hands washed, and a broth
by myself is made.
What my husband's mother
likes to eat I never know,
I ask his young sister to taste,
see if it were fine so.

The first finite verb in this translation – "went" – is in simple past tense, then the tense is changed to simple present ("is made", "likes", "know" and "ask"), and finally the tense is changed back to simple past ("were"). Such a change of tense is similar to the aforementioned change in Example (1).

As pointed out in our previous discussion, when translating LI Bai's *Jing Ye Si* ("床前明月光/疑是地上霜/举头望明月/低头思故乡"

[*chuáng qián míng yuè guāng / yí shì dì shàng shuāng / jǔ tóu wàng míng yuè / dī tóu sī gù xiāng*; bed before bright moon light / wonder be ground on frost / raise head see bright moon / lower head think hometown]) into English, most translators apply simple present tense, while a small number of them apply simple past tense. Among the English translations we collected, W.J. Fletcher's rendition (see Lü 1980: 104) especially deserves our attention because the first and second lines of the original are translated in simple past tense, while the third and fourth lines are translated in simple present tense.

Example (20)

The Moon Shines Everywhere

Seeing the Moon before my couch so bright
I though hoar frost had fallen from the night.
On her clear face I gaze with lifted eyes:
Then hide them full of Youth's sweet memories.

In Example (20), no finite verb is found in the first line; in the second line, two finite verbs are both in past tense – that is, "thought" in present past tense and "had fallen" in past perfect tense; in the third line, the two finite verbs – "gaze" and "hide" – are both in simple present tense.

The uses of simple present tense in Examples (19) and (20) are all categorized as historical present tense and are not totally the same as the uses of simple present tense in Example (3). This is because the purpose of applying simple present tense in Example (3) is to convert the personal experience restricted by time and space to the universal, constant and "impersonal" experience unrestricted by time and space; in Examples (19) and (20), simple present tense and other tenses (especially simple past tense) are used interchangeably in the poem, with simple past tense being found before simple present tense. This use of simple present tense mainly contributes to the vivid description of past events and to the creation of a lifelike scenery. Such alternate uses of simple past tense and simple present tense are frequently seen in various literary and non-literary narrative descriptions. For instance, the above-mentioned Example (1) is a narration in a non-literary work: "I **couldn't believe** it! Just as we **arrived**, up *comes* Ben and slaps me on the back as if we'*re* life-long friends. "Come on, old pal," he *says*, "Let me buy you a drink!" I'<u>m telling</u> you, I nearly **fainted** on the spot." (Quirk et al. 1985: 181) (simple past tense highlighted in bold, simple present tense in italic, present progressive tense underlined).

We have already investigated several translations of *Song Bie* by WANG Wei in the Tang Dynasty. The following translation is rendered by Herbert Giles (see Lü 1980: 148).

Example (21) Translation by Herbert Giles (see Lü 1980: 148)
Goodbye to Meng Hao-jan
Dismounted o'er wine we had said our last say;
Then I whisper, "Dear friend, tell me whither away."
"Alas!" he replied, "I am sick of life's ills
"And I long for repose on the slumbering hills.
"But oh seek not to pierce where my footsteps may stray.
"The white clouds will soothe me for ever and ay."

In Example (21), the verb "had said" in the first line is in past perfect tense and "whisper" in the second line is in simple present tense. With regard to the choice of tense, there can be two explanations: first, the tense in the second line is a historical present one, hence simple present tense should be adopted in the second line despite the fact that past perfect tense is used in the first line; second, "whisper" is a typo and should have been spelled as "whispered". In our opinion, the second explanation is more reasonable.

13.7 On the change of tense

As pointed out in our discussion, by choosing simple present tense, the English translations can sometimes convert the personal experience restricted by time and space to the universal, constant and "impersonal" experience unrestricted by time and space; alternatively, by alternately applying simple present tense and other tenses, the English translations can describe past events more vividly, hence creating a lifelike scenery. In most cases, when translating ancient poems into English the choice of tense selection and the expression of meaning will be involved. In some translations (e.g. Zhang 2001), simple past tense tends to be applied, while in others (e.g. Xu 2000a, 2000b, 2003a, 2003b, 2003c), simple present tense is often adopted. In a functional linguistic perspective, choosing form means choosing and expressing meaning. We will here analyse an English translation of *Jie Fu Yin* (节妇吟) by ZHANG Ji (张籍), composed in the Tang Dynasty ("君知妾有夫，/赠妾双明珠。/感君缠绵意，/系在红罗襦。/妾家高楼连苑起，/良人执戟明光里。/知君用心如日月，/事夫誓拟同生

死。/还君明珠双泪垂，/恨不相逢未嫁时。" [*jūn zhī qiè yǒu fū, / zèng qiè shuāng míng zhū. / gǎn jūn chán mián yì, / xì zài hóng luó rú. / qiè jiā gāo lóu lián yuàn qǐ, / liáng rén zhí jǐ míng guāng lǐ. / zhī jūn yòng xīn rú rì yuè, / shì fū jǐng nǐ tóng shēng sǐ. / huán jūn míng zhū shuāng lèi chuí, / hèn bù xiāng féng wèi jià shí.*; you know I have husband, / give me two bright pearl. / feel your touching intention, / fasten to red short dress. / my home high building connect palace stand, / husband hold halberd bright light in. / know you attentive be like sun moon, / serve husband danger compare together life death. / return you bright pearl both tear shed, / regret not each other meet not married time.]).

Example (22) Xiaolong Qiu's (2003: 33) translation

A Virtuous Wife

Knowing I am married, you gave me (1)
a pair of lustrous pearls. (2)
Beholden to you for your kindness, (3)
I fastened them to my red slip. (4)

My house is close to the Mingguang Palace, (5)
where my husband serves as a guard. (6)

Your intention is as lofty (7)
as the sun and the moon, I know. (8)
Having sworn to be with him (9)
in life and death, I have (10)
to return the glistening pearls to you (11)
with tears in my eyes. (12)
Oh, if we could have met (13)
before I married. (14)

The original of *Jie Fu Yin* includes ten lines. By regarding it as a narrative poem, we can interpret it in the following way: lines 1 to 4 mainly discuss the happenings in the past, lines 5 and 6 inform the current situation in her home, lines 7 and 8 introduce her position on love affairs, line 9 deals with her decision at present or in the future, and the last line includes some thoughts on the affair. Qiu (2003) renders the poem into 12 lines. In terms of the tense selection of verbs, Qiu has done a successful job in his translation. When discussing happenings in the past, simple past tense is used (i.e. "gave" in line 1 and "fastened" in line 4); when narrating current situation, simple present tense is applied (i.e. "is" in line 5, "serves" in line 6, "is" in line 7 and "know" in line 8); when relating a decision, the "have to do" structure is adopted (i.e. "have to return" in lines 10–11); finally, subjunctive mood is used to indicate exclamation (i.e. "if we could have met" in line 13).

In Qiu's (2003) English translation of ancient poem, it would also be possible to change the tense of "gave" in line 1 and "fastened" in line 4 to simple present, but the contrast in meaning would then be less effective. Also, if we translate "未 嫁 时" (*wèi jià shí*; not married time) in the original as a finite clause, the verb should not be in simple present tense. We further note that Qiu (2003: 33) renders it as "before I married", while Yuanchong Xu renders it as "before I was made a wife".

13.8 Conclusion

The use of tense in poetry is a topic that deserves further exploration. In English translations of ancient poems, the selection of tense form can reflect the translators' understanding of the original poem and their control over artistic conception. Under certain conditions, it is possible to select two or more tenses, while in other situations the selection of tense will be restrained, and sometimes no choice will be available.

We can summarize our discussion in this chapter as follows. First, the selection of tense will inevitably be involved when translating ancient poems into English. When present tense and past tense both serve as options, past tense mainly focuses on personal experience restricted by time and space, while present tense functions to convert the experience restricted by time and space to the universal and constant experience. Second, when lines explicitly indicating the past or future are found in the original, the selection of tense has to be determined by meaning; under such circumstances, one specific tense will normally be the most suitable. Third, when exploring the use of tense in English translations of ancient poems, we should differentiate narration and quotation and note that the choice of tense in quotation will normally not be restricted by the tense in narration. Fourth, the change of tense or the interchangeable use of tense in a poem is often for rhetorical considerations, with purposes of vividly recreating the depiction.

Chapter 14

Epilogue: A functional linguistic approach to translation studies

14.1 Introduction: The academic game and its rules

As stated previously, translation activity is an important component of human activities. Wherever human communication takes place, translation activities will exist. Without translation activities, it would be difficult or impossible for both cultural transmission and interpersonal communication to be carried out. Translation activity involves various subtypes and definition of translation can take various forms. As an activity, translation involves a wide range of perspectives. Through translation practice, a large number of established translators have accumulated abundant experiences in translation and have summarized different methods of translation, thus providing a theoretical basis for the exploration and formulation of translation theory. Various translation scholars have attempted to construct a scientific theory of translation, with one of their aims being the hope of breaking away from the traditional methods of translation criticism that are commentative, casual and impressionistic. With a scientific theory of translation, we can then investigate translation in a different perspective, which enables us to analyse translated texts from multidimensional, stereoscopic, qualitative, quantitative and scientific approaches.

Currently, most scholars study translation mainly in the perspectives of literary studies and literary criticism. As maintained by various scholars, literary language is emotional rather than scientific; therefore, comments on literary translation and translated works can only be made from the approaches of literary studies and literary criticism. There are many scholars who support this approach, due to its *raison d'être*. As a researcher in the field of linguistics and applied linguistics, I like to view academic research as a collection of games. Scholars from literary studies and literary criticism, as well as from linguistics and applied linguistics, are simply playing different games with the same playing cards. Although they are interested in the same phenomenon (e.g. translation issues and translated works), they are not playing the same game, and different games have different rules. When exploring translation, different scholars have different views but their discussions must be based on certain scopes and premises. In recent years, I have investigated English translations of Chinese poems in the functional linguistic perspective, but I am incapable of evaluating the advantages and disadvantages of studying translation in the perspectives of literary studies and literary criticism. Since we are playing different games, we should all enjoy the game. The principle is then to live and to let live.

I have made these comments because I am fully aware that some scholars would comment on my functional approach in their perspectives of literary studies and literary criticism.

14.2 A linguistic approach to translation studies

As early as 1965, J.C. Catford (1965) attempted to apply M.A.K. Halliday's (1956, 1961) Scale and Category Grammar with the aim of constructing a theoretical model of translation based on linguistics. Catford's (1965) concepts, such as context and contextual meaning, originate from the linguistic theories of M.A.K. Halliday and J.R. Firth – Halliday's teacher and the founder of the London School. As stated by Catford (1965: 1), "The general linguistic theory made use of in this book is essentially that developed at the University of Edinburgh, in particular by M.A.K. Halliday and influenced to a large extent by the work of the late J.R. Firth." In China, Catford's (1965) book has not only been translated into Chinese and published (Catford 1991), but has also been collected by Yuping Shen in his *Selection of Western Translation Theories* (Shen 2002: 280–363).

In the decade before Shen's (2002) book was published, various papers and monographs on translation that were guided by functional linguistics[1] were published abroad. In the United Kingdom, several monographs were published (e.g. Baker 1992; Bell 1991; Hatim 1998; Hatim & Mason 1990, 1997; Munday 2001). From the literature, we have found an increasing number of scholars applying functional linguistic theories to translation studies, with one of the most important theories being Halliday's (1985, 1994) Systemic Functional Linguistics (SFL).[2] In the works on translation studies empowered by SFL, the concepts in

SFL, such as context, metafunction, cohesion, coherence and theme, are of crucial importance.

I know little about formal linguistics, but I do know that E.A. Nida (1964; Nida & Taber 1969) applied linguistic theories to translation in general and proposed a three-phase model in translation process. According to this model, the surface structure (including grammar, meaning, and implication) in the source text has to be transformed in the translated text and reorganized as the central and subcentral structures in the surface structure of the target language. This linguistic-based model of translation is very much informed by Chomsky's (1957, 1965) generative grammar and has had a profound influence on the development of translation studies in Europe and on dynamic equivalence in the 1960s and 1970s (see Nord 1997: 5). Therefore, we can certainly say that the exploration of translation, whether in the perspective of functional linguistics or formal linguistics, has certainly inspired and promoted translation studies. In fact, modern translation studies has actively absorbed the contributions from linguistic theories, thus leading to the foundation of the linguistic school in translation studies. At present, linguistic-based translation studies seems to have given its once-dominant role to cultural-based studies, whereas the significance of linguistic-based research in translation studies can never be replaced.

14.3 Exploring English translations of ancient Chinese poems

In recent years, I have been especially interested in English translations of Chinese poems. According to the literature, translation scholars in China have done plenty of work on English translations of Chinese poems (especially ancient poems), with some scholars focusing mainly on translation practice, some mainly investigating translated texts and some both researching and commenting on translation. Until the present time, the comments on English translations of Chinese poems published in China have mostly been subjective, impressionistic, experience-based and commentative, with no replicable and reusable method or theory being applied. I have neither gained a thorough understanding of translation, nor tended to evaluate the translations and essays by famous translators. Hence, I only attempt to investigate the issue in the perspective of functional linguistics and meanwhile test the applicability of functional linguistics in translation studies and translation analysis. However, since we mainly conduct functional analysis of poems, our focus is linguistic analysis and text analysis, rather than reading and analysing poems based on literary appreciation and artistic conception. For this reason, we inevitably have to overlook an important aspect of poetry evaluation.

As previously stated, to provide a good translation of a source text – especially a literary text such as ancient Chinese poems and lyrics – we should first interpret the source text, find out the intention of the original author, understand the implications and artistic conception, then choose specific linguistic forms to convey the meanings in the source text. The form chosen by the translator (including macro-structure, clause, group and word in a text) must maximally convey the meanings and artistic conceptions of the source text. Certain forms will indicate certain meanings, with form being the realization of meaning (Huang 1999: 106–15). An experienced translator may not deliberately consider the selection of form, but as discourse analysts we should investigate why certain forms rather than others are selected to convey the meaning in the source text. No matter whether the translators have chosen these forms intentionally, their choices have largely determined the effect, as choices are meaningful.

Exploration of translations of ancient Chinese poems in a linguistic (especially SFL) perspective is a new attempt. In our research, we proceed from "observation" to "interpretation", "description", "analysis", "explanation" and finally "evaluation". By conducting such research, we aim to achieve the following two goals: (1) to re-examine some issues in translation in a new perspective and (2) to test the applicability and operationality of functional linguistics in discourse analysis and translation studies.

14.4 Steps in functional discourse analysis

We hold that there are generally six steps in doing functional discourse analysis: (1) observation, (2) interpretation, (3) description, (4) analysis, (5) explanation and (6) evaluation (see also Huang 2002b). These six steps constitute a methodology that can be applied to the investigation of issues in translation or translated texts.

Like discourse analysis, studying translation requires certain abilities of *observation*, as well as of determining whether a text (a translation) has the value of being analysed and researched. Theoretically, all translation issues or all translated texts have the value of being studied and can be studied, and all translations can be commented on. However, in practice, not all translation issues or translated texts will draw researchers' attention or fall within researchers' aims or scopes of investigation. A scholar and artist may create an artwork due to their love of a person, place or event; by the same token, a discourse analyst may choose a text/discourse as data for analysis because of their love of the text. The beginning of research lies in the capability of observing translated texts or translation issues that are in line with one's research interests, goals or scope.

During the process of observation and after selecting research objects, one should have the ability of *interpreting* the text (translated text) or the translation issue, managing to identify the meanings and implications of texts or the key to the translation issue or other related issues. If a researcher is incapable of interpreting and exploring the translation issues or is incapable of providing an illustrative analysis of a certain translated text, the researcher would not be able to conduct further research.

To *describe* a translated text or a translation issue, one must have certain theoretical foundations and explore issues within a certain theoretical framework, including the use of certain terminology. If one cannot do this, the analysis will be impressionistic, experience-based and unsystematic, and others cannot repeat the analysis with the same procedure. Naturally, the analysis cannot be tested and it is thus unscientific. We can say that most English learners have the ability of "observing" and "interpreting" a certain translated text, but not all of them can carry out a systematic description of a translated text or translation issue under a certain theoretical framework.

After "interpreting" and "describing" a translated text or a translation issue, one has to find ways of *analysing* and *explaining* it. Such an analysis should be based on one's research goals and scopes, while explanation has to ascertain whether the translated text or translation issues fall in this way rather than others; explanation is usually based on analysis.

Following Halliday (1994: xv), linguistic analysis involves two goals at different levels. At the lower level, we interpret the meaning of a text, explaining why the text means what it intends to mean by conducting a linguistic analysis. If the analysis at this level is based on a certain grammatical system, the goal would not be difficult to attain. However, by comparison, the goal at a higher-level is to *evaluate* a text. By carrying out a linguistic and text-based analysis, we can explain why a text has (or has not) attained its goals; we can also explain the respects in which the text is successful or unsuccessful. This goal is difficult to attain, as it not only involves analysis of the text itself, but also requires us to take the context of culture and context of situation of the text into consideration; meanwhile, we also need to explore the different relations between text and context. Thus, the final step is the most difficult.

The above-mentioned six steps can be situated along a continuum from "objective" to "subjective", with "observation" being the most objective and "evaluation" being the most subjective. In the following section, I will illustrate how to follow these six steps in translation studies, with the help of two examples.

14.5 Two examples

In this section, we will discuss how the six steps can be applied using two examples. Our first example is SU Shi's (苏轼) poem *Ti Xi Lin Bi* (题西林壁). The original is as follows:

题 西林 壁
tí xī lín bì
write Xilin (west-forest) wall

（宋）苏轼
(sòng) sū shì
(Song Dynasty) SU Shi

横 看 成 岭 侧 成 峰，
héng kàn chéng lǐng cè chéng fēng,
horizontal look become ridge side become peak,

远 近 高 低 各 不 同。
yuǎn jìn gāo dī gè bù tóng.
far near high low each not same.

不 识 庐 山 真 面 目，
bù shí lú shān zhēn miàn mù,
not recognize Mount-Lu real appearance,

只 缘 身 在 此 山 中。
zhǐ yuán shēn zài cǐ shān zhōng.
only because body be in this mountain in.

In Chapter 1, we proved the following two points by analysing SU Shi's *Ti Xi Lin Bi*: (1) a linguistic analysis of English translations of Chinese poems can raise further questions and shed light on translation studies and comparative studies of English-Chinese discourse and (2) the analysis of a poem can be multidimensional and multidirectional.

Written by SU Shi, this poem elucidates a life philosophy:

> The poem is about the poet's enriched understanding after his visit to Mount Lu. To tell the true shape of Mount Lu, the poet must carry out an all-round observation, incorporating views from the front, the sides, afar, nearby, above, and below. If one merely views Mount Lu in one perspective, one side, or one direction, he cannot have an overall image of the mountain. (Zhu 2000: 211–12, our translation)

The philosophy further provides a foundation for our linguistic exploration of English translations of Chinese poems. Since this book examines English translations of Chinese poems, it is also a coincidence that this poem is used to support the claims in this book. The philosophy of life in this poem is both simple and universal. By extending its meaning, we hold that different translators can interpret a poem differently. Translators all attempt to express the meanings encoded in one code with another code, thus they all have to elaborate, interpret and reconstruct the original poem from their own standpoints (which are also restricted by their knowledge and proficiency). As widely acknowledged, poetry translators and researchers of poetry translation are all scholars in translation studies. In that sense, would it be likely that their investigations and comments be restricted by their standpoints, like viewing Mount Lu when being inside the mountain? This is why we attempt to explore and analyse English translations of ancient Chinese poems in a linguistic perspective (*viz.* from "outside the mountain").

Another reason for choosing this poem in the introductory chapter was that its four English translations could serve as a starting point for our discussions in Chapters 2–13, in which various issues related to the English translations were examined in detail. As a result, the analysis of the English translations in Chapter 1 served as an outline of the whole book and functioned as a gateway to the analyses in the following chapters.

In our study, the choice of SU Shi's poem was due to the researcher's observation and interpretation. After observing and interpreting, the next step will then be description. Since this book is a study in the functional linguistic perspective, the analytical framework, terminology, and focus of discussion are all closely related to functional linguistics.

The focus of our analysis lies in the aspects that are strongly associated with our research goals and scopes, involving not only the choice and use of language, but also the narrative perspective or other rhetorical devices.

After describing and analysing the examples (translations), we need to explain the analytical results. The description and analysis of translations can be relatively objective, but the explanation of analytical results somehow involves subjective factors. That problem exists in all disciplines of the humanities and social sciences. In terms of evaluation, the subjective factors are even more obvious.

We can illustrate with another example. In Chapter 8, we analysed MA Zhiyuan's (马致远) *Tian Jing Sha Qiu Si* (天净沙·秋思) from the Yuan Dynasty and its three English translations in terms of "formal equivalence". I am particularly fond of this short lyric because it is a masterpiece among the short lyrics in the Yuan Dynasty as well as a very popular and widely read work. During my process of "observation", I found that many translators were interested in this lyric and had rendered it into English. I also noticed that the renditions reflected two different views on translation: resemblance in form and resemblance in spirit.

By means of *observation*, I selected three English translations of *Tian Jing Sha Qiu Si* as my research object and attempted to *interpret* and discuss the original and the three translations. Then I *analysed* and *described* the language of the original and the translations. Since my study is an attempt to investigate English translations of Chinese classics, the focus is thus on the analysis and description of the translations. In fact, we can conduct an exhaustive functional analysis of the translations, which is plausible in theory, but is uneconomical in practice – indeed, sometimes even meaningless or impossible (see also Huang 1988, 2001a). The most effective and realistic method is to focus on the perspectives that match the researcher's goals and interests. For the same translation, different researchers may identify different perspectives worthy of exploration.

By means of linguistic analysis and description, we can provide some *explanations* in terms of research goals and scopes:

> Xianliang Weng's translation has reflected his views on translation: "We only need to reproduce the image in the original, rather than imitating its composition," we can "totally abandon the word order and syntactic structure in the original", and by "abandoning the form and retaining the spirit", we can "abandoning the form and retaining the spirit". (Yang & Liu 1994: 47–50, our translation).

However, in Schlepp's translation, he adopts his language and linguistic organization to indicate static "things". Composed of 11 sceneries, the whole lyric forms "a dynamic picture" with the things that are loosely interrelated. This explanation is based on our linguistic analysis and description.

Finally, we attempt to *evaluate* the different translations. According to our analysis, in terms of formal equivalence, Schlepp's translation, compared with the other two, is more faithful to the original and is better at rendering the artistic conception of the original, thus providing readers with more space for imagination and allowing for more interpretations. By following the ideas in functional linguistics, form is regarded as the realization of meaning. Thus, in translating a well-known lyric such as *Tian Jing Sha Qiu Si*, we should try to maintain equivalence in both form and meaning. It is exactly for this reason that we prefer Schlepp's translation to the other two (see also Chapter 8). During "evaluation", the following comments are made. Formal equivalence, as merely one standard of assessing translation quality, may not be suitable to assess other translations. This standard is suitable for analysing our three selected translations of *Tian Jing Sha Qiu Si*, but it may not be suitable for analysing other translations of the lyric, nor will it be suitable for analysing other originals and their corresponding English translations. I state this clearly so as not to be mistaken for always regarding "formal equivalence" as the standard of evaluating translation quality.

As seen from the two examples above, during our process of exploring translation issues or evaluating and analysing translated works, we need to undergo the steps of observation, interpretation, description, analysis, explanation and evaluation. In this way, both objective description and subjective hypothesis will be involved.

14.6 Conclusion

As pointed out in our previous discussion, exploring translation issues or translated texts in a functional linguistic perspective is a relatively new attempt that has seldom been seen both inside and outside Chinese academia. Through our efforts, we have re-examined some translation issues in new perspectives based on our linguistic analysis; we also hope that our linguistic analysis has been able to test the applicability and operationality of functional linguistics in discourse analysis and translation studies. As a science and an art, translation has its own regular patterns (including the inexplicable issues of inspiration in translation). There are certainly limitations in the evaluation and judgement of translation. We are aware of these and hope our readers can also realize that this is the case.

After seeing the publication of my research papers on English translations of ancient Chinese poems in several academic journals in China, I am deeply encouraged; hence I have an impetus to explore this area further. My efforts have also drawn the attention of experts and scholars in the area of translation studies. Of course, some scholars are opposed to my linguistic attempt, questioning whether it suitable to interpret and analyse English translations of Chinese poems in the perspectives of functional linguistics and discourse analysis. This deserves further investigation. Readers can judge whether our analysis has been successful in attaining the stated objectives.[3]

Notes

1. "Functional" is here used in a "macro" sense, in contrast to Noam Chomsky's formalism, and such functional theory of language has been applied to areas such as discourse/text analysis, sociolinguistics, cognitive linguistics, pragmatics and cognitive linguistics.
2. "Functional" is here used in a "micro" sense.
3. Additionally, in recent years I have found several works on English translations of ancient Chinese poems and lyrics being published in China (for monographs published in around 2003, see Gu 2003; Mu 2004; Zhang 2003; Zhuo 2003).

Appendix 1

The English translations of ancient Chinese poems and lyrics discussed in this book

长相思
cháng xiāng sī
everlasting longing

（唐）白居易
(táng) bái jū yì
(Tang Dynasty) BAI Juyi

汴水流，
biàn shuǐ liú,
Bian River flow,

泗水流，
sì shuǐ liú,
Si River flow,

流到瓜州古渡头。
liú dào guā zhōu gǔ dù tóu.
flow to Guazhou (melon-shoal) ancient ferry.

吴山点点愁。
wú shān diǎn diǎn chóu.
Wu-mountain dot dot woe.

思悠悠，
sī yōu yōu,
thought endlessly,

恨悠悠，
hèn yōu yōu,
regret endlessly,

恨到归时方始休。
hèn dào guī shí fāng shǐ xiū.
regret till return time then begin stop.

月 明 人 倚 楼。
yuè míng rén yǐ lóu.
moon bright person lean tower.

Jinghao Gong's (1999: 5) translation
Chang Xiang Si
The River Pian flows,
The River Si flows,
They flow to the ancient ferry at Melon Shoal,
With the Wu Mountains dotted with gall.
The thought of you lingers,
My regret meanders.
They will only cease when you return.
In a bright moon I lean up high against the window.

Yuanchong Xu's (1990b: 21) translation
Everlasting Longing
See the Bian River flow
And the Si River flow!
By Ancient Ferry, mingling waves, they go;
The Southern hills reflect my woe.
My thought stretches endlessly;
My grief wretches endlessly.
Oh, when will my beloved come back to me?
Alone I lean on moonlit balcony.

《红 楼 梦》卷头 诗
hóng lóu mèng juàn tóu shī
red chamber dream volume header poem

（清）曹雪芹
(qīng) cáo xuě qín
(Qing Dynasty) CAO Xueqin

满 纸 荒唐 言，
mǎn zhǐ huāng táng yán,
full paper absurd word,

一 把 辛酸 泪！
yì bǎ xīn suān lèi!
one handful bitter tear!

都 云 作者 痴，
dōu yún zuò zhě chī,
all say author foolish,

谁解其中味?
shuí jiě qí zhōng wèi?
who understand inside message?

David Hawkes's translation (see Cao & Gao 1999: 51)
Pages full of idle words
Penned with hot and bitter tears:
All men call the author fool;
None his secret messages hears.

Xinqu Huang's (2002: 197) translation
Pages full of absurd words
Soaked with bitter tears;
All say he is a fool in love,
But who his message hears!

Zhongde Liu's (2003: 100) translation
The story is full of words that sound queer,
Which imply a handful of bitter tear.
"The author is silly," all people say,
But, oh, its true meaning who can explain?

Xianyi Yang and Gladys Yang's (2001a: 11) translation
Pages full of fantastic talk
Penned with bitter tears;
All men call the author mad,
None his message hears.

长干曲
cháng gān qǔ
Changgan song

（唐）崔颢
(táng) cuī hào
(Tang Dynasty) CUI Hao

（其一）"君家何处住?
(qí yī) "jūn jiā hé chù zhù?
(one) "your home which place live?

妾住在横塘。"
qiè zhù zài héng táng."
I live be at sideward pond."

停船暂借问，
tíng chuán zàn jiè wèn,
stop boat moment may ask,

或恐是同乡。
huò kǒng shì tóng xiāng.
also perhaps be same village.

（其二）"家临九江水，
(qí èr) "jiā lín jiǔ jiāng shuǐ,
(two) "home be close to Jiujiang (nine-river) water,

来去九江侧。
lái qù jiǔ jiāng cè.
come go Jiujiang (nine-river) side

同是长干人，
tóng shì cháng gān rén,
same be Changgan people,

生小不相识。"
shēng xiǎo bù xiāng shí."
born little not each other know."

Burton Watson's translation (see Wen 1989: 76)
Songs of Changgan
She:
Tell me, where is your home?
I live at Sloping Banks myself –
Stop the boat, let me ask a minute –
who knows but maybe we're from the same town!

He:
My home looks over the Nine River waters:
up and down the rivers I go.
True, I came from Changgan like you,
but I was a boy then – we never met.

Juntao Wu's (1997: 283) translation
A Song of Long Vale, Four Poems (Two Selections)
I
"Where do you live? Tell me, man, if you like;
And I, a girl, live at the Sideward Dyke.
I ask briefly with my boat slowing down,
Because I think we were from the same town."

II
"My home is also by the lower reaches;
My boat frequents both sides to the beaches.
We're from the same town, my maid coy,
Why I didn't know you when I was a boy!"

Yuanchong Xu's translation (see Xu, Lu & Wu 1988: 139)
A Riverside Song
I The woman's Song
"Tell me where you are from!
On riverbank's my home.
Let us stop rowing down!
Maybe we're from same town?"
II The man's Song
"I live by riverside
And sail on river tide.
We dwell on the same shore,
But didn't know it before."

Yuanchong Xu's (2000b: 205) translation
Songs on the River
(I) The Woman's Song
Where are you coming from?
On the shore I've my home.
Will you rest on your oar?
Are we from the same shore?
(II) The Man's Song
I dwell by riverside,
And sail on river wide.
We live on the same shore,
Not knowing it before.

题 都城 南庄
tí dū chéng nán zhuāng
inscription capital-city south-village

（唐）崔护
(táng) cuī hù
(Tang Dynasty) CUI Hu

去年今日此门中，
qù nián jīn rì cǐ mén zhōng,
last year this day this gate in,

人面桃花相映红。
rén miàn táo huā xiāng yìng hóng.
human face peach blossom each other mirror red.

人面不知何处去，
rén miàn bù zhī hé chù qù,
human face not know which place go,

桃花依旧笑春风。
táo huā yī jiù xiào chūn fēng.
peach blossom still smile spring wind.

Kenneth Rexroth's translation (see Wen 1989: 137)
By the City Gate
A year ago today by
This very gate your face and
The peach blossoms mirrored each
Other. I do not know where
Your beautiful face has gone.
There are only peach blossoms
Flying in the spring wind.

Dayu Sun's (1997: 395) translation
In the Capital's Southern Village
On the same day last year within this door,
A comely face and peach blooms together did glow.
She I've admired has gone I know not where,
Th' peach blooms are smiling still in th' breeze to blow.

Dalian Wang's (1997: 113) translation
Written in a Village South of the Capital
Within this door and on this day last year,
Peach flowers and fair face both shone pink right here.
Though no one knows where fair face is today,
Peach flowers in spring wind still smile in same way.

Yuanchong Xu's (2000b: 463) translation
Written in a Village South of the Capital
In this house on this day last year, a pink face vied
In beauty with the pink peach blossoms side by side.
I do not know today where the pink face has gone;
In vernal breeze still smile pink peach blossoms full-blown

泊秦淮
bó qín huái
moor Qinhuai River

（唐）杜牧
(táng) dù mù
(Tang Dynasty) DU Mu

烟笼寒水月笼沙，
yān lǒng hán shuǐ yuè lǒng shā,
mist veil cold water moon veil sand,

夜泊秦淮近酒家。
yè bó qín huái jìn jiǔ jiā.
night moor Qinhuai River near wineshop

商女不知亡国恨，
shāng nǚ bù zhī wáng guó hèn,
singsong-girl not know subjugate nation hatred,

隔江犹唱《后庭 花》。
gé jiāng yóu chàng hòu tíng huā.
across river still sing backyard flower.

Zhiyu Luo's translation (see Wu 1997: 639)
Berthed at Qinhuai River
Over the river so cold is the mist
and over the sand the moonlit so bright,
I moor my boat by the river,
a wineshop is near, at night.
The singing girls in the merchant's ship
no sense of the conquered's spite,
Sing still *Blooms in Backyard*, a love song,
from the other side of the river, out of sight.

Dalian Wang's (1997: 141) translation
Mooring on Qinhuai River
Cold stream's embraced by mists and moon's caressing sands with light;
We anchor by wineshops along Qinhuai Canal at night.
Some singsong girls who know no sorrow of a nation's fall
Are still singing the decadent song "Back Court Flower" in hall.

Yuanchong Xu's translation (see Xu, Lu & Wu 1988: 316)
Mooring on River Qinhuai
Cold water veiled in mist and shores steeped in moonlight,
I moor on River Qinhuai near wineshops at night,

Where songgirls knowing not the grief of conquered land
Are singing songs composed by a captive ruler's hand.

Yuanchong Xu's (2000b: 524) translation
Moored on River Qinhuai
Cold water and sand bars veiled in misty moonlight,
I moor on River Qinhuai near wineshops at night.
The songstress knows not the grief of the captive king,
By riverside she sings his song of Parting Spring.

Xianyi Yang and Gladys Yang's (2001a: 270) translation
Mooring on the Qinhuai River
The chilly water is shrouded in mist and the sand bathed in moonlight,
As I moor at night on the Qinhuai River near the taverns.
The singsong girls are ignorant of the tragedy of a lost regime,
They are still singing the Backyard Flowers beyond the river!

遣怀
qiǎn huái
express thought

（唐）杜牧
(táng) dù mù
(Tang Dynasty) DU Mu

落魄 江 湖 载 酒 行，
luò pò jiāng hú zǎi jiǔ xíng,
down and out river lake carry wine roam,

楚 腰 纤细 掌 中 轻。
chǔ yāo xiān xì zhǎng zhōng qīng.
Chu waist slim palm in light.

十 年 一 觉 扬州 梦，
shí nián yí jiào yáng zhōu mèng,
ten year one sleep Yangzhou dream,

赢 得 青楼 薄倖 名。
yíng dé qīng lóu bó xìng míng.
obtain VPART brothel unfaithful name.

Zhiye Luo's translation (see Wu 1997: 645)
Self-thought
So penniless and luckless I live
In a boat on the rivers with wine,
Here girls so tender and slender.

As if they can dance in the palm of mine.
Since ten years ago I came here in Yangzhou
I have been dreaming a dream so bad.
What I get from these girls of brothels,
Is the fickle lover, a name so sad.

Dalian Wang's (1997: 151) translation
A Regret
Lacking success in life, I used to roam and drink around
With some sweet, slender southern maidens here and there I found.
My ten years life in Yangzhou is a dream of but one night;
I've only earned a name of faithless swain at brothel site.

Yuanchong Xu's translation (see Xu, Lu & Wu 1988: 321)
A Confession
Luckless, I roved the lakes and rivers with my wine
And spent my life with slender Southern girls so fine.
Having dreamed ten years in Yangzhou, I woke a rover
Who earned in mansions green the name of fickle lover.

Yuanchong Xu's (2000b: 529) translation
A Confession
I roved the rivers, indulged in pleasure and wine
With slender Southern girls who'd dance on palms of mine.
Having dreamed happy dreams ten years, I woke a rover
Who earned in mansions green the name of fickle lover.

Shi Zong's (1999: 214) translation
Thoughts About My Past
In the South my life was dissolute – soaked in wine;
Wasp-waisted girls danced around me constantly.
Those days, ten years ago in Yangzhou, now seem like dream,
With nothing gained but the reputation of being a dandy.

清明
qīng míng
Qingming

（唐）杜牧
(táng) dù mù
(Tang Dynasty) DU Mu

清明 时节 雨 纷纷，
qīng míng shí jiē yǔ fēn fēn,
Qingming season rain succession,

路上行人欲断魂。
lù shàng xíng rén yù duàn hún.
road on pedestrian about to lose soul.

借问酒家何处有，
jiè wèn jiǔ jiā hé chù yǒu,
may ask tavern which place have,

牧童遥指杏花村。
mù tóng yáo zhǐ xìng huā cūn.
herd child far point apricot flower village.

Tinggan Cai's translation (see Wen 1989: 174)
All Souls' Day
The rain falls thick and fast on All Souls' festive day,
The men and women sadly move along the way.
They ask where wineshops can be found or where to rest –
And there the herdboy's fingers Almond-Town suggest.

Zuxin Ding's (2001: 267) translation
Qingming Festival
Qingming Rains never seem to end.
The traveler along this road is overcome by dejection.
"Where can I find a tavern?"
"Apricot village, way down the road."
A cowboy replies pointing his finger.

Dayu Sun's (1997: 435) translation
The Clear-and-Bright Feast
Upon the Clear-and-Bright Feast of spring
  The rain drizzleth down in spray.
Pedestrians on country-side ways
  In gloom are pining away.
When asked "Where a tavern fair for rest
  Is hereabouts to be found",
The shepherd boy the Apricot Bloom Vill
  Doth point to afar and say.

Changsheng Wan and Xianzhong Wang's (2000: 166) translation
The Tomb-visiting Day
The ceaseless drizzle drips all the dismal day,
So broken-hearted fares the traveler on the way.
When asked where could be found a tavern bower,
A cowboy points to yonder village of the apricot flower.

Juntao Wu's translation (see Zhang 1996: 30)
The Pure Brightness Day
It drizzles thick on the Pure Brightness Day;
I travel with my heart lost in dismay.
"Is there a public house somewhere, cowboy?"
He points at Apricot Bloom Village faraway.

Yuanchong Xu's (2000b: 537) translation
The Mourning Day
A drizzling rain falls like tears on the Mourning Day;
The mourner's heart is going to break on his way.
Where can a wineshop be found to drown his sad hours?
A cowherd points to a cot 'mind apricot flowers.

Xianyi Yang and Gladys Yang's (2000a: 266) translation
In the Rainy Season of Spring
It drizzles endlessly during the rainy season in spring,
Travelers along the road look gloomy and miserable.
When I ask a shepherd boy where I can find a tavern,
He points at a distant hamlet nestling amidst apricot blossoms.

回乡偶书
huí xiāng ǒu shū
return hometown incidental write

（唐）贺知章
(táng) hè zhī zhāng
(Tang Dynasty) HE Zhizhang

少小离家老大回，
shào xiǎo lí jiā lǎo dà huí,
young-small leave home old-big return,

乡音无改鬓毛衰。
xiāng yīn wú gǎi bìn máo cuī.
hometown accent not change sideburns hair gray.

儿童相见不相识，
ér tóng xiāng jiàn bù xiāng shí,
child each other see not each other recognize,

笑问客从何处来？
xiào wèn kè cóng hé chù lái?
laugh ask guest from which place come?

Witter Bynner and Kanghu Jiang's translation (see Wen 1989: 53)
Coming Home
I left home young. I return old.
Speaking as then, but with hair grown thin;
And my children, meeting me, do not know me.
They smile and say: "Stranger, where do you come from?"

Zhongde Liu's (2003: 67) translation
Homecoming
I left home quite young. I come back home very old.
My accent remains the same, but my hair turns gray.
Kids don't know me when one another we behold.
"Where do you come from?" with a smile to me they say.

Changsheng Wan and Xianzhong Wang's (2000: 23) translation
Homecoming
I left home when young, now returned, I become old,
My accent as before, yet thin and grey grows my hair.
The children recognize me not when me they behold,
And inquire from where have I come, from where?

Dalian Wang's (1997: 5) translation
On Homecoming
I left home young and now return when I am old;
Not in my speech but thin hair my change would be told.
Boys meet but know me not. They look at me awhile;
"Stranger, where are you from?" they ask me with a smile.

Juntao Wu's (1997: 33) translation
A Casual Homecoming Song
I left home when I was a lad;
  Now old, and home's again in sight.
I have my native tongue as I had,
  But my temple hair is sparse and white.
Confronted by the children small,
  I am a stranger to the place.
"And where do you come from at all?"
  One asks with a brightly smiling face.

寻隐者不遇
xún yǐn zhě bú yù
seek hermit not encounter
（唐）贾岛
(táng) jiǎ dǎo
(Tang Dynasty) JIA Dao

松下问童子，
sōng xià wèn tóng zǐ,
pine under ask boy,

言师采药去。
yán shī cǎi yào qù.
say master gather herb go.

只在此山中，
zhǐ zài cǐ shān zhōng,
only be in this mountain in,

云深不知处。
yún shēn bù zhī chù.
cloud deep not know place.

Witter Bynner's translation (see Wen 1989: 166–67)
A Note Left for an Absent Recluse
When I questioned your pupil, under a pine tree,
"My master," he answered, "went for herbs,
but toward which corner of the mountain,
How can I tell, through all these clouds?"

Dayu Sun's (1997: 427) translation
A Call on the Recluse Who Is Just Out
I asked the boy beneath the pine tree,
Who said, "The master's gone herbs to pick;
He must be some where around these cliffs,
Concealed unseen in the clouds thick"

Changsheng Wan and Xianzhong Wang's (2000: 160) translation
A Hermit Visited but Not Encountered
About the hermit I ask a boy under a pine,
And he answers that his master is gone out,
Into the mountains to gather herbs for medicine,
Yet for the heavy clouds he knows not his whereabout.

Dalian Wang's (1997: 129) translation
An Unsuccessful Visit to an Absent Recluse
Beneath pine trees I asked your lad nearby;
"My master's gone for herbs," was the reply.
"He's only in this mountain somewhere 'round.
In heavy mists he's nowhere to be found."

Burton Watson's translation (see Wen 1989: 167)
Looking for a Recluse but Failing to Find Him
Under the pines I questioned the boy.
"My master's off gathering herbs.
All I know is he's here on the mountain
clouds are so deep, I don't know where

Juntao Wu's (1997: 621) translation
Missing the Hermit when Visiting Him
"Where is your Master?" under pines I ask a lad;
"He's gathering medicinal herbs," so he says,
"Deep in the mountains, where all things are clad
With clouds, and no one can grope out the ways."

Yuanchong Xu's translation (see Xu, Lu & Wu 1988: 308)
Looking for a Hermit Without Finding Him
I ask your lad 'neath a pine-tree.
"My master's gone for herbs," says he,
"Amid the hills I know not where,
For clouds have veiled them here and there."

Yuanchong Xu's (2000b: 479) translation
For an Absent Recluse
I ask your lad 'neath a pine tree.
"My master's gone for herbs," says he.
You hide amid the mountains proud,
I know not where deep in the cloud.

黄鹤楼 送 孟浩然 之 广陵
huáng hè lóu sòng mèng hào rán zhī guǎng líng
yellow-crane-tower see off Meng Haoran to Guangling

（唐）李白
(táng) lǐ bái
(Tang Dynasty) LI Bai

故人 西 辞 黄鹤楼，
gù rén xī cí huáng hè lóu,
old friend west leave yellow-crane-tower

烟花三月下扬州。
yān huā sān yuè xià yáng zhōu.
misty flower third month go to Yangzhou.

孤帆远影碧空尽，
gū fān yuǎn yǐng bì kōng jìn,
lonely sail distant shadow azure sky end,

惟见长江天际流。
wéi jiàn cháng jiāng tiān jì liú.
only see Yangtze River sky end flow.

Witter Bynner and Kanghu Jiang's translation (see Wen 1989: 83)
A Farewell to Meng Haoran on His Way to Yangzhou
You have left me behind, old friend, at the Yellow Crane Terrace,
On your way to visit Yangzhou in the misty month of flowers;
Your sail, a single shadow, becomes one with the blue sky.
Till now I see only the river, on its way to heaven.

Dayu Sun's (1997: 223) translation
Seeing Meng Haoran off to Guangling on the Yellow Crane Tower
Mine old friend leaveth the West
From the Yellow Crane Tower.
In this flowery April clime
For thickly peopled Yangzhou.
A solitary sail's distant speck
Vanisheth in the clear blue:
What could be seen heavenward
Flowing is but the Long River.

Di Tu and An Tu's translation (see Wu 1997: 193)
Seeing Meng Haoran off to Guangling
My friend leaves Yellow Crane Tower towered in the west,
Going to Yangzhou in the third moon when blooms are vying their best.
His lonely sailing boat floats far away into the azure sky,
Only the Yangtze River flowing towards heaven on high.

Changsheng Wan and Xianzhong Wang's (2000: 69) translation
Seeing off Meng Haoran at Tower of Yellow Crane
From Tower of Yellow Crane my friend is going away to
Yangzhou in the month of glowing blooms and dimming willows.
The distant shadow of a lonely sail now melts into the blue,
And I can see yonder only a mighty river idly flows.

Dalian Wang's (1997: 49) translation
A Farewell Song to Meng Haoran at Yellow Crane Tower
From west Crane Tower my friend is on his way
Down to Yangzhou in misty, flowery May.
A sail's faint figure dots the blue sky's end
Where's seen but River rolling till its bend.

Xianyi Yang and Gladys Yang's (2000a: 266) translation
Seeing Meng Haoran off from Yellow Crane Tower
At Yellow Crane Tower in the west
My old friend says farewell;
In the mist and flowers of spring
He goes down to Yangzhou;
Lonely sail, distant shadow,
Vanish in blue emptiness;
All I see is the great river
Flowing into far horizon.

Bingxing Zhang (2001: 41) translation
Seeing Meng Haoran off to Guangling
When my old friend left the Yellow Crane Tower,
it was just March of the lovely spring full of flower.
A lonely sail and a distant shadow
gradually disappeared in the blue zone.
I saw only the Yangtze River flowing on the horizon.

金陵 酒肆 留别
jīn líng jiǔ sì liú bié
Jinling tavern parting

（唐）李白
(táng) lǐ bái
(Tang Dynasty) LI Bai

风 吹 柳 花 满 店 香，
fēng chuī liǔ huā mǎn diàn xiāng,
wind blow willow flower whole shop fragrant,

吴 姬 压 酒 劝 客 尝，
wú jī yā jiǔ quàn kè cháng,
Wu woman squeeze wine bid guest taste,

金陵 子弟 来 相送，
jīn líng zǐ dì lái xiāng sòng,
Jinling junior come see off,

欲行不行各尽觞。
yù xíng bù xíng gè jìn shāng.
plan go not go all great extent wine cup.

请君试问东流水。
qǐng jūn shì wèn dōng liú shuǐ.
please you try ask east flow water.

别意与之谁短长?
bié yì yǔ zhī shuí duǎn cháng?
part thought and it who short long?

Di Tu and An Tu's translation (see Wu 1997: 203)
Parting at an Inn in Jinling
The inn is so sweet with the willow catkins in the wind aflying.
The maid from Wu bids us the flavour of the vintage trying.
Here come my young friends from Jinling to see me off.
I drink my fill and to their hearts' content they quaff.
O my friend, please ask this river eastward going,
Is my grief of parting longer than its ceaseless flowing?

Yuanchong Xu's (2000b: 137) translation
Parting at a Tavern in Jinling
The tavern's sweetened when wind blows in willow-down;
A southern maiden urges guests to taste her wine.
My dear young friends have come to see me leave the town;
They who stay drink their cups and I who leave drink mine.
O ask the river flowing to the east, I pray,
Whether its parting grief or mine will longer stay!

静夜思
jìng yè sī
quiet night thought

（唐）李白
(táng) lǐ bái
(Tang Dynasty) LI Bai

床前明月光,
chuáng qián míng yuè guāng,
bed before bright moon light,

疑是地上霜。
yí shì dì shàng shuāng.
wonder be ground on frost.

举头望明月，
jǔ tóu wàng míng yuè,
raise head see bright moon,

低头思故乡。
dī tóu sī gù xiāng
lower head think hometown

Witter Bynner's translation (see Ma 2000: 193)
So bright a gleam on the foot of my bed –
Could there have been a frost already?
Lifting up my head to look, I found that it was moonlight.
Sinking back again, I thought suddenly of home.

Arthur Cooper's translation (see Ma 2000: 196)
Before my bed
/ there is bright moonlight
So that it seems
/ like frost on the ground;
Lifting my head
I watch the bright moon,
Lowering my head
I dream that I'm home.

L. Cranmer-Byng's translation (see Ma 2000: 195)
Athwart the bed
I watch the moonbeams cast a trail
So bright, so cold, so frail,
That for a space it gleams
Like hoar-frost on the margin of my dreams.
I raise my head, –
The splendid moon I see;
Then droop my head,
And sink to dreams of thee –
My fatherland, of thee!

W.J. Fletcher's translation (see Ma 2000: 194)
Seeing the Moon before my couch so bright
I thought hoar frost had fallen from the night.
On her clear face I gaze with lifted eyes:
Then hide them full of Youth's sweet memories.

Herbert A. Giles's translation (see Ma 2000: 193)
I wake, and moonbeams play around my bed,
Glittering like hoar-frost to my wandering eyes;

Up towards the glorious moon I raise my head.
Then lay me down – and thoughts of home arise.

Xinqu Huang's (2002: 229) translation
Thoughts on a Silent Night
A gleam of light streams down over my bed,
Could it be the real frost on the ground.
Raising my eyes, I gaze at the bright moon,
Lowering my head, my sweet home comes around.

Amy Lowell's translation (see Ma 2000: 194)
In front of my bed the moonlight is very bright.
I wonder if that can be frost on the floor?
I lift up my head and look at the full moon, the dazzling moon.
I drop my head, and think of the home of old days.

Junping Liu's (2002: 59) translation
Homesick at a Still Night
A silver moon hangs by the balustrade,
I fancy moonlight as frost on the ground.
Gazing up of the bright moon I'm looking,
Lowering my head of my native land I'm missing

Hongjun Ma's (2000: 198) translation
Before my bed the moon gleams bright,
And frosts the floor with a hoary light.
My eyes to the fair moon o'erhead roam –
Head bent, I'm lost in dreams of home.

S. Obata's translation (see Ma 2000: 194)
I saw the moonlight before my couch,
And wondered if it were not the frost on the ground.
I raised my head and looked out on the mountain moon,
I bowed my head and thought of my far-off home.

Dayu Sun's (1997: 189) translation
Thoughts in a Still Night
The luminous moonshine before my bed,
Is thought to be the frost fallen on the ground.
I lift my head to gaze at the cliff moon,
And then bow down to muse on my distant home.

Di Tu and An Tu's translation (see Wu 1997: 251)
Homesickness in a Silent Night
Before my bed the silver moonbeams spread –

I wonder if it is the frost upon the ground.
I see the moon so bright when raising my head,
Withdrawing my eyes my nostalgia comes around.

Dalian Wang's (1997: 53) translation
Homesickness in a Quiet, Moonlit Night
What bright beams are beside my bed in room!
Could on the ground there be the frost so soon?
Lifting my head, I see a big, full moon,
Only to bend to think of my sweet home.

Changsheng Wan and Xianzhong Wang's (2000: 57) translation
Reflections on a Quiet Night
Before my bed shine bright the silver beams,
It seems the autumn frost on the ground so gleams.
I gaze upwards toward the moon in the skies,
And downwards look when a nostalgia does arise.

Burton Watson's translation (see Wen 1989: 77)
Still Night Thoughts
Moonlight in front of my bed –
I took it for frost on the ground!
I lift my eyes to watch the mountain moon,
lower them and dream of home.

Xianliang Weng's (1985: 19) translation
Nostalgia
A splash of white on my bedroom floor. Hoarfrost?
I raise my eyes to the moon, the same moon.
As scenes long past come to mind, my eyes fall again on the splash of white, and my heart aches for home.

Yuanchong Xu's (2000b: 141) translation
Thoughts on a Tranquil Night
Before my bed a pool of light –
Can it be hoar-frost on the ground?
Looking up, I find the moon bright;
Bowing, in homesickness I'm drowned.

Zhongjie Xu's translation (see Ma 2000: 192)
I descry bright moonlight in front of my bed.
I suspect it to be hoary frost on the floor.
I watch the bright moon, as I tilt back my head.
I yearn, while stooping, for my homeland more.

Zhentao Zhao's (1999: 37) translation
Quiet Night Thought
Moonlight before my bed,
Could it be frost instead?
Head up, I watch the moon;
Head down, I think of home.

Bingxing Zhang's (2001: 41) translation
Longing in the Night
Before the bed shone the bright moonlight at hand,
I fancied it was frost on the ground.
I raised my head to look at the bright moon,
and lowered my head to think of my native land.

Zhenying Zhuo's (1996: 114) translation
In the Quiet of the Night
The ground before my bed presents a stretch of light,
Which seems to be a track of frost that's pure and bright.
I raise mine head; a lonely moon is what I see;
I stoop, and homesickness is crying loud in me!

苏台览古
sū tái lǎn gǔ
Su terrace view past

（唐）李白
(táng) lǐ bái
(Tang Dynasty) LI Bai

旧苑荒台杨柳新，
jiù yuàn huāng tái yáng liǔ xīn,
old garden deserted terrace willow new,

菱歌清唱不胜春。
líng gē qīng chàng bú shèng chūn.
caltrap song clear chant not surpass spring.

只今惟有西江月，
zhǐ jīn wéi yǒu xī jiāng yuè
now only have west-river moon,

曾照吴王宫里人。
céng zhào wú wáng gōng lǐ rén.
once shine Wu-king palace in person.

Dalian Wang's (1997: 61) translation
The Ruin of the Gusu Palace
In the deserted gardens willows swing;
Sweet water-nut songs fail to praise the spring.
Over West River now remains but moon
That once shone on Wu King's fair ladies boon.

Burton Watson's translation (see Wen 1989: 86)
At Su Terrace Viewing the Past
Old gardens, a ruined terrace, willow trees new;
caltrap gatherers, clear chant of songs, a spring unbearable;
and now there is only the west river moon
that shone once on a lady in the palace of the king of Wu.

Yuanchong Xu's (2000b: 171) translation
The Ruin of the Wu Palace
Deserted garden, crumbling terrace, willows green,
Sweet notes of lotus songs cannot revive old spring.
All are gone but the moon o'er West River that's seen
The ladies fair who won the favor of the king.

越 中 览 古
sū tái lǎn gǔ
Yue in view past

（唐）李白
(táng) lǐ bái
(Tang Dynasty) LI Bai

越王 勾践 破 吴 归，
yuè wáng gōu jiàn pò wú guī,
Yue-king Goujian destroy Wu return,

战士 还 家 尽 锦 衣。
zhàn shì huán jiā jìn jǐn yī.
warrior return home all brocade robe.

宫 女 如 花 满 春 殿，
gōng nǚ rú huā mǎn chūn diàn,
palace maid be like flower fill spring court,

只今 惟 有 鹧鸪 飞。
zhǐ jīn wéi yǒu zhè gū fēi.
now only have partridge fly.

Dayu Sun's (1997: 241) translation
Looking Back to Olden Times in Yue
When Goujian King of Yue,
had crushed his state foe Wu,
His homing warriors were dressed in brocade all.
Then beauties held captive, lush like flowers, thronged the spring court;
Now only partridges are flying and each to each call.

Burton Watson' translation (see Wen 1989: 8)
In Yue Viewing the Past
Goujian, king of Yue, came back from the broken land of Wu;
his brave men returned to their homes. all in robes of brocade.
Ladies in waiting like flowers filled his spring palace
Where now only the partridges fly.

Yuanchong Xu's (2000b: 173) translation
The Ruin of the Capital of Yue
The king of Yue returned, having destroyed the foe;
His loyal men came home, with silken dress aglow.
His palace thronged with flower-like ladies fair;
Now we see but a frock of partridges flying there.

无 题
wú tí
no title

（唐）李商隐
(táng) lǐ shāng yǐn
(Tang Dynasty) LI Shangyin

相 见 时 难 别 亦 难，
xiāng jiàn shí nán bié yì nán,
each other meet time difficult part also difficult,

东 风 无 力 百 花 残。
dōng fēng wú lì bǎi huā cán.
east wind no force hundred flower wither.

春 蚕 到 死 丝 方 尽，
chūn cán dào sǐ sī fāng jìn,
spring silkworm until death thread just end,

蜡炬 成 灰 泪 始 干。
là jù chéng huī lèi shǐ gān.
candle become ash tear just dry.

晓镜但愁云鬓改，
xiǎo jìng dàn chóu yún bìn gǎi,
morning mirror only worry cloud-like hair change,

夜吟应觉月光寒。
yè yín yīng jué yuè guāng hán.
night hum should feel moonlight chill.

蓬山此去无多路，
péng shān cǐ qù wú duō lù,
Penglai mountain here go not have much distance,

青鸟殷勤为探看。
qīng niǎo yīn qín wèi tàn kàn.
green bird (messenger) attentively for visit see.

Innes Herdan's translation (see Ma 2000: 166–67)
Hard it was to see each other –
  hard still to part!
The east wind has no force,
  the hundred flowers wither.
The silkworms die in spring
  when her thread is spun;
The candle dries its tears
  only when burnt to the end.

Grief at the morning mirror –
  cloud-like hair must change;
Verses hummed at night,
  feeling the chill of moonlight ...
Yet from here to Paradise
  the way is not so far:
Helpful bluebird,
  bring me news of her!

Changsheng Wan and Xianzhong Wang's (2000: 178–79) translation
An Untitled Poem
To meet makes one sad, sad too the parting hours,
The east wind languishes, and wither all the flowers.
The silkworm emits silk threads till its breath stops,
To ashes burnt, the candle sheds tears to the last drop.
She'll fear to see in the morning glass some hairs white,
And feel, as I read aloud at night, the chilly moonlight.
As the fairy hill from here will not be far apart,
May the messenger bird bring there the love of my heart!

Yuanchong Xu's translation (see Xu, Lu & Wu 1988: 347)
Poem without a Title
It's difficult for us to meet and hard to part,
The east wind is too weak to revive flowers dead.
The silkworm till its death spins silk from love-sick heart;
The candle only when burned has no tears to shed.
At dawn she'd be afraid to see mirrored hair gray;
At night she would feel cold while I croon by moonlight.
To the three fairy hills it is not a long way.
Would the blue-bird oft fly to see her on their height?

Yuanchong Xu's (2000b: 565) translation
To One Unnamed
It's difficult for us to meet and hard to part,
The east wind is too weak to revive flowers dead.
Spring silkworm till its death spins silk from lovesick heart;
The candle only when burned has no tears to shed.
At dawn she'd be afraid to see mirrored hair gray;
At night she would feel cold while I croon by moonlight.
To the three fairy hills it is not a long way.
Would the blue-bird oft fly to see her on their height?

Bingheng Zeng's translation (see Wu 1997: 677, 679)
No Title
Meeting chance is hard to get and parting time's hard to bear;
The east wind languid, faded flowers appear everywhere.
Silkworm's threads, like men's longing thought, end only when death comes;
Candles shed tears like men till they burn to their bottoms.
In the morning mirror you grieve at your dishevelled hair;
In the moonlight, humming poems, you stand in the cold air.
From here to Mount Penglai it is not a long way to go;
Let Bluebird be my messenger to tell you all my woe.

Tingchen Zhang and Bruce M. Wilson's (1994: 221) translation
Untitled
Difficult it was for us to meet, and difficult to part.
Now the east wind has failed, and all the flowers wither.
The silkworm labors until death its fine thread severs;
The candle's tears are dried when it itself consumes.

Before the mirror, you will fret to find those cloudlike tresses changing.
Making rhymes at night, you'll find the moonlight has grown chill.
The fairy mountain Peng is not so far from here:
Might the Blue Bird become our go between?

江雪
jiāng xuě
river snow

（唐）柳宗元
(táng) liǔ zōng yuan
(Tang Dynasty) LIU Zongyuan

千山鸟飞绝，
qiān shān niǎo fēi jué,
thousand mountain bird fly die out,

万径人踪灭。
wàn jìng rén zōng miè.
ten thousand path man footprint wipe out

孤舟蓑笠翁，
gū zhōu suō lì wēng,
lonely boat bamboo cape bamboo hat old man,

独钓寒江雪。
dú diào hán jiāng xuě.
alone fish cold river snow.

Witter Bynner's translation (see Wen 1989: 162)
River Snow
A hundred mountains and no bird,
A thousand paths without a footprint;
A little boat, a bamboo cloak,
An old man fishing in the cold river-snow.

Soame Jenyns' translation (see Zhu 2000: 10)
On a thousand hills all birds life is cut off,
On ten thousand paths there is no trace of human footsteps;
In a lonely boat the old man with the bamboo hat and cape
Sits by himself fishing the river in the winter snow.

Dayu Sun's (1997: 423) translation
Snowing on the River
Not a bird o'er the hundreds of peaks,
Not a man on the thousands of trails.
An old angler alone in a boat,
With his rod and line, in raining outfit,
Is fishing on the river midst th' snowdrift.

Dalian Wang's (1997: 127) translation
River Snowfall
Amidst all mountains, birds no longer fly;
On all roads, no more travelers pass by.
Straw hat and cloak, old man's in boat, head low,
Fishing alone on river cold with snow.

Shouyi Wang and John Knoepfle's (1989: 45) translation
snow on the river
no singing of birds in the mountain ranges
no footprints of men on a thousand trails
there is only one boat on the water
with an old man in a straw rain cape
who stands on deck and fishes by himself
where the snow falls on the cold river

Burton Watson's translation (see Wen 1989: 163)
River Snow
From a thousand hills, bird flights have vanished;
on ten thousand paths, human traces wiped out;
lone boat, an old man in straw cape and hat,
fishing alone in the cold river snow.

Xianliang Weng's (1985: 51) translation
Snow
No sign of birds in the mountains; nor of men along the trails;
nor any craft on the river but a little boat, with an old man in rustic hat
and cape dangling a line in the frigid waters – a solitary figure veiled in
silent snow.

John C.H. Wu's translation (see Zhu 2000: 10)
River Snow
Myriad mountains – not a bird flying.
Endless roads – not a trace of men.
Only an old fisherman in a lonely boat,
Angling silently in the river covered with snow.

Juntao Wu's (1997: 607) translation
The Snowbound River
O'er mountains and mountains no bird is on the wing;
On thousand lines of the pathways there's no footprint.
In a lone boat on the snowbound river, an old man,
In palm-bark cape and straw hat, drops his angle string.

Yuanchong Xu's translation (see Xu, Lu & Wu 1988: 305)
Fishing in Snow
From hill to hill no bird in flight;
From path to path no man in sight.
A straw-cloak'd man in a boat, lo!
Fishing on river clad in snow.

Yuanchong Xu's (2000b: 457) translation
Fishing in Snow
From hill to hill no bird in flight;
From path to path no man in sight.
A lonely fisherman afloat
Is fishing snow in lonely boat.

采桑子
cǎi sāng zǐ
pick mulberry

（宋）吕本中
(sòng) lǚ běn zhōng
(Song Dynasty) LÜ Benzhong

恨 君 不 似 江 楼 月，
hèn jūn bú sì jiāng lóu yuè,
grieve you not be like river tower moon,

南 北 东 西。
nán běi dōng xī.
south north east west

南 北 东 西，
nán běi dōng xī.
south north east west

只有 相随 无 别离。
zhǐ yǒu xiāng suí wú bié lí.
only-have companion no separation.

恨 君 却 似 江 楼 月，
hèn jūn què sì jiāng lóu yuè,
grieve you yet be like river tower moon,

暂 满 还 亏。
zàn mǎn huán kuī.
brief wax then wane.

暂满还亏，
zàn mǎn huán kuī,
brief wax then wane.

待得团圆是几时？
dài dé tuán yuán shì jǐ shí.
wait VPART union be what time?

Jinghao Gong's (1999: 137–38) translation
Cai Sang Zi
I wish you were the moon,
Shining on the river from behind the waterside lodge.
North, South, East, West;
North, South, East, West,
You always follow and will never never me.
But then,
I wish you wouldn't be that moon:
Temporarily full but soon waning;
Temporarily full but soon waning,
How long have I got to wait
Before it is again full?

Robert Kotewell and Norman Smith's translation (see Wen 1989: 280)
To "Picking Mulberries"
I grieve that my love is not like the moon over the riverside tower:
South and North, East and West,
South and North, East and West,
Only constant companionship and no separation.
I grieve that my love is all too like the moon over the riverside tower:
A brief waxing, and then a waning,
A brief waxing, and then a waning,
I wait for the full circle of union – but how short-lived!

Xiaolong Qiu's (2003: 159) translation
Not Like the Moon (to the Tune of Caisangzi)
A pity – you are not like the moon
above the river pavilion:
east, west, north, south,
east, west, north, south ...
following me everywhere
without separation.
A pity – you are like the moon
above the river pavilion:

waxing and waning,
waxing and waning ...
when will be the full circle
of our union?

Yuanchong Xu's (1996: 335) translation
Tune: "Gathering Mulberry Leaves"
I regret you could not be like the full moon bright,
  Shining all night.
  Shining all night,
It is ever in view and never out of sight.

I regret that you are just like the fickle moon,
  Waning too soon.
  Waning too soon,
When will you wax again to turn my night to noon?

天 净 沙 · 秋 思
tiān jìng shā qiū sī
sky clear sand autumn thought

（元）马致远
(yuán) mǎ zhì yuǎn
(Yuan Dynasty) MA Zhiyuan

枯 藤 老 树 昏 鸦，
kū téng lǎo shù hūn yā,
withered vine old tree dusk crow,

小 桥 流 水 人家，
xiǎo qiáo liú shuǐ rén jiā,
small bridge running water household,

古 道 西 风 瘦 马。
gǔ dào xī fēng shòu mǎ.
ancient road west wind thin horse.

夕阳 西 下，
xī yáng xī xià,
setting sun west descend,

断肠 人 在 天涯。
duàn cháng rén zài tiān yá.
heartbroken man be at skyline.

Zuxin Ding and Burton Raffel's translation (see Gu 1993: 13)
Tune: Tian Jing Sha
Withered vines hanging on old branches,
Returning crows croaking at dusk.
A few houses hidden past a narrow bridge,
And below the bridge quiet creek running.
Down a worn path, in the west wind,
A lean horse comes plodding.
The sun dips down in the west,
And the lovesick traveler is still at the end of the world.

Wayne Schlepp's translation (see Wen 1989: 331)
Tune to "Sand and Sky"
– Autumn Thoughts
Dry vine, old tree, crows at dusk,
Low bridge, stream running, cottages,
Ancient road, west wind, lean nag,
The sun westering
And one with breaking heart at the sky's edge.

Xianliang Weng's (1985: 101–02) translation
Autumn
Crows hovering over rugged trees wreathed with rotten vine – the day is about done. Yonder is a tiny bridge over a sparkling stream, and on the far bank, a pretty little village. But the traveler has to go on down this ancient road, the west wind moaning, his bony horse groaning, trudging towards the sinking sun, farther and farther away from home.

题西林壁
tí xī lín bì
write Xilin wall

（宋）苏轼
(sòng) sū shì
(Song Dynasty) SU Shi

横看成岭侧成峰，
héng kàn chéng lǐng cè chéng fēng,
horizontal look become ridge side become peak,

远近高低各不同。
yuǎn jìn gāo dī gè bù tóng.
far near high low each not same.

不识庐山真面目，
bù shí lú shān zhēn miàn mù,
not recognize Lu-Mount real appearance,

只缘身在此山中。
zhǐ yuán shēn zài cǐ shān zhōng.
only because body be in this mountain in.

Changsheng Wan and Xianzhong Wang's (2000: 212) translation
An Inscription on the Wall of Xilin Temple
The sidelong ranges become steep peaks in a vertical view,
The scenes so vary when seen from high or low, from far or near.
The genuine features of Lushan Mountain are strange to you,
Because your situation is within this mountain's bounding sphere.

Shouyi Wang and John Knoepfle's translation (1989: 88)
written on the wall of xilin monastery
behold this world horizontally
and it appears all ranges
or stare at it vertically
and peaks scrape the clouds

high or low
far or near
all this individuality
teeming in diversity

how can we recognize
the real face of lushan
we who wander here
so deep in the mountains

Burton Watson's translation (see Wen 1989: 251)
Written on the Wall at West Forest Temple
From the side, a whole range; from the end, a single peak:
Far, near, high, low, no two parts alike.
Why can't I tell the true shape of Lu-shan?
Because I myself am in the mountain.

Yuanchong Xu's (2000a: 139) translation
Written on the Wall of West Forest Temple
It's a range viewed in face and peaks viewed from one side,
Assuming different shapes viewed from far and wide.
Of Lu Mountains we cannot make out the true face,
For we are lost in the heart of the very place.

芙蓉楼送辛渐
fú róng lóu sòng xīn jiàn
hibiscus-tower see off Xin Jian

（唐）王昌龄
(táng) wáng chāng líng
(Tang Dynasty) WANG Changling

寒雨连江夜入吴，
hán yǔ lián jiāng yè rù wú,
cold rain mingle river night enter Wu,

平明送客楚山孤。
píng míng sòng kè chǔ shān gū.
daybreak see off guest Chu mountain lonely

洛阳亲友如相问，
luò yáng qīn yǒu rú xiāng wèn,
Luoyang relative friend if ask,

一片冰心在玉壶。
yí piàn bīng xīn zài yù hú.
one piece ice heart be in jade jar.

Jie Tao's translation (see Wu 1997: 119)
Seeing Xin Jian off at Hibiscus Pavilion
Along the river that merged with a cold rain,
We entered the Wu city late at night.
Early at daybreak I bid you farewell,
With only the lone Chu Mountain in sight.
If my kinsfolk in Luoyang should feel concerned,
Please tell them for my part,
Like a piece of ice in a crystal vessel,
Fore'er aloof and pure remains my heart.

Changsheng Wan and Xianzhong Wang's (2000: 37) translation
Send-off to Xin Jian at Hibiscus Tower
Amid the nightly haze of cold rains and streams I came to Wu,
And saw my friend in dawn leave the lonely mountain of Chu.
Oh, Friend, when folks in Luoyang inquires, let it be said,
My heart is as bright as crystal ice in the jar of jade.

Dalian Wang's (1997: 23) translation
Bidding Farewell to Xin Jian at Lotus Pavilion
Cold rains reigning the stream last eve, I got in Wu;
Seeing friend off this dawn, I saw forlorn Mount Chu.

In Luoyang should my folks and friends ask after me,
Tell them a heart's in jade pot, pure as it can be.

Yuanchong Xu's (2000a: 85) translation
Farewell to Xin Jian at Lotus Tower
A cold rain mingled with Eastern Stream at night;
At dawn you leave the Southern hills lonely in haze.
If my friends in the North should ask if I'm all right,
My heart is free of stain as ice in crystal vase.

Yuanchong Xu's (2000b: 83) translation
Farewell to Xin Jian at Lotus Tower
A cold rain mingled with East Stream invades the night;
At dawn you leave the Southern hills lonely in haze.
If my friends in the North should ask if I'm all right,
My heart is free of stain as ice in crystal vase.

新 嫁 娘 词
xīn jià niáng cí
newly wedded bride lyric

（唐）王建
(táng) wáng jiàn
(Tang Dynasty) WANG Jian

三 日 入 厨下，
sān rì rù chú xià,
three day go to kitchen,

洗 手 作 羹汤。
xǐ shǒu zuò gēng tāng.
wash hand make broth-soup.

未 谙 姑 食 性，
wèi ān gū shí xìng,
not know mother-in-law food habit,

先 遣 小姑 尝。
xiān qiǎn xiǎo gū cháng.
first dispatch sister-in-law taste.

W.J. Fletcher's translation (see Wen 1989: 140–41)
The Daughter-in-law
Now married three days, to the kitchen I go,
And washing my hand, a find broth I prepare.

But what kind of taste auntie likes, I don't know.
So send to my sister-in-law the first share.

Zhiye Luo's translation (see Wu 1997: 523)
A Bride's Song
On the third day being a bride
I went to cook as a maid;
My hands washed, and a broth
by myself is made.
What my husband's mother
likes to eat I never know,
I ask his young sister to taste,
see if it were fine so.

Dalian Wang's (1997: 117) translation
A Newly Wedded Daughter-in-law
She comes to kitchen, married but three days;
Having washed hands, she makes some consommés.
Knowing her mother-in-law's taste not yet,
She let young sis have first, a clue to get.

Burton Watson's translation (see Wen 1989: 140–41)
Words of the Newly-wed Wife
The third day I went into the kitchen,
Washed my hands and made the soup.
Not yet sure of my mother-in-law's tastes,
I sent some first for sister-in-law to try.

Yuanchong Xu's (2000b: 375) translation
A Bride
Married three days, I go shy-faced
To cook a soup with hands still fair.
To meet my mother-in-law's taste,
I send to her daughter the first share.

鹿柴
lù zhài
deer fence

（唐）王维
(táng) wáng wéi
(Tang Dynasty) WANG Wei

空山不见人，
kōng shān bú jiàn rén,
empty mountain not see man,

但闻人语响。
dàn wén rén yǔ xiǎng.
but hear man voice sound.

返景入深林，
fǎn jǐng rù shēn lín,
dusk sunlight enter deep wood,

复照青苔上。
fù zhào qīng tái shàng.
again shine green moss on.

C.J. Chen and Michael Bullock's translation (see Wen 1989: 69)
The Deer Enclosure
On the lonely mountain
I met no one,
I hear only the echo
of human voices.
At an angle the sun's rays
enter the depth of the wood,
And shine
upon the green moss.

Burton Watson's translation (see Wen 1989: 70)
Deer Fence
Empty hills, no one in sight,
only the sound of someone talking;
late sunlight enters the deep wood,
shining over the green moss again.

送别
sòng bié
farewell

（唐）王维
(táng) wáng wéi
(Tang Dynasty) WANG Wei

下马饮君酒
xià mǎ yǐn jūn jiǔ
dismount horse drink your wine

问君何所之
wèn jūn hé suǒ zhī
ask you which place to

君言不得意
jūn yán bù dé yì
you say not achieve ambition

归卧南山陲
guī wò nán shān chuí
return lie south mountain foot

但去莫复问
dàn qù mò fù wèn
just go not again ask

白云无尽时
bái yún wú jìn shí
white cloud no end time

Witter Bynner's translation (see Lü 1980: 148)
At Parting
I dismount from my horse and I offer you wine.
And I ask you where you are going and why.
And you answer: "I am discontent
And would rest at the foot of the southern mountain.
So give me leave and ask me no questions.
White clouds pass there without end."

W.J. Fletcher's translation (see Lü 1980: 148)
"So farewell. And if for ever, still for ever fare ye well."
Quitting my horse, a cup with you I drank.
And drinking, asked you whither you were bound.
Your hopes unprospered, said you, turned you round.
You went. I asked no more. The white clouds pass,
And never yet have any limit found.

Herbert A. Giles's translation (see Lü 1980: 148)
Goodbye to Meng Hao-jan
Dismounted o'er wine we had said our last say;
Then I whisper, "Dear friend, tell me whither away."
"Alas!" he replied, "I am sick of life"s ills
"And I long for repose on the slumbering hills.
"But oh seek not to pierce where my footsteps may stray.
"The white clouds will soothe me for ever and ay."

Dayu Sun's (1997: 139) translation
Bidding Adieu to a Friend
As thou alight from thy horse,
I greet thee with a stoup of wine,

And ask thee whither thou wouldst tend.
Thy answer thou givest disheartened
Saying thou wouldst go to retire
As a recluse by the South Mount.
Go but thither without a query;
White clouds are there at all times.

Baotong Wang's translation (see Wu 1997: 131)
Farewell
Dismounting, I asked you to have a draught,
"And where to, my friend?" I inquired.
"My hopes are shattered," you bitterly laughed,
"To the southern hills. I'm retired."
Then go ahead, say no more, my dear.
The fleecy clouds have endless cheer.

Yuanchong Xu's (2000b: 87) translation
At Parting
Dismounted, I drink with you
And ask what you've in view.
"I can't do what I will,
So I'll go to south hill.
Be gone, ask no more, friend,
Let cloud drift without end!"

Xianyi Yang and Gladys Yang's (2001a: 28) translation
A Farewell
I dismount from my horse and drink your wine.
I ask where you're going.
You say you are a failure.
And want to hibernate at the foot of Deep South Mountain.
Once you're gone no one will ask about you.
There are endless white clouds on the mountain.

寄 李儋 元锡
jì lǐ dān yuán xī
to Li Dan Yuan Xi

（唐）韦应物
(táng) wéi yīng wù
(Tang Dynasty) WEI Yingwu

去 年 花 里 逢 君 别，
qù nián huā lǐ féng jūn bié,
last year flower in meet you part,

今日花开又一年。
jīn rì huā kāi yòu yì nián
this day flower blossom another one year

世事茫茫难自料，
shì shì máng máng nán zì liào,
world affair boundless difficult self expect,

春愁黯黯独成眠。
chūn chóu àn àn dú chéng mián.
spring sorrow gloomy alone fall asleep.

身多疾病思田里，
shēn duō jí bìng sī tián lǐ,
body more illness miss hometown,

邑有流亡愧俸钱。
yì yǒu liú wáng kuì fèng qián.
town have exile shame salary-money.

闻道欲来相问讯，
wén dào yù lái xiàng wèn xùn,
hear want come VPART ask message,

西楼望月几回圆。
xī lóu wàng yuè jǐ huí yuán.
west tower watch moon how many time round.

Peixian Lu's translation (see Wu 1997: 479)
To Li Dan
In the month of flowers we met last year, then parted;
Today they bloom again, to mark another year.
Man contrives in vain, in this riddling, changeful world;
Spring to my lonely nights brings dreams both dim and drear.
An ailing body sets my thoughts all homeward bound;
My fee shames me when hungry people flee their land.
How many full moons I've watched from my western bower,
E'er since I got the tidings of your visit planned!

丑奴儿
chǒu nú er
ugly slave

（宋）辛弃疾
(sòng) xīn qì jí
(Song Dynasty) XIN Qiji

少年不识愁滋味，
shào nián bù shí chóu zī wèi,
young age not know sorrow taste,

爱上层楼。
ài shàng céng lóu.
love climb storey tower.

爱上层楼，
ài shàng céng lóu.
love climb storey tower,

为赋新词强说愁。
wèi fù xīn cí qiáng shuō chóu
to compose new lyric manage talk sorrow.

而今识尽愁滋味，
ér jīn shí jìn chóu zī wèi,
now know all sorrow taste,

欲说还休。
yù shuō huán xiū.
want talk but refrain.

欲说还休，
yù shuō huán xiū,
want talk but refrain,

却道天凉好个秋。
què dào tiān liáng hǎo gè qiū.
but say day cool good such autumn.

Jinghao Gong's (1999: 160–61) translation
Chou Nu Er
As a young man, I'd not really tasted sadness.
I liked to climb the stairs.
I liked to climb the stairs,

To mimic the telling of deep sorrow
By composing new poems.

Now I've known only too much sadness,
What is the point of telling?
What is the point of telling?
I merely say: What a cool nice autumn!

Robert Kotewell and Norman Smith's translation (see Wen 1989: 305–06)
To "The Ugly Slave"
In youth, not knowing the taste of sorrow,
I loved to ascend the storeyed towers,
I loved to ascend the storeyed towers,
And, to fashion new verses, I made myself speak of sorrow.

But now, having all the taste of sorrow,
I should speak of it but refrain,
I should speak of it but refrain,
Instead, I say: "A cool day, a fine Autumn."

Yuanchong Xu's (1986: 201) translation
Tune: "Song of Ugly Slave"
While young, I knew no grief I could not bear,
  I'd like to go upstair.
  I'd like to go upstair
To write new verses, with a false despair.
I know what grief is now that I am old,
  I would not have it told.
  I would not have it told
But only say I'm glad that autumn's cold.

Xianyi Yang and Gladys Yang's (2001b: 231) translation
Chou Nu Er
Written on My Way to Boshan
As a lad I never knew the taste of sorrow,
But loved to climb towers,
Loved to climb towers,
And drag sorrow into each new song I sang.

Now I know well the taste of sorrow,
It is on the tip of my tongue,
On the tip of my tongue,
But instead I say, "What a fine, cool autumn day!"

节妇吟
jié fù yín
chaste wife song

（唐）张籍
(táng) zhāng jí
(Tang Dynasty) ZHANG Ji

君知妾有夫，
jūn zhī qiè yǒu fū,
you know I have husband,

赠妾双明珠。
zèng qiè shuāng míng zhū.
give me two bright pearl.

感君缠绵意，
gǎn jūn chán mián yì,
feel your touching intention,

系在红罗襦。
xì zài hóng luó rú.
fasten to red short dress.

妾家高楼连苑起，
qiè jiā gāo lóu lián yuàn qǐ,
my home high building connect palace stand,

良人执戟明光里。
liáng rén zhí jǐ míng guāng lǐ.
husband hold halberd bright light in.

知君用心如日月，
zhī jūn yòng xīn rú rì yuè,
know you attentive be like sun moon,

事夫誓拟同生死。
shì fū jǐng nǐ tóng shēng sǐ.
serve husband danger compare together life death.

还君明珠双泪垂，
huán jūn míng zhū shuāng lèi chuí,
return you bright pearl both tear shed,

恨不相逢未嫁时。
hèn bù xiāng féng wèi jià shí.
regret not each other meet not married time.

Xiaolong Qiu's (2003: 33) translation
A Virtuous Wife
Knowing I am married, you gave me
a pair of lustrous pearls.
Beholden to you for your kindness,
I fastened them to my red slip.

My house is close to the Mingguang Palace,
where my husband serves as a guard.

Your intention is as lofty
as the sun and the moon, I know.
Having sworn to be with him
in life and death, I have
to return the glistening pearls to you
with tears in my eyes.
Oh, if we could have met
before I married.

Yuanchong Xu's (2000b: 371) translation
Reply of a Chaste Wife
You know I love my husband best,
Yet you send me two bright pearls still.
I hang them within my red silk vest,
So grateful I'm for your good will.
You see my house o'erlooks the garden and
My husband guards the palace, halberd in hand.
I know your heart as noble as the sun in the skies,
But I have sworn to serve my husband all my life.
With your twin pearls I send back two tears from my eyes.
Why did we not meet before I was made a wife?

枫 桥 夜 泊
fēng qiáo yè bó
maple bridge night anchor

（唐）张继
(táng) zhāng jì
(Tang Dynasty) ZHANG Ji

月 落 乌 啼 霜 满 天，
yuè luò wū tí shuāng mǎn tiān,
moon set crow cry frost fill sky,

江枫渔火对愁眠。
jiāng fēng yú huǒ duì chóu mián.
river maple fishing fire to sorrow sleep.

姑苏城外寒山寺，
gū sū chéng wài hán shān sì,
Gusu (Suzhou) city outside cold-hill temple,

夜半钟声到客船。
yè bàn zhōng shēng dào kè chuán.
midnight (night-half) bell sound reach boat.

Tinggan Cai's translation (see Wen 1989: 125)
Anchored at Night by the Maple Bridge
The moon is setting, rooks disturb the frosty air,
I watch by mapled banks the fishing-torches flare.
Outside the Suzhou wall, from Hanshan Temple's bell,
I hear its sound aboard and feel its midnight spell.

Dalian Wang's (1997: 95) translation
A Night Mooring by Maple Bridge
Moon's down, crows cry and frosts fill all the sky;
By maples and boat light, I sleepless lie.
Outside Gusu Cold-Hill Temple's in sight;
Its ringing bells reach my boat at midnight.

Yuanchong Xu's translation (see Xu, Lu & Wu 1988: 224)
Mooring at Night by Maple Bridge
The moon goes down, crows cry under the frosty sky,
Dimly-lit fishing boats 'neath maples sadly lie.
Beyond the Gusu walls the Temple of Cold Hill
Rings bells which reach my boat, breaking the midnight still.

Yuanchong Xu's (2000b: 329) translation
Mooring by Maple Bridge at Night
At moonset cry the crows, streaking the frosty sky;
Dimly lit fishing boats 'neath maples sadly lie.
Beyond the city wall, from Temple of Cold Hill
Bells break the ship-borne roamer's dream and midnight still.

Appendix 2

An interview with Guowen Huang

Interviewee: Guowen Huang[1]
Interviewers: Bo Wang and Yuanyi Ma
Date: 3 September 2022
Place: Online

1. Motivation for applying Systemic Functional Linguistics to translation studies

Bo Wang: What motivated you to apply Systemic Functional Linguistics (SFL) to translation studies?

Guowen Huang: As a teacher of English and linguistics, I am devoted to SFL because I am fascinated by many of the systemic and functional ideas about language and linguistics. I am interested in exploring the use of language in relation to language choice and one of my research interests has been the study of translation issues in an SFL perspective. Briefly, there have been three main reasons for undertaking studies of translation in relation to SFL. The first reason is that I fully accept the Hallidayan functional view of language and I want to explore translation issues in a systemic functional perspective. The second reason is that although SFL is both a general linguistics and an appliable linguistics, the focus of recent studies has been on appliable linguistics because the latter is more closely related to discourse studies and solving practical problems, and studying translation is an example of applying SFL to solving practical problems related to language use. This is in line with Halliday's (2009a) statement that SFL is a problem-oriented theory. The third reason is that about 20 years ago when I first began to pay attention to translation studies, there were few studies and publications in systemic functional translation studies, so I published a number of research papers in this area (e.g. Huang 2002a, 2002b, 2002c, 2002d, 2002e, 2002f, 2002g, 2002i, 2003b, 2003c, 2003d).

Over the last two decades, the situation has changed dramatically. We now have a number of scholars carrying out research on this topic, and there have been many publications both in China and abroad – I have noticed that you two have done a lot of work in this area (e.g. Wang & Ma 2020, 2021, 2022).

2. Advantages of applying SFL theory to translation studies

Bo Wang: As a linguistic theory, what are the advantages of applying SFL to issues of translation?

Guowen Huang: Although translation issues can be studied in different perspectives and different levels of detail, a linguistic approach based on a particular theory of language is necessary. In 1962, Halliday published an article on linguistics and machine translation, arguing that any description of language and language use, including that on translation studies, should be based on a theory of some kind. As he noted:

> It is impossible to describe language without a theory, since some theory, however inadequate, is implicit in all descriptions; but it is quite possible to make a description that is in practice unsystematic, with categories neither clearly interrelated nor consistently assigned. (Halliday 1962: 147)

He later identified the nature of a linguistic theory of translation by saying that "for a linguist, translation theory is the study of how things are: what is the nature of the translation process and the relation between texts in translation" (Halliday 2001: 13). According to Halliday, an SFL theory of translation is a "declarative" theory rather than an "imperative" theory, which studies how things are rather than how things should be. This defines the nature of a linguistic theory of translation and distinguishes it from other theories of translation.

As I said a few years ago (see Huang 2017), over the past few decades, scholars of different ideological, social, cultural, educational and professional backgrounds have approached translation issues in many different perspectives with different motivations and purposes, and proposed different theoretical models for studying translation. The literature to date shows that there are a number of approaches to the study of translation issues, linguistic approaches being one. When

Halliday's theory of language was in its initial stages – that is, in the era of Scale and Category Grammar (Halliday 1961), there were already scholars who had set out to apply his theory to translation studies, one of whom was J.C. Catford, who proposed "a theory of translation which may be drawn upon in any discussion of particular translation-problems" (Catford 1965: vii). Catford acknowledged that his approach to translation was a linguistic one and "the general linguistic theory made use of in this book is essentially that developed at the University of Edinburgh, in particular by M.A.K. Halliday and influenced to a large extent by the work of the late J.R. Firth" (1965: 1). In terms of his theoretical support, Catford (1965: 1) referred readers to Halliday's "Categories of the Theory of Grammar" (Halliday 1961) and Halliday, McIntosh and Strevens (1964). If we agree that translation is translating meaning, then a meaning-oriented and function-oriented approach such as SFL would have more advantages in studying translation issues, and to me SFL is the most appropriate theoretical model. Many years ago, after receiving a PhD in applied linguistics from the University of Edinburgh in 1992, I did a second PhD with Professor Robin Fawcett at Cardiff University. I was influenced by Robin's ideas about language and linguistics and I totally agreed with him when he said that, "Halliday has given us more insights into the nature of language and its use than any other linguist since Saussure – and probably even more than him" (Fawcett 2008: 10).

3. Studying translations of ancient Chinese poems

Bo Wang: Why would you choose to study the translations of ancient Chinese poetry? What is so specific about this register?

Guowen Huang: Classical literature plays an essential role in education. There is now a general assumption that ancient Chinese poetry should be taught, read, memorized and recited by every Chinese child. But I was brought up in the years when China experienced the so-called "Cultural Revolution" (1966–76), when this was not the case. I always feel that my primary and secondary education was inadequate, and one reason was that I did not have the chance to learn the classics at school. After so many years of reading academic works on language and linguistics, I began to read the Chinese classics in my spare time, to make up for those lost years and to enrich myself as a Chinese scholar. One by-product of this activity was that I began to study the translation of classics in an SFL perspective, which was a way of combining my present research interests with the readings and writings that I was not able to experience when I was young. Another reason is that the Chinese poems have attracted numerous scholars, both in China and abroad, to translate them into English, and as a result there are many poems that have many different translated versions. This allows the academic comparison of the different translated versions. Another practical reason is that Tang poems are usually very short and so lend themselves to detailed text analysis, which is my most favourite research method.

4. Studying translations of the *Lun Yu* (*The Analects*)

Bo Wang: What motivated you to study *The Analects* (*Lun Yu*) by Confucius and its translations? What have been your major findings?

Guowen Huang: The *Lun Yu* by Confucius is generally known in English as *The Analects* (of Confucius), and it is a collection of different sayings, descriptions and activities concerned with Confucius (551–479 BCE) during his lifetime. This work has strongly influenced the Chinese people in terms of their understanding of the world and the relationships between people on the one hand, and between people and nature on the other hand. Also, the work has influenced people's behaviors and their social practices. Both the general teaching and learning of the *Lun Yu* and the academic study of this classic have a history of more than 2000 years, and there are numerous academic writings on this work. As I said earlier, I was born and brought up in a special period of the Chinese history when ancient Chinese poetry was not taught in schools and people were not allowed to read and memorize the classics. Therefore, one reason for me to pay attention to the *Lun Yu* is that I wanted to learn and study it so I could see what an "intelligentleman" (Xu 2005) was like in ancient times. A second reason for me to carry out research into this great work is to see how an SFL approach can be applied in the analysis of this text and its different translations. These two reasons are closely related to my own interest in understanding and analysing this canonical text. The third reason is that there are many different approaches to the study of the English translations of this text and to me an SFL approach would be more desirable; thus, an SFL analysis of this work is a way to illustrate the applicability and powerfulness of SFL.

The *Lun Yu* is generally taken not to be a book in the sense usually understood by modern readers, because it is generally assumed that there is not a coherent argument or storyline presented by a single author, to be read page by page, or to be digested alone in the quiet of one's study; and thus the way the sayings and descriptions are put together is not textually cohesive in the Hallidayan sense (Halliday 1985; Halliday & Hasan 1976). As a text analyst, I was interested in exploring the issues of coherence and cohesive ties in this book.

Halliday (1985: 318; 1994: 339) argues that "for a text to be coherent, it must be cohesive", but some people in text analysis circles have criticized this argument by quoting Widdowson's (1978: 29) invented example to illustrate that a text can be coherent without being cohesive:

A: That's the telephone.

B: I'm in the bath.

A: Okay.

After analysing the text of the *Lun Yu*, one of the arguments I make is that Widdowson's invented example is both cohesive and coherent. The three utterances or conversation turns are cohesive because they occur in the context of the same communicative activity. "That's the telephone" is a statement by the initiator of the communication and it expects a response from the addressee, who thus gives a reason for not being able to answer the telephone – "I'm in the bath", which the initiator acknowledges and accepts by saying "Okay". Therefore, it seems to me that Widdowson's invented example is both coherent and cohesive, and this argument supports Halliday's (1985: 318; 1994: 339) statement that cohesion and coherence work together to ensure texture in a text.

The text of the *Lun Yu* contains 20 chapters in which most of the quotations, sayings or descriptions are independent, in that most of them are not locally coherent and cohesive. But my argument is that even if two utterances are not coherent in terms of their propositional meanings, they become coherent and cohesive if they are used as two turns in a conversational pair. Therefore, "That's the telephone" and "I'm in the bath" are cohesive because the latter is used as a response (answer) to the former's request (question). By the same token, if two things are put together in a particular context, they automatically become "cohesive" because they form a pair of some kind in that context. As far as the textual organization of the *Lun Yu* is concerned, it is clear that most of the individual quotations, sayings or descriptions are not propositionally related to each other, even though all of them are concerned with Confucius's teaching. However, as I argued in one of my articles (i.e. Huang 2011), the quotations, sayings or descriptions in the *Lun Yu* are cohesive because they were put together to form different chapters of the same book.

One of the findings of my research has been the importance of using commentaries and notes in the translated version, which helps to make the meaning of the source text clear to the reader. We argued that more attention should be paid to the context of culture in which the text needs to be interpreted. More so than for the translation of other texts, the rendering of the *Lun Yu* needs more interpretations and commentaries, without which the translation is often not to be understood by the target audience.

In the field of translation studies, the nature of translation has been discussed at different times by different people from different research areas. As Hartmann and Stork (1972: 713; see also Bell 1991: 6) put it, "translation is the replacement of a representation of a text in one language by a representation of an equivalent text in a second language". Moreover, as observed by a number of different scholars, since the 1950s the issue of equivalence, which is "a central concept in translation theory" (Chesterman 1989: 99), has been one of the most discussed issues in translation studies (Munday 2001: 35) and the concept is incorporated into most theoretical approaches to translation studies. In Yallop's (2001: 241) words, equivalence is regarded as "a clear aim of translation", so almost everyone in the field of translation, no matter whether they are more interested in issues relating to theory or those of practice, has a stake in understanding this issue. In discussing "the environments of translation" in relation to translation equivalence, Matthiessen (2001) proposes that, in line with what SFL recognizes as the main organizing principles of human language, these environments can be defined by the various dimensions of stratification, rank, instantiation, metafunction, delicacy and axis, and these six dimensions have been discussed and illustrated by Halliday in relation to translation in a number of places (e.g. Halliday 2001, 2009b, 2010).

In translation studies, equivalence is widely regarded as the ultimate goal of translation, and different types of equivalence have been proposed – for example, "translation equivalence" in contrast to "formal correspondence" (Catford 1965), and "dynamic equivalence"

(Nida & Taber 1969). In studying this issue in an SFL perspective, we can apply a metafunctional perspective to characterizing translation equivalence; thus, we can examine the target text in the perspectives of ideational (experiential and logical), interpersonal or textual equivalence. I (Huang 2017) have argued that experiential equivalence is the fundamental element in any instance of good translation because other kinds of equivalence cannot operate without an experiential basis. By comparing a number of source texts and their corresponding target texts, we hypothesized that in evaluating target texts from certain registers (e.g. *The Analects*), the order of importance would be as follows: the experiential metafunction is the most important and the textual metafunction the least important, with the interpersonal metafunction being less important than the experiential metafunction but more important than the logical metafunction, as illustrated in Figure 16.1.

Most Importance of equivalence

↓ Experiential metafunction

↓ Interpersonal metafunction

↓ Logical metafunction

↓ Textual metafunction

Least Importance of equivalence

Figure 16.1. Order of importance of metafunctional equivalence (Huang 2017)

However, I understand that apart from metafunctional equivalence, other kinds of equivalence exist that need to be studied further. For an SFL approach, Matthiessen's (2001) notion of "the environments of translation" in defining equivalence in terms of the parameters of stratification, rank, instantiation, metafunction, delicacy and axis can serve as theoretical guidance.

5. PhD supervision in this area

Yuanyi Ma: Professor Huang, you have trained many PhD students in applying SFL to translation, many of whom have become important and productive scholars in this area in China. Could you briefly introduce their work and their contributions?

Guowen Huang: In the Chinese educational context, the teacher generally influences his students in different ways, no matter whether they are young or old, junior or senior, because traditionally the teacher was regarded as the student's life guide. As I have said on a number of occasions, I have been greatly influenced in my academic studies by systemicists such as Halliday and Fawcett, and I have to say that I have equally influenced my students in applying SFL to translation studies. Up to the present I have supervised nine PhD students who did their PhD studies on translation, and they now have become well-known in the field. These students fall into two categories. One group (four students) explored general translation issues and the others (five students) worked on the analysis of the translation of the *Lun Yu*: most of these PhD theses have been published as monographs (see also Table 0.1 in the Translators' Preface for information about monographs published in Mainland China).

Yuanyuan Shang (尚媛媛) (2003, 2005) studied the phenomenon of translation shifts in an SFL perspective, focusing on the translation of political speeches from English into Chinese. The aim of her research was to use SFL as an analytical tool for text description and analysis. Peng Wang (王鹏) (2004, 2007) explored the translation of fiction using the Harry Potter books; her focus was on the equivalence between the source text and the target text in relation to the influence of the speaker's gender and age on their use of modality, in particular the modal operators *can* and *could* in English as translated in Chinese. Fagen Li (李发根) (2005, 2007) investigated the expression of interpersonal meanings in Chinese poetry as translated into English, with special reference to equivalence. The focus of his studies was on the linguistic realizations of interpersonal meanings in both source and target texts, using as data the lyric poem *Shu Dao Nan* (蜀道难) by famous Tang Dynasty poet Li Bai, and five English renderings. Xianzhu Si (司显柱) (2006, 2007) studied quality assessment in translation and proposed a text-based translation quality assessment model based on SFL, focusing on issues such as the nature and quality of translation and the dialectic correlation between form, function and context within a framework of translation as verbal behaviour.

Guoxiang Wu (吴国向) (2013) investigated grammatical complexity in multiple English translations of the *Lun Yu*, examining the versions by Legge (1861), Ku (1898), Waley (1938) and Pound (1951), with a special focus on the balance between lexical density and grammatical intricacy. Yang Chen (陈旸) (2014, 2020) compared different translations of the *Lun Yu* in the light of their respective communicative functions, with the aim of identifying the translator's aims in translating the text, and finding methods of translation quality assessment that would be applicable to the case of classics such as the *Lun Yu*. Ying Chen (陈莹) (2014, 2020) studied various English versions of the *Lun Yu* produced in different periods of time by translators from different social, cultural, linguistic and geographical backgrounds, focusing on register variation. Her study was an instance of functional discourse analysis, as illustrated by Huang (2001b, 2006). Shengwen Gao (高生文) (2014, 2016) also took a register analysis approach, in this case comparing Legge's (1861) and Ku's (1898) translations of the *Lun Yu* in a metafunctional perspective, linking the analysis of ideational, interpersonal and textual meanings to his characterization of the field, tenor and mode of discourse respectively. Juan Yu (余娟) (2015) investigated the occurrence of explicitation in Chinese–English translations of the *Lun Yu* and, like Ying Chen (2014), worked within the framework of functional discourse analysis (Huang 2001b, 2006). Her study showed that the ideational explicitation of participants and circumstances was salient, as reflected in the translators' addition of participants and circumstances that were only implicit in the source text.

Apart from these nine PhD theses, many of my students, including quite a number of my MA and MTI students, have applied an SFL framework to the study of translation issues and have published quite a number of research papers, most of which have appeared in Chinese journals of linguistics and applied linguistics.

6. Applying ecolinguistics to translation studies

Yuanyi Ma: Ecolinguistics, as discussed in Stibbe's (2015: 1) book *Ecolinguistics: Language, Ecology and the Stories We Live By*, deals with "critiquing forms of language that contribute to ecological destruction, and aiding in the search for new forms of language that inspire people to protect the natural world". We also find that ecolinguistics "has been used to describe studies of language interaction and diversity; studies of texts such as signposts which are outdoors; analysis of texts that happen to be about the environment; studies of how words in a language relate to objects in the local environment; studies of the mix of languages surrounding pupils in multicultural schools; studies of dialects in particular geographical locations, and many other diverse areas" (Stibbe 2015: 8). Can ecolinguistics be applied to translation studies?

Guowen Huang: Thank you for your interest in what I have been doing these past seven years in applying Halliday's (2007) systemic functional ecolinguistics to the study of language and translation. Halliday (1990: 145) states that language does not passively reflect reality but actively creates reality, and that our ways of meaning and saying have an impact on the environment. Halliday (1990, 2007) also characterizes the function of language as doing things, including construing experiences, maintaining social relationships and organizing language and discourse. Our behavior, whether ecological or not, is influenced or determined by our conception of the relationship between man and nature, and our ways of expressing meaning have certainly impacted the ecosystem of which the human beings and their languages are a part. In terms of translation, a systemic ecolinguistic approach can indicate whether a particular translation is characterized more by ecocentrism or by anthropocentrism. Let me illustrate this by analysing two English translations of the poem *Chun Xiao* (春晓; "Spring Dawn") by a well-known Tang poet, MENG Haoran (孟浩然):

春 眠 不 觉 晓
chūn mián bù jué xiǎo
spring sleep not feel dawn

处处 闻 啼 鸟
chù chù wén tí niǎo
everywhere (place-place) hear sing bird

夜 来 风 雨 声
yè lái fēng yǔ shēng
night come wind rain sound

花 落 知 多 少
huā luò zhī duō shǎo
flower fall know how many (many-few)

As is evident from the interlinear glossing (IG), this poem is about nature (i.e. the season – "spring"; the times of day – "dawn", "night"; location – "everywhere"; animals – "birds"; weather – "wind", "rain"; plants – "flowers") and the actions related to nature: "sleep", "feel", "hear", "sing", "come", "fall", "know". There are a number of ways to translate this well-known poem and there exist at least 30 English versions (Tan & Huang 2019): we will compare two of them here. The first version was translated by Peter Jingcheng Xu (see Tan & Huang 2019: 75):

> ***Spring Morn***
> Spring sleep, coming morn, unaware.
> Awake, hearing birds' song everywhere.
> After last night's wind 'n rain,
> how many flowers fallen fair?

In this version, life forms other than humans and their actions are represented in the way they occur in the source text. Like the source text, some of the implicit actors are understood but not explicitly represented or expressed in the target text (TT):

> IGa: spring sleep not feel dawn
> TT1a: spring sleep, coming morn, unaware
> IGb: everywhere hear sing bird
> TT1b: awake, hearing birds' song everywhere
> IGc: night come wind rain sound
> TT1c: after last night's wind 'n rain
> IGd: flower fall know how many
> TT1d: how many flowers fallen fair

In an ecolinguistic perspective, Xu's translation reflects the description of the events on one morning in spring and the focus of attention is on other forms of life and their actions rather than on man and his actions. We now look at another version, translated by Witter Bynner and Kanghu Jiang (see Wen 1989: 63):

> ***A Spring Morning***
> I awake light-hearted this morning of spring,
> Everywhere round me the singing of birds.
> But now I remember the night, the storm,
> And I wonder how many blossoms were broken.

If we compare the interlinear glossing with this second translation, we can see the differences between this translated version and the source text on the one hand and between this second translation and the previous one by Xu:

IGa: spring sleep not feel dawn
TT2a: I awake lighxt-hearted this morning of spring
IGb: everywhere hear sing bird
TT2b: everywhere round me the singing of birds
IGc: night come wind rain sound
TT2c: but now I remember the night, the storm
IGd: flower fall know how many
TT2d: and I wonder how many blossoms were broken

In this translation, "I / me" appears in every line of the poem, which indicates that the focus of attention is on the speaker experiencing the different situations, which gives the impression that the poem is not about nature but rather about a man's experiences in a morning in spring, and hence what this translation provides is a self-centred image of the speaker.

If we carry out a metafunctional analysis of the source text and the two target texts, we can see how powerful a tool SFL can be in revealing the relationships between the participants and circumstances involved in the processes in the texts, as well as in organizing the messages.

7. Development of systemic functional translation studies in China

Yuanyi Ma: How has the application of SFL to translation been developed in China?

Guowen Huang: When I first tried to apply SFL to translation studies about 20 years ago, there were only few studies in this area in China, although there were quite a number of good articles discussing translation issues in an SFL perspective (e.g. Halliday 2001; Matthiessen 2001; Steiner & Yallop 2001). The past two decades have witnessed a great number of Chinese scholars working on translation studies in an SFL perspective, and many articles and monographs have been published in China. When I typed the keywords "系统功能语言学" (*xì tǒng gōng néng yǔ yán xué*; Systemic Functional Linguistics) and "翻译研究" (*fān yì yán jiū*; translation studies) into the CNKI (China National Knowledge Infrastructure) webpage, there were 142 entries (retrieved on 14 September 2022). There have also been a number of review articles on the SFL approach to translation studies, one of which was written by Si and Tao (2014), which reviews the literature on this topic between 2004 and 2014 and discusses the theoretical and applied value of SFL theory in translation studies, focusing on different aspects of the theory in relation to translation studies: metafunctions, context, appraisal analysis and grammatical metaphor. There have also been articles written in English on applying SFL to translation studies published outside China, and I have contributed two of them (Huang 2014, 2017). You two (e.g. Wang & Ma 2020, 2021, 2022) have also done a great job in recent years, and I have enjoyed reading your publications on systemic functional translation studies.

8. Future studies needed in this area

Yuanyi Ma: What future studies involving the application of SFL to translation are needed in China?

Guowen Huang: I have read the collection you edited with Dr Bo Wang (Wang & Ma 2022) and I very much agree with what those well-known SFL scholars say about the key themes and new directions in systemic functional translation studies. They have clearly mapped the new directions for us in SFL studies of translation issues, and all the new directions predicted by these scholars, it seems to me, are also applicable in the Chinese context. Here I would like to emphasize one point: since translation studies can be dealt with from a number of different perspectives going across a number of different disciplines, we have to remember that a linguistic approach is only one possibility in our endeavor. In my opinion, an interdisciplinary approach with the SFL approach as its core will be a good choice for future work in this area.

Bo Wang: Thank you, Professor Huang. The purpose of editing *Key Themes and New Directions in Systemic Functional Translation Studies* (Wang & Ma 2022) is not only to summarize the contributions of this research area by interacting with important scholars, but also to offer some directions for future research. The interview with you is also conducted by following the same principle. In the near future, we hope we can collect this transcript in the second volume of *Key Themes and New Directions in Systemic Functional Translation Studies*, which is still in preparation.

Note

1. I would like to express my heartfelt thanks to Dr Bo Wang and Dr Yuanyi Ma for translating my interview with them into English. They are not only outstanding translation researchers but also skilful translation practitioners. I hope readers of this book will appreciate what they have done in connecting not only SFL and translation studies but also in systemic functional translation studies in China and in English-speaking countries.

References

Baker, Mona. 1992. *In other words: A coursebook on translation*. London: Routledge.

Bell, Roger T. 1991. *Translation and translating: Theory and practice*. London: Longman.

Biber, Douglas, Stig Johansson, Geoffrey Leech, Susan Conrad & Edward Finegan. 1999. *Longman grammar of spoken and written English*. London: Pearson.

Bloor, Thomas & Meriel Bloor. 1995. *The functional analysis of English: A Hallidayan approach*. London: Arnold.

Cao, Xueqin. 1973. *The story of the stone (vol. 1)* (trans. David Hawkes). Harmondsworth: Penguin.

Cao, Xueqin [曹雪芹] & E Gao [高鄂]. 1999. 红楼梦 [A dream of red mansions]. (trans. 杨宪益 [Xianyi Yang] & 戴乃迭 [Gladys Yang]). 北京/长沙 [Beijing/Changsha]: 外文出版社/湖南人民出版社 [Foreign Languages Press/Hunan People's Publishing House].

Catford, J.C. 1965. *A linguistic theory of translation*. Oxford: Oxford University Press.

Catford, J.C. 1991. 翻译的语言学理论 [A linguistic theory of translation] (trans. 穆雷 [Lei Mu]). 北京 [Beijing]: 旅游教育出版社 [Travel and Education Press].

Chen, Dandan [陈丹丹]. 2022. 先秦儒家典籍《尚书》之传译研究 [Research on translation of *Book of history* – a Pre-Qin Confucius classic]. 南京 [Nanjing]: 南京大学出版社 [Nanjing University Press].

Chen, Yang [陈旸]. 2014.《论语》英译研究的功能语篇分析途径 [A functional discourse analysis of translated texts of Confucius's *Lun Yu* (*The analects*)]. PhD thesis, Sun Yat-sen University, Guangzhou.

Chen, Yang [陈旸]. 2020.《论语》英译研究的功能语篇分析途径 [A functional discourse analysis of translations of the *Lun Yu* (*The analects of Confucius*)]. 广州 [Guangzhou]: 暨南大学出版社 [Jinan University Press].

Chen, Ying [陈莹]. 2014.《论语》英译变异的功能语篇分析 [A functional discourse analysis of variation in English translations of Confucius's *Lun Yu*]. PhD thesis, Sun Yat-sen University, Guangzhou.

Chen, Ying [陈莹]. 2020.《论语》英译变异的功能语篇分析 [A functional discourse analysis of variation in English translations of the *Lun Yu*]. 北京 [Beijing]: 中国社会科学出版社 [China Social Sciences Press].

Chen, Xuejun [陈雪军] & Jie Huang [黄洁]. 2000. 唐宋名篇赏析 [Appreciating and analysing famous works in Tang and Song Dynasty]. 杭州 [Hangzhou]: 浙江古籍出版社 [Zhejiang Chinese Classics Publishing House].

Cheng, Jintao [程瑾涛]. 2020. 系统功能语言学视阈下的翻译研究 [Translation studies: A systemic functional linguistic approach]. 北京 [Beijing]: 北京交通大学出版社 [Beijing Jiao Tong University Press].

Chesterman, Andrew. (ed). 1989. *Readings in translation theory*. Helsinki: Finn Lectura.

Chomsky, Noam. 1957. *Syntactic structures*. The Hague: Mouton.

Chomsky, Noam. 1965. *Aspects of the theory of syntax*. Cambridge, MA: MIT Press.

Chu, Zhida [楚至大]. 1992. "浅论中国古典诗歌英译问题 [A brief discussion on English translations of ancient Chinese poems]." 外国语 [Journal of Foreign Languages] 4: 62–66.

de Waard, Jan & Eugene A. Nida. 1986. *From one language to another: Functional equivalence in Bible translating*. New York: Thomas Nelson.

Ding, Zuxin [丁祖馨]. 2001. 中国诗歌集：英汉对照 [An anthology of Chinese poetry: English–Chinese] (edited and translated). 沈阳 [Shenyang]: 辽宁大学出版社 [Liaoning University Press].

Fang, Li [方立], Zhuanglin Hu [胡壮麟] & Kerong Xu [徐克容]. 1977. "谈谈现代英语语法的三大体系和交流语法学 [On the three systems in modern English grammar and communicative grammar]." 语言教学与研究 [Language Teaching and Research] 6: 1–28.

Fawcett, Robin P. 1988. "The English personal pronouns: An exercise in linguistic theory." In James D. Benson, Michael Cummings & William S. Greaves (eds), *Linguistics in a systemic perspective*. Amsterdam: John Benjamins, 185–220.

Fawcett, Robin P. 2008. *Invitation to Systemic Functional Linguistics through the Cardiff Grammar: An extension and simplification of Halliday's Systemic Functional Grammar*. 3rd ed. London: Equinox.

Fei, Zhengang [费振刚]. (ed.). 2001. 古诗 [Classical Chinese poems]. 北京 [Beijing]: 人民文学出版社 [People's Literature Publishing House].

Gao, Shengwen [高生文]. 2014. 翻译研究的语域视角——理雅各和辜鸿铭《论语》英译比较 [Translation studies from the registerial perspective: Comparison between the translations of *Lun Yu* (*The analects*) by James Legge and Ku Hung-ming]. PhD thesis, Sun Yat-sen University, Guangzhou.

Gao, Shengwen [高生文]. 2016. 语域视角下的翻译研究——理雅各和辜鸿铭《论语》英译比较 [Translation studies from the perspective of register: Comparison between the translations of the *Lun Yu* (*The analects*) by James Legge and Ku Hung-ming]. 北京 [Beijing]: 对外经济贸易大学出版社 [University of International Business and Economics Press].

Goddard, Angela. 1998. *The language of advertising*. London: Routledge.

Gong, Jinghao [龚景浩]. 1999. 英译中国古词精选 [Rendition of selected old Chinese ci-poems]. 北京 [Beijing]: 商务印书馆 [Commercial Press].

Gu, Yanling [顾延龄]. 1993. "马致远《天净沙》英译赏析 [An appreciation of the English translations of *Tian Jing Sha* by MA Zhiyuan]." 外国语 [Journal of Foreign Languages] 2: 14–16. Reprinted in Yanling Gu. 1999. 译海探秘 [Diving into the translocean]. Edited by 彭长江 [Changjiang Peng] & 顾延龄

[Yanling Gu]. 长沙 [Changsha]: 湖南师范大学出版社 [Hunan Normal University Press], 347–53.

Gu, Zhengyang [顾正阳]. 2003. 古诗词曲英译论稿 [Notes on English translations of ancient poem, lyric and verse]. 上海 [Shanghai]: 百家出版社 [Baijia Publishing House].

Guo, Peizhong [郭培忠]. 2002. "古典诗歌中的地名特点初探 [A preliminary exploration of place names in ancient Chinese poetry]." 中山大学学报（社会科学版）[Journal of Sun Yat-sen University (Social Sciences Edition)] 42(1): 70–75.

Halliday, M.A.K. 1956. "Grammatical categories in modern Chinese." *Transactions of the Philosophical Society* 1956: 177–224. Reprinted in part in M.A.K. Halliday. 1976. *Halliday: System and function in language*. Edited by Gunther Kress. London: Oxford University Press, 36–51.

Halliday, M.A.K. 1961. "Categories of the theory of grammar." *WORD* 17: 241–92. Reprinted in M.A.K. Halliday. 2002. *On grammar. Volume 1* in the *Collected works of M.A.K. Halliday*. Edited by Jonathan J. Webster. New York: Continuum, 37–94.

Halliday, M.A.K. 1962. "Linguistics and machine translation." *Zeitschrift für Phonetik, Sprachwissenschaft und Kommunikationsforschung* 15: 145–58. Reprinted in M.A.K. Halliday. 2005. *Computational and quantitative studies. Volume 6* in the *Collected works of M.A.K. Halliday*. Edited by Jonathan J. Webster. New York: Continuum, 20–36.

Halliday, M.A.K. 1985. *An introduction to functional grammar*. London: Edward Arnold.

Halliday, M.A.K. 1990. "New ways of meaning: A challenge to applied linguistics." *Journal of Applied Linguistics* 6: 7–36. Reprinted in M.A.K. Halliday. 2005. *On language and linguistics. Volume 3* in the *Collected works of M.A.K. Halliday*. Edited by Jonathan J. Webster. New York: Continuum, 139–74.

Halliday, M.A.K. 1994. *An introduction to functional grammar*, 2nd ed. London: Edward Arnold.

Halliday, M.A.K. 2001. "Towards a theory of good translation." In Erich Steiner & Colin Yallop (eds), *Exploring translation and multilingual text production: Beyond content*. Berlin: Mouton de Gruyter, 13–18.

Halliday, M.A.K. 2007. "Applied linguistics as an evolving theme." In *Language and education. Volume 9* in the *Collected works of M.A.K. Halliday*. Edited by Jonathan J. Webster. New York: Continuum, 1–19.

Halliday, M.A.K. 2009a. "Method – techniques – problems." In M.A.K. Halliday & Jonathan J. Webster (eds), *Continuum companion to Systemic Functional Linguistics*. New York: Continuum, 59–86.

Halliday, M.A.K. 2009b. "The gloosy ganoderm: Systemic Functional Linguistics and translation." *Chinese Translators Journal* [中国翻译] 1: 17–26. Reprinted in M.A.K. Halliday. 2013. *Halliday in the 21st century. Volume 11* in the *Collected works of M.A.K. Halliday*. Edited by Jonathan J. Webster. London: Bloomsbury. 105–26.

Halliday, M.A.K. 2010. "Pinpointing the choice: Meaning and the search for equivalents in a translated text." In Ahmar Mahboob & Naomi K. Knight (eds), *Appliable linguistics*. New York: Continuum, 13–24. Reprinted in M.A.K. Halliday. 2013. *Halliday in the 21st century. Volume 11* in the *Collected works of M.A.K. Halliday*. Edited by Jonathan J. Webster. London: Bloomsbury. 143–154.

Halliday, M.A.K. & Ruqaiya Hasan. 1976. *Cohesion in English*. New York: Longman.

Halliday, M.A.K. & Christian M.I.M. Matthiessen. 2014. *Halliday's introduction to functional grammar*. 4th ed. London: Routledge.

Halliday, M.A.K., Angus McIntosh & Peter Strevens. 1964. *The linguistic sciences and language teaching*. London: Longman.

Han, Jian [韩健]. 2013. 功能语言学视阈下的法律文本对比分析 [A comparative study of legal texts in the perspective of functional linguistics]. 上海 [Shanghai]: 上海交通大学出版社 [Shanghai Jiaotong University Press].

Hartmann, Reinhard R.K. & Francis C. Stork. 1972. *Dictionary of language and linguistics*. London: Applied Science Publishers.

Hatim, Basil. 1998. *Communication across culture: Translation theory and contrastive text linguistics*. Exeter: University of Exeter Press.

Hatim, Basil & Ian Mason. 1990. *Discourse and the translator*. London: Longman.

Hatim, Basil & Ian Mason. 1997. *The translator as communicator*. London: Routledge.

Hu, Honghui [胡红辉]. 2019.《论语》及其英译本的投射语言对等研究 [A study on the equivalence of projection in *The Lunyu* (*The analects*) and its translations]. 广州 [Guangzhou]: 中山大学出版社 [Sun Yat-sen University Press].

Hu, Zhuanglin [胡壮麟]. 1983. "韩礼德 [M.A.K. Halliday]." 国外语言学 [Foreign Linguistics] 2: 60–63.

Hu, Zhuanglin [胡壮麟]. 1984. "韩礼德的语言观 [M.A.K. Halliday's views on language]." 外语教学与研究 [Foreign Language Teaching and Research] 1: 23–29.

Hu, Zhuanglin [胡壮麟]. 1986. "韩礼德的功能语法 [M.A.K. Halliday's functional grammar]." 现代英语研究 [Studies on Modern English] 1: 50–58.

Hu, Zhuanglin [胡壮麟]. 1994. 语篇的衔接与连贯 [Cohesion and coherence in discourse]. 上海 [Shanghai]: 上海外语教育出版社 [Shanghai Foreign Language Education Press].

Hu, Zhuanglin [胡壮麟], Yongsheng Zhu [朱永生] & Delu Zhang [张德禄]. 1989. 系统功能语法概论 [An introduction to Systemic Functional Grammar]. 长沙 [Changsha]: 湖南教育出版社 [Hunan Education Press].

Huang, Guowen [黄国文]. 1988. 语篇分析概要 [Essentials of text analysis]. 长沙 [Changsha]: 湖南教育出版社 [Hunan Education Press].

Huang, Guowen [黄国文]. 1999. 英语语言问题研究 [Research on problems of the English language]. 广州 [Guangzhou]: 中山大学出版社 [Sun Yat-sen University Press].

Huang, Guowen [黄国文]. 2001a. 语篇分析的理论与实践——广告语篇研究 [Theory and practice of discourse analysis: A study in advertising discourse].

上海 [Shanghai]: 上海外语教育出版社 [Shanghai Foreign Language Education Press].

Huang, Guowen [黄国文]. 2001b. "功能语篇分析纵横谈 [Some discussions on functional discourse analysis]." 外语与外语教学 [Foreign Languages and Their Teaching] 153(12): 1–4+19.

Huang, Guowen [黄国文]. 2002a. "功能语言学分析对翻译研究的启示——《清明》英译文的经验功能分析 [The inspiration of functional linguistic analysis on translation studies: A functional analysis of the experiential meaning in the English version of the poem *Qing Ming*]." 外语与外语教学 [Foreign Languages and Their Teaching] 158(5): 4–9+14.

Huang, Guowen [黄国文]. 2002b. "杜牧《清明》英译文的逻辑功能分析 [A functional analysis of logical meaning in the English versions of DU Mu's *Qing Ming*]." 外语与翻译 [Foreign Languages and Translation] 32(1): 1–6.

Huang, Guowen [黄国文]. 2002c. "《清明》一诗英译文的人际功能探讨 [An interpersonal analysis of *Qing Ming* and its translated versions]." 外语教学 [Foreign Language Education] 23(3): 34–38.

Huang, Guowen [黄国文]. 2002d. "从语篇功能的角度看《清明》的几种英译文 [Exploring the English translations of *Qing Ming* in the perspective of textual metafunction]." In 钱军 [Jun Qian] (ed.), 语言学：中国与世界同步——祝贺胡壮麟教授70诞辰学术论文集 [Linguistics in China: Keeping pace with the world – a festschrift in honor of Professor Zhuanglin Hu's 70th birthday]. 北京 [Beijing]: 外语教学与研究出版社 [Foreign Language Teaching and Research Press], 172–85.

Huang, Guowen [黄国文]. 2002e. "对唐诗《寻隐者不遇》英译文的功能语篇分析 [A functional discourse analysis of the English versions of the Tang poem *Xun Yin Zhe Bu Yu*]." 解放军外国语学院学报 [Journal of the PLA University of Foreign Languages] 25(5): 70–73+118.

Huang, Guowen [黄国文]. 2002f. "唐诗英译文中的引述现象分析 [An analysis of quoting-reporting in translating ancient Tang poems into English]." 外语学刊 [Foreign Languages Research] 110(3): 1–6.

Huang, Guowen [黄国文]. 2002g. "关于语篇与翻译 [On discourse and translation]." 外语与外语教学 [Foreign Languages and Their Teaching] 7: 70–73+118.

Huang, Guowen [黄国文]. 2002h. "功能语篇分析面面观 [Perspectives from functional discourse analysis]." 国外外语教学 [Foreign Language Teaching Abroad] 4: 25–32.

Huang, Guowen [黄国文]. (ed.). 2002i. 语篇·语言功能·语言教学 [Discourse, language function and language teaching]. 广州 [Guangzhou]: 中山大学出版社 [Sun Yat-sen University Press].

Huang, Guowen [黄国文]. 2003a. "汉英语篇比较研究的功能语言学尝试——对唐诗《芙蓉楼送辛渐》及其英译文的功能分析 [A functional linguistic attempt on the comparison of Chinese–English discourse: A functional analysis of Tang poem *Fu Rong Lou Song Xin Jian* and its English translations]." 外语与外语教学 [Foreign Languages and Their Teaching] 2: 21–25.

Huang, Guowen [黄国文]. 2003b. "古诗英译文里的时态分析 [An analysis of tense in the translations of ancient Chinese poems]." 四川外语学院学报 [Journal of Sichuan International Studies University] 19(1): 95–100.

Huang, Guowen [黄国文]. 2003c. "从《天净沙·秋思》的英译文看'形式对等'的重要性 [The importance of formal equivalence: A study of the English versions of the poem *Tian Jing Sha Qiu Si*]." 中国翻译 [Chinese Translators Journal] 24(2): 21–23.

Huang, Guowen [黄国文]. 2003d. "静态和动态在翻译中的表现——柳宗元的《江雪》英译文分析 [Realizations of dynamic and static states in translation: An analysis of the English translations of *Jiang Xue* by LIU Zongyuan]." 外语与翻译 [Foreign Languages and Translation] 36(1): 1–6.

Huang, Guowen [黄国文]. 2006. 翻译研究的语言学探索——古诗词英译本的语言学分析 [Linguistic explorations in translation studies: Analyses of English translations of ancient Chinese poems and lyrics]. 上海 [Shanghai]: 上海外语教育出版社 [Shanghai Foreign Language Education Press].

Huang, Guowen [黄国文]. 2011. "《论语》的篇章结构及英语翻译的几个问题 [The textual structure of Confucius's *Lun Yu* (*The analects*) in relation to the English translation of the book title and chapter headings]." 中国外语 [Chinese Translators Journal] 6: 88–95.

Huang, Guowen. 2014. "Analysing the reporting clause in translating Confucius's *Lun Yu* (*The analects*)." In Yan Fang & Jonathan J. Webster (eds), *Developing Systemic Functional Linguistics: Theory and application*. London: Equinox, 256–70.

Huang, Guowen. 2017. "Searching for metafunctional equivalence in translated texts." In Jonathan J. Webster & Xuanwei Peng (eds), *Applying Systemic Functional Linguistics: The state of the art in China today*. London: Bloomsbury. 285–306.

Huang, Guowen [黄国文] & Junhong Xiao [肖俊洪]. 1996. 英语复合句——从句子到语篇 [Aspects of English complex sentences – from sentence to text]. 厦门 [Xiamen]: 厦门大学出版社 [Xiamen University Press].

Huang, Guowen [黄国文] & Junhong Xiao [肖俊洪] (eds). 1999. 大中学生简明英语语法词典 [A concise dictionary of English grammar for students]. 广州 [Guangzhou]: 广东教育出版社 [Guangdong Education Press].

Huang, Xinqu [黄新渠]. 2002. 汉译英基本技巧 [Basic skills of Chinese–English translation]. 成都 [Chengdu]: 四川人民出版社 [Sichuan People's Publishing House].

Ji, Xianlin [季羡林]. (ed.). 2001. 古诗歌读本 [A textbook of ancient poems and lyrics]. 天津 [Tianjin]: 百花文艺出版社 [Baihua Literature & Art Publishing House].

Ku, Hung-Ming. 1898. *The discourses and sayings of Confucius*. Shanghai: Kelly and Walsh.

Labov, William. 1972. *Language in the inner city: Studies in the Black English vernacular*. Philadelphia: University of Pennsylvania Press.

Legge, James. 1861. *The Chinese classics with a translation, critical and exegetical notes, prolegomena, and copious indexes (vol. I)*. London: Trübner & Co.

Li, Fagen [李发根]. 2005. 人际意义与等效翻译:《蜀道难》及英译文的功能语言学分析 [Interpersonal meanings and equivalence in translation: A functional linguistic analysis of "Shu Dao Nan" and its English version]. PhD thesis, Sun Yat-sen University, Guangzhou.

Li, Fagen [李发根]. 2007. 人际意义与等效翻译:《蜀道难》及英译文的功能语言学分析 [Interpersonal meanings and equivalence in translation: A functional linguistic analysis of "Shu Dao Nan" and its English version]. 南昌 [Nanchang]: 江西人民出版社 [Jiangxi People's Publishing House].

Li, Pingshou [李平收] & Geng Zhang [张耕]. 2001. 学生版唐诗三百首 [A collection of three hundred Tang poems for students]. 北京 [Beijing]: 华语教学出版社 [Sinolingua Press].

Li, Xi [李晰]. 2023. 文学翻译中的连贯模式研究：以《红楼梦》及其英译本为例 [Research on the patterns of coherence in literary translation: Examples from *Hongloumeng* and its English translations]. 上海 [Shanghai]: 上海交通大学出版社 [Shanghai Jiao Tong University Press].

Lian, Shuneng [连淑能]. 1993. 英汉对比研究 [Contrastive studies of English and Chinese]. 北京 [Beijing]: 高等教学出版社 [Higher Education Press].

Liu, Junping [刘军平]. (trans.). 2002. 新译唐诗英韵百首 [New translations of 100 Tang poems]. 北京 [Beijing]: 中华书局 [Zhonghua Book Company].

Liu, Yingkai [刘英凯]. 1982. "'形美'、'音美'杂议——与许渊冲教授商榷 [A discussion on 'beauty in form' and 'beauty in sound' with Professor Xu Yuanchong]." 外语学刊 [Foreign Languages Research] 3: 59–63.

Liu, Yingkai [刘英凯]. 1986. "许渊冲教授'音美'理论与实践质疑 [Some doubts on Professor Xu Yuanchong's theory and practice of 'beauty in sound']." 现代外语 [Modern Foreign Languages] 3: 47–57.

Liu, Yingkai [刘英凯]. 1989. "关于'音美'理论的再商榷 [Another discussion on the theory of 'beauty in sound']." 现代外语 [Modern Foreign Languages] 2: 37–43.

Liu, Yingkai [刘英凯]. 1994. "英语形合传统观照下的汉语意合传统 [The meaning-oriented tradition of Chinese in view of the form-oriented tradition of English]." In 刘重德 [Zhongde Liu] (ed.), 英汉语比较研究：中国英汉语比较研究会首届学术研讨会论文选辑 [Comparative Chinese–English studies: Collection of papers in the First Symposium of China Association for Comparative Studies of English and Chinese]. 长沙 [Changsha]: 湖南科学技术出版社 [Hunan Science and Technology Press]. 163–73.

Liu, Zhongde [刘重德]. 1994. 英汉语比较研究：中国英汉语比较研究会首届学术研讨会论文选辑 [Comparative Chinese–English studies: Collection of papers in the First Symposium of China Association for Comparative Studies of English and Chinese]. 长沙 [Changsha]: 湖南科学技术出版社 [Hunan Science and Technology Press].

Liu, Zhongde [刘重德]. 2003. 寒窗草——刘重德诗文选集 [Grass before "a cold window": Selected poems and essays by Zhongde Liu]. Edited by 刘超先

[Chaoxian Liu] & 蔡平 [Ping Cai]. 长沙 [Changsha]: 湖南师范大学出版社 [Hunan Normal University Press].

Lü, Shuxiang [吕叔湘]. (ed.). 1980. 中诗英译比录 [A comparative study on English translations of classical Chinese poems]. 上海 [Shanghai]: 上海外语教育出版社 [Shanghai Foreign Language Education Press].

Ma, Hongjun [马红军]. 2000. 翻译批评散论 [A collection of papers on translation criticism]. 北京 [Beijing]: 中国对外翻译出版公司 [China Translation and Publishing Corporation].

Martin, J.R. 1992. *English text: System and structure*. Amsterdam: John Benjamins.

Matthiessen, Christian M.I.M. 2001. "The environments of translation." In Erich Steiner & Colin Yallop (eds), *Exploring translation and multilingual text production: Beyond content*. Berlin: Mouton de Gruyter, 41–124.

Matthiessen, Christian M.I.M. 2014. "Registerial cartography: Context-based mapping of text types and their rhetorical-relational organization." In *Proceedings of the 28th Pacific Asia Conference on Language, Information and Computation*, 5–26.

Matthiessen, Christian M.I.M. 2015. "Modelling context and register: The long-term project of registerial cartography." *Letras, Santa Maria* 25(50): 15–90. https://doi.org/10.5902/2176148520205

Matthiessen, Christian M.I.M., Bo Wang, Yuanyi Ma & Isaac N. Mwinlaaru. 2022. *Systemic functional insights on language and linguistics*. Singapore: Springer.

Mu, Shixiong [穆诗雄]. 2004. 跨文化传播——中国古典诗歌英译论 [Cross-cultural transmission: On English translation of classic Chinese poetry]. 合肥 [Hefei]: 中国科学技术大学出版社 [University of Science and Technology of China Press].

Mu, Xuqin [牟许琴]. 2015. 隐喻的态度意义——基于英语诗歌语篇的系统研究 [Attitudinal meanings of metaphors: A systematic study based on English poetry]. 四川 [Sichuan]: 四川大学出版社 [Sichuan University Press].

Munday, Jeremy. 2001. *Introducing translation studies*. London: Routledge.

Nida, Eugene. A. 1964. *Toward a science of translating*. Leiden: E.J. Brill.

Nida, Eugene A. & Charles R. Taber. 1969. *The theory and practice of translation*. Leiden: E.J. Brill.

Nord, Christiane. 1997. *Translating as a purposeful activity*. Manchester: St Jerome.

Ouyang, Qianhua [欧阳倩华]. 2015. 口译质量评估：功能语言学新途径 [Assessing the quality of interpreting: A new perspective from functional linguistics]. 广州 [Guangzhou]: 世界图书出版公司 [World Publishing Corporation].

Pan, Wenguo [潘文国]. 1994. "单数乎？复数乎？——唐诗英译二十四品之一 [Singular or plural? A paper on 24 qualities in English translations of Tang poems]." In 刘重德 [Zhongde Liu] (ed.), 英汉语比较研究：中国英汉语比较研究会首届学术研讨会论文选辑 [Comparative Chinese-English studies: Collection of papers in the First Symposium of China Association for

Comparative Studies of English and Chinese]. 长沙 [Changsha]: 湖南科学技术出版社 [Hunan Science and Technology Press], 85–100.

Pound, Ezra (trans.). 1951. *The Confucian analects*. Washington DC: Square Series.

Qiu, Xiaolong [裘小龙]. (trans.). (ed.). 2003. 中国古典爱情诗词选 [A selection of classical Chinese love poems]. 上海 [Shanghai]: 上海社会科学院出版社 [Shanghai Academy of Social Sciences Press].

Quirk, Randolph, Sidney Greenbaum, Geoffrey Leech & Jan Svartvik. 1985. *A comprehensive grammar of the English language*. London: Longman.

Sanqin Press [三秦出版社]. (ed.). 2000. 小学古诗词背诵 [Poems for recitation in primary school]. 西安 [Xi'an]: 三秦出版社 [Sanqin Press].

Shang, Yuanyuan [尚媛媛]. 2001. "语境配置与语篇体裁之间的关系——从功能语法谈新闻标题语的语言表达特点 [Contextual configuration and genre: A functional approach to English news headlines]." 解放军外国语学院学报 [Journal of PLA University of Foreign Languages] 24(6): 37–41.

Shang, Yuanyuan [尚媛媛]. 2003. 英汉政治语篇翻译研究 [Translation shifts in political texts from English into Chinese]. PhD thesis, Sun Yat-sen University, Guangzhou.

Shang, Yuanyuan [尚媛媛]. 2005. 英汉政治语篇翻译研究 [Translation shifts in political texts from English into Chinese]. 成都 [Chengdu]: 四川人民出版社 [Sichuan People's Publishing House].

Shen, Yuping [申雨平]. (ed.). 2002. 西方翻译理论精选 [A selection of western translation theories]. 北京 [Beijing]: 外语教学与研究出版社 [Foreign Language Teaching and Research Press].

Si, Jianguo [司建国]. 2004. 系统功能语言学与小说文体研究——《在冷血中》的功能主义分析 [Systemic Functional Linguistics and the style of novels – a modified functional analysis of *In cold blood*]. 广州 [Guangzhou]: 暨南大学出版社 [Jinan University Press].

Si, Xianzhu [司显柱]. 2005. 翻译研究：理论·方法·评估 [Translation studies: Theory, method and evaluation]. 北京 [Beijing]: 中国文史出版社 [China Literature and History Press].

Si, Xianzhu [司显柱]. 2006. 功能语言学与翻译研究——翻译质量评估模式建构 [Translation studies: A functional linguistic approach – constructing a translation quality assessment model]. PhD thesis, Sun Yat-sen University, Guangzhou.

Si, Xianzhu [司显柱]. 2007. 功能语言学与翻译研究——翻译质量评估模式建构 [Translation studies: A functional linguistic approach – constructing a translation quality assessment model]. 北京 [Beijing]: 北京大学出版社 [Peking University Press].

Si, Xianzhu [司显柱]. 2016. 功能语言学与翻译研究——翻译质量评估模式建构 [Translation studies in the perspective of Systemic Functional Linguistics: Constructing a translation quality assessment model]. 北京 [Beijing]: 外语教学与研究出版社 [Foreign Language Teaching and Research Press].

Si, Xianzhu [司显柱] & Yuhou Pang [庞玉厚]. 2019. 英译汉翻译研究功能途径 [Studies of English into Chinese translation: A systemic functional linguistic approach]. 北京 [Beijing]: 外语教学与研究出版社 [Foreign Language Teaching and Research Press].

Si, Xianzhu [司显柱], Yuhou Pang [庞玉厚] & Jintao Cheng [程瑾涛]. 2017. 汉译英翻译研究功能途径 [Studies of Chinese into English translation: A systemic functional linguistic approach]. 北京 [Beijing]: 外语教学与研究出版社 [Foreign Language Teaching and Research Press].

Si, Xianzhu [司显柱] & Yang Tao [陶阳]. 2014. "中国系统功能语言学视角翻译研究十年探索：回顾与展望 [A decade of the systemic functional linguistic approach to translation studies in China: Retrospect and prospect]." 中国外语 [Chinese Translators Journal] 11(3): 99–105.

Steiner, Erich & Colin Yallop (eds). 2001. *Exploring translation and multilingual text production: Beyond content*. Berlin: Mouton de Gruyter.

Stibbe, Arran. 2015. *Ecolinguistics: Language, ecology and the stories we live by*. London: Routledge.

Sun, Dayu [孙大雨]. (trans.). 1997. 古诗文英译集 [An anthology of ancient Chinese poetry and prose]. 上海 [Shanghai]: 上海外语教育出版社 [Shanghai Foreign Language Education Press].

Tan, Xiaochun [谭晓春] & Guowen Huang [黄国文]. 2019. "自然诗歌翻译的功能语言学解读——以孟浩然《春晓》为例 [A functional linguistic interpretation of a nature poem: A case study of MENG Haoran's *Chun Xiao*]." 外语教学 [Foreign Language Education] 5: 72–77.

Tao, Yang [陶炀]. 2002. "《列车上的对话》功能文体分析 [A functional-stylistic analysis of *Conversation on the train*]." In Guowen Huang [黄国文] (ed.), 语篇·语言功能·语言教学 [Discourse, language functions and language teaching]. 广东 [Guangdong]: 中山大学出版社 [Sun Yat-sen University Press], 114–24.

Thompson, Geoff. 1996. *Introducing functional grammar*. London: Arnold.

Thompson, Geoff [汤普森]. 2000. 转述法 [Reporting] (trans. 王之光 [Zhiguang Wang]). 北京 [Beijing]: 外文出版社 [Foreign Languages Press].

Waley, Arthur. 1938. *The analects of Confucius*. London: George Allen & Unwin.

Wan, Changsheng [万昌盛] & Xianzhong Wang [王僩中]. (trans.) 2000. 中国古诗一百首 [A selection of one hundred ancient Chinese poems]. Edited by 朱丽云 [Liyun Zhu]. 郑州 [Zhengzhou]: 大象出版社 [Elephant Press].

Wang, Bo & Yuanyi Ma. 2020. *Lao She's Teahouse and its two English translations: Exploring Chinese drama translation with Systemic Functional Linguistics*. London: Routledge.

Wang, Bo & Yuanyi Ma. 2021. *Systemic functional translation studies: Theoretical insights and new directions*. Sheffield: Equinox.

Wang, Bo & Yuanyi Ma (eds). 2022. *Key themes and new directions in systemic functional translation studies*. London: Routledge.

Wang, Dalian [王大濂]. (trans.). 1997. 英译唐诗绝句百首 [English translation of 100 Chinese quatrains by the Tang poets]. 天津 [Tianjin]: 百花文艺出版社 [Baihua Literature and Art Press].

Wang, Hongyang [王红阳]. 2010. 中国语境下的系统功能语言学研究 [Studies on Systemic Functional Linguistics in the Chinese context]. 北京 [Beijing]: 海洋出版社 [Ocean Press].

Wang, Hongyang [王红阳] & Guowen Huang [黄国文]. 2010. "系统功能语言学在中国的三十年 [Thirty years of Systemic Functional Linguistics in China]." In 黄国文 [Guowen Huang] & 常晨光 [Chenguang Chang] (eds), 功能语言学年度评论：第*1*卷 [Annual review of functional linguistics (I)]. 北京 [Beijing]: 高等教育出版社 [Higher Education Press], 51–91.

Wang, Peng [王鹏]. 2004.《哈利·波特》与其汉语翻译——以系统功能语言学分析情态系统 [*Harry Potter* and its Chinese translation: An examination of modality system in systemic functional approach]. PhD thesis, Sun Yat-sen University, Guangzhou.

Wang, Peng [王鹏]. 2007.《哈利·波特》与其汉语翻译——以系统功能语言学分析情态系统 [*Harry Potter* and its Chinese translation: Analysis of modality system in the perspective of Systemic Functional Linguistics]. 重庆 [Chongqing]: 重庆大学出版社 [Chongqing University Press].

Wang, Shouyi & John Knoepfle (trans.). 1989. 唐宋诗词英译 [English translation of poems from Tang and Song Dynasties]. 哈尔滨 [Harbin]: 黑龙江人民出版社 [Heilongjiang People's Publishing House].

Wang, Shouyuan [王守元] & Delu Zhang [张德禄] (eds). 1996. 文体学辞典 [A dictionary of stylistics]. 济南 [Jinan]: 山东教育出版社 [Shandong Education Press].

Wang, Zhenzhen [王珍珍]. 2014. 试论系统功能语言学在日汉翻译分析中的作用 [On the effect of systemic functional linguistic analysis in Japanese-Chinese translation]. 北京 [Beijing]: 世界图书出版公司 [World Publishing Corporation].

Wang, Zongyan [王宗炎]. 1980. "伦敦学派奠基人弗斯的语言理论 [The linguistic theories of J.R. Firth – founder of the London School]." 国外语言学 [Foreign Linguistics] 5: 1–8.

Wang, Zongyan [王宗炎]. 1981. "评哈利迪的《现代汉语语法范畴》[A Review of Halliday's 'Grammatical categories in Modern Chinese']." 国外语言学 [Foreign Linguistics] 2: 48–54.

Wen, Shu [文殊]. (ed.). 1989. 诗词英译选 [Anthology of English translations of ancient Chinese poems and lyrics]. 北京 [Beijing]: 外语教学与研究出版社 [Foreign Language Teaching and Research Press].

Weng, Xianliang [翁显良]. 1982. "本色与变相 [True coloring and false complexion]." 外国语 [Journal of Foreign Languages] 1: 22–25. Reprinted in 翻译新论 [A series of translation studies in China]. Edited by 杨自俭 [Zijian Yang] & 刘学云 [Xueyun Liu]. 武汉 [Wuhan]: 湖北教育出版社 [Hubei Education Press], 43–56.

Weng, Xianliang [翁显良]. (trans.). 1985. 古诗英译 [An English translation of ancient Chinese poems]. 北京 [Beijing]: 北京出版社 [Beijing Publishing House].

Widdowson, H.G. 1978. *Teaching language as communication*. Oxford: Oxford University Press.

Wu, Guoxiang [吴国向]. 2013.《论语》翻译版本的语法复杂性研究 [On the grammatical complexity of the translations of Confucius's *The analects*]. PhD thesis, Sun Yat-sen University, Guangzhou.

Wu, Juntao [吴钧陶]. (trans.). (ed.). 1997. 唐诗三百首（汉英对照、文白对照）[300 Tang poems (Chinese–English) (classical Chinese – modern Chinese)]. 长沙 [Changsha]: 湖南出版社 [Hunan Publishing House].

Wu, Yaqing [伍雅清]. 1994. "论英语与汉语的形合和意合的差异 [On the differences between form-orientation and meaning-orientation in English and Chinese]." In 刘重德 [Zhongde Liu] (ed.), 英汉语比较研究：中国英汉语比较研究会首届学术研讨会论文选辑 [Comparative Chinese–English studies: Collection of papers in the First Symposium of China Association for Comparative Studies of English and Chinese]. 长沙 [Changsha]: 湖南科学技术出版社 [Hunan Science and Technology Press], 152–62.

Xiao, Difei [萧涤非] et al. 1983. 唐诗鉴赏辞典 [A dictionary for appreciating poems of the Tang Dynasty]. 上海 [Shanghai]: 上海辞书出版社 [Shanghai Lexicographical Publishing House].

Xiao, Liming [萧立明]. 2001. 新译学论稿 [A new collection of papers on translation studies]. 北京 [Beijing]: 中国对外翻译出版公司 [China Translation and Publishing Corporation].

Xie, Jianping [谢建平] et al. 2008. 功能语境与专门用途英语语篇翻译研究 [*Functional context and ESP discourse translation*]. 杭州 [Hangzhou]: 浙江大学出版社 [Zhejiang University Press].

Xu, Jun [徐珺]. 2002. "《儒林外史》英汉语语篇对比研究—系统功能语言学的尝试 [A comparative study of Chinese–English texts from *The scholars*: Perspective from Systemic Functional Linguistics]." 外语与外语教学 [Foreign Languages and Their Teaching] 12: 1–5.

Xu, Min [徐敏]. (ed.). 1990. 儿童古诗300首 [300 ancient poems for children]. 北京 [Beijing]: 语文出版社 [Language & Culture Press].

Xu, Yuanchong [许渊冲]. 1979a. "'毛主席诗词'译文研究 [A study on the translations of Chairman Mao's poems and lyrics]." 外国语 [Journal of Foreign Languages] 1: 1–4.

Xu, Yuanchong [许渊冲]. 1979b. "如何译毛主席诗词 [How to translate Chairman Mao's poems and lyrics]." 外语教学与研究 [Foreign Language Teaching and Research] 2: 1–6.

Xu, Yuanchong [许渊冲]. (trans.). 1986. 唐宋词一百首（汉英对照）[100 Tang and Song ci poems (Chinese–English)]. 北京 [Beijing]: 中国对外翻译出版公司 [China Translation and Publishing Corporation] / 香港 [Hong Kong]: 商务印书馆（香港）有限公司 [The Commercial Press (H.K.)].

Xu, Yuanchong [许渊冲]. 1987. "三谈意美、音美、形美 [The third discussion on beauty in meaning, beauty in sound and beauty in form]." 深圳大学学报 [Journal of Shenzhen University] 2: 70–77.

Xu, Yuanchong [许渊冲]. (trans.). 1988. 唐诗三百首新译（英汉对照） [A new translation of 300 Tang poems (Chinese–English)]. 北京 [Beijing]: 中国对外翻译出版公司 [China Translation and Publishing Corporation].

Xu, Yuanchong [许渊冲]. 1990a. "文学翻译1+1=3 [1+1=3 in literary translation]." 外国语 [Journal of Foreign Languages] 1: 8–12.

Xu, Yuanchong [许渊冲]. (trans.). 1990b. 唐宋词一百五十首 [150 Tang and Song lyrics]. 北京 [Beijing]: 北京大学出版社 [Peking University Press].

Xu, Yuanchong [许渊冲]. (trans.). 1996. 宋词三百首 [300 Song lyrics]. 长沙 [Changsha]: 湖南出版社 [Hunan Publishing House].

Xu, Yuanchong [许渊冲]. (trans.). 2000a. 新编千家诗 [Gem of classical Chinese poetry]. 北京 [Beijing]: 中华书局 [Zhonghua Book Company].

Xu, Yuanchong [许渊冲]. (trans.). 2000b. 唐诗三百首 [300 Tang poems]. 北京 [Beijing]: 高等教育出版社 [Higher Education Press].

Xu, Yuanchong [许渊冲]. 2002. "谈《唐宋词三百首》英译 [On the English translation of *300 Tang and Song lyrics*]." 外语论坛 [Forum of Foreign Languages] 2.

Xu, Yuanchong [许渊冲]. (trans.). 2005. 汉英对照论语 [Thus spoke the master]. 北京 [Beijing]: 高等教育出版社 [Higher Education Press].

Xu, Yuanchong [许渊冲] et al. (trans.) 2003a. 小学生必背古诗词（汉英对照） [Ancient poems and lyrics that must be recited by primary school students (Chinese–English)]. 石家庄 [Shijiazhuang]: 河北人民出版社 [Hebei People's Publishing House].

Xu, Yuanchong [许渊冲] et al. (trans.) 2003b. 初中生必背古诗词（汉英对照） [Ancient poems and lyrics that must be recited by junior high school students (Chinese–English)]. 石家庄 [Shijiazhuang]: 河北人民出版社 [Hebei People's Publishing House].

Xu, Yuanchong [许渊冲] et al. (trans.) 2003c. 高中生必背古诗词（汉英对照） [Ancient poems and lyrics that must be recited by senior high school students (Chinese–English)]. 石家庄 [Shijiazhuang]: 河北人民出版社 [Hebei People's Publishing House].

Xu, Yuanchong [许渊冲], Peixian Lu [陆佩弦] & Juntao Wu [吴钧陶] (eds). 1988. 唐诗三百首新译（英汉对照） [A new translation of 300 Tang poems (Chinese–English)]. 北京 [Beijing]: 中国对外翻译出版公司 [China Translation and Publishing Corporation] / 香港 [Hong Kong]: 商务印书馆（香港）有限公司 [The Commercial Press (H.K.)].

Yallop, Colin. 2001. "The construction of equivalence." In Erich Steiner & Colin Yallop (eds), *Exploring translation and multilingual text production: Beyond content*. Berlin: Mouton de Gruyter, 229–46.

Yang, Xianyi [杨宪益] & Gladys Yang [戴乃迭]. (trans.). 2001a. 唐诗 [Tang poems]. 北京 [Beijing]: 外文出版社 [Foreign Languages Press].

Yang, Xianyi [杨宪益] & Gladys Yang [戴乃迭]. (trans.). 2001b. 宋词 [Song lyrics]. 北京 [Beijing]: 外文出版社 [Foreign Languages Press].

Yang, Zijian [杨自俭] & Xueyun Liu [刘学云] (eds). 1994. 翻译新论 [A series of studies on translation in China]. 武汉 [Wuhan]: 湖北教育出版社 [Hubei Education Press].

Yip, Wai-lim [叶维廉]. 1992. 中国诗学 [Chinese poetics]. 北京 [Beijing]: 三联书店 [Joint Publishing Bookstore].

Yu, Juan [余娟]. 2015. 功能语篇视角下的《论语》英译本之显化研究 [On meaning explicitation in Chinese to English translations of *The analects* of Confucius]. PhD thesis, Sun Yat-sen University, Guangzhou.

Zhang, Baohong [张保红]. 1996. "汉诗英译中意象的处理 [Rendering the images in English translations of Chinese poems]." 外语与翻译 [Foreign Language and Translation] 3.

Zhang, Baohong [张保红]. 2003. 汉英诗歌翻译与比较研究 [A study on Chinese–English poetry translation and comparison]. 武汉 [Wuhan]: 中国地质大学出版社 [China University of Geosciences Press].

Zhang, Bingxing [张炳星] (trans.). 2001. 英译中国古典诗词名篇百首 [100 famous Chinese classical poems and their English translations]. 北京 [Beijing]: 中华书局 [Zhonghua Book Company].

Zhang, Delu [张德禄]. 1998. 功能文体学 [Functional stylistics]. 济南 [Jinan]: 山东教育出版社 [Shandong Education Press].

Zhang, Haiou [张海鸥]. 2000. 唐名家诗导读 [An introduction to poems by famous Tang poets]. 广州 [Guangzhou]: 广东人民出版社 [Guangdong People's Publishing House].

Zhang, Haiou [张海鸥]. 2001. 宋名家诗导读 [An introduction to poems by famous Song poets]. 广州 [Guangzhou]: 广东人民出版社 [Guangdong People's Publishing House].

Zhang, Jin [张今] & Yunqing Chen [陈云清]. 1981. 英汉比较语法纲要 [An outline of English–Chinese comparative grammar]. 北京 [Beijing]: 商务印书馆 [Commercial Press].

Zhang, Meifang [张美芳]. 2003. "诺德及其功能翻译理论 [Nord and her functional translation theory]." 外语与翻译 [Foreign Languages and Translation] 4: 74–76.

Zhang, Meifang [张美芳]. 2005. 翻译研究的功能途径 [Functional approaches to translation studies]. 上海 [Shanghai]: 上海外语教育出版社 [Shanghai Foreign Language Education Press].

Zhang, Meifang [张美芳]. 2015. 功能途径论翻译：以英汉翻译为例 [Functional approaches to English–Chinese translation]. 北京 [Beijing]: 外文出版社 [Foreign Languages Press].

Zhang, Tingchen [张廷琛] & Bruce M. Wilson (trans.). 1994. 唐诗一百首（汉英对照）[100 Tang poems (Chinese–English)]. 北京 [Beijing]: 中国对外翻译出版公司 [China Translation and Publishing Corporation].

Zhang, Zhenbang [章振邦] (ed.). 1997. 新编英语语法 [A new English grammar]. 3rd ed. 上海 [Shanghai]: 上海外语教育出版社 [Shanghai Foreign Education Press].

Zhao, Dequan [赵德全]. 2007. 纯理功能的传译–功能语言学理论框架下的翻译研究 [Transferring the metafunctions between English and Chinese: A functional linguistic approach to translation studies]. 保定 [Baoding]: 河北大学出版社 [Hebei University Press].

Zhao, Haihu [赵海湖]. 2021. 系统功能语言学视域下的旅游翻译研究 [A study of tourism translation from the perspective of Systemic Functional Linguistics]. 广州 [Guangzhou]: 广东人民出版社 [Guangdong People's Publishing House].

Zhao, Jing [赵晶]. 2017. 跨语际再实例化视角下的及物性翻译转换研究 [Transitivity translation shifts in the perspective of interlingual re-instantiation]. 北京 [Beijing]: 清华大学出版社 [Tsinghua University Press].

Zhao, Shikai [赵世开]. (ed.). 1999. 汉英对比语法论集 [A collection of studies on Chinese–English contrastive grammar]. 上海 [Shanghai]: 上海外语教育出版社 [Shanghai Foreign Language Education Press].

Zhao, Zhentao [赵甄陶] (trans.). 1999. 中国诗词精选英译 [English translations of the selected Chinese poems]. 长沙 [Changsha]: 湖南师范大学出版社 [Hunan Normal University Press].

Zhu, Chunshen [朱纯深]. 2000. "感知、认知与中国山水诗翻译：从诗中有'画'看《江雪》诗的翻译 [Perception, cognition and translation of Chinese landscape poetry: On the translation of *Jiang Xue* in the perspective of 'painting' in poetry]." 外语与翻译 [Foreign Languages and Translation] 2: 1–10.

Zhu, Hui [朱徽]. 1990. "中英诗歌的语法问题比较研究 [A comparative study of grammar in Chinese and English poems]." 外国语 [Journal of Foreign Languages] 1: 48–55.

Zhu, Liyun [朱丽云]. (ed.). 2000. 中国古诗一百首 [A selection of one hundred ancient Chinese poems] (trans. Changsheng Wan [万昌盛] & Xianzhong Wang [王僴中]). 郑州 [Zhengzhou]: 大象出版社 [Elephant Press].

Zhu, Yongsheng [朱永生] & Shiqing Yan [严世清]. 2001. 系统功能语言学多维思考 [Reflections on Systemic Functional Linguistics]. 上海 [Shanghai]: 上海外语教育出版社 [Shanghai Foreign Language Education Press].

Zhuo, Zhenying [卓振英]. 1996. 华夏情怀——历代名诗英译及探微 [The Chinese sentiments – as expressed in 128 oft-quoted poems (1100BC–AD1910)]. 广州 [Guangzhou]: 中山大学出版社 [Sun Yat-sen University Press].

Zhuo, Zhenying [卓振英]. 2003. 汉诗英译论要 [A theoretical outline of Chinese verse translation]. 北京 [Beijing]: 中国科学文化出版社 [China Science and Culture Press].

Zong, Shi [偬仕] (ed.). 1999. 唐诗选（英汉对照）[Selected poems from the Tang Dynasty (Chinese–English)]. 北京 [Beijing]: 中国文学出版社 [Chinese Literature Press] / 外语教学与研究出版社 [Foreign Language Teaching and Research Press].

Author biographies

Guowen Huang is a Chair Professor of the Changjiang Programme selected by the Ministry of Education of the People's Republic of China. He was a Professor of Functional Linguistics during 1996–2016 at Sun Yat-sen University, PRC and a Professor of Ecolinguistics at South China Agricultural University during 2016–2024. He is now a Professor of Applied Linguistics at City University of Macau. He was educated in Britain and received two PhD degrees from two British universities (1992, Applied Linguistics, Edinburgh; 1996, Functional Linguistics, Cardiff). He was a Fulbright Scholar during 2004–2005 at Stanford University. Since 2010, he has served as the editor-in-chief of the journal *Foreign Languages in China* (bimonthly), published by Higher Education Press, China. He publishes extensively both in China and abroad and serves/served as an editorial/advisory committee member for a number of journals. His research interests include Systemic Functional Linguistics, Ecolinguistics, Applied Linguistics, Discourse Analysis, and Translation Studies.

Bo Wang and **Yuanyi Ma** received their doctoral degrees from the Hong Kong Polytechnic University. Bo Wang is Research Assistant Professor, Faculty of Arts and Humanities, University of Macau. Yuanyi Ma is a researcher in the Faculty of Education, Vancouver Island University, Canada. Their research interests include Systemic Functional Linguistics, translation studies, discourse analysis and language description. They are co-authors of *Lao She's* Teahouse *and Its Two English Translations: Exploring Chinese Drama Translation with Systemic Functional Linguistics* (Routledge, 2020), *Systemic Functional Translation Studies: Theoretical Insights and New Directions* (Equinox, 2021), *Translating Tagore's* Stray Birds *into Chinese: Applying Systemic Functional Linguistics to Chinese Poetry Translation* (Routledge, 2021), *Systemic Functional Insights on Language and Linguistics* (Springer, 2022, with Christian M.I.M. Matthiessen and Isaac N. Mwinlaaru), *Introducing M.A.K. Halliday* (Routledge, 2022), *Introducing Chinese Discourse* (Routledge, forthcoming), *Mini-explorations of Systemic*

Functional Grammar (Equinox, forthcoming) and *Mini-explorations of Language* (Equinox, forthcoming). They are co-editors of *Key Themes and New Directions in Systemic Functional Translation Studies* (Routledge, 2022), *Theorizing and Applying Systemic Functional Linguistics: Developments by Christian M.I.M. Matthiessen* (Routledge, 2024), and *Readings in Systemic Functional Translation Studies (Vols 1 & 2)* (Equinox, in press). They are translators of Wang Li's *Modern Chinese Grammar (Volumes 1–4)* (Routledge, 2023) and co-editors of the Chinese Culture section of *The Routledge Encyclopedia of Chinese Studies.*

Index